MH

math expressions

Common Core

Dr. Karen C. Fuson

Watch the platypus come alive in its watery world as you discover and solve math challenges.

Download the *Math Worlds AR* app available on Android or iOS devices.

Grade 2

Volume 1

This material is based upon work supported by the
National Science Foundation
under Grant Numbers
ESI-9816320, REC-9806020, and RED-935373.

Any opinions, findings, and conclusions, or recommendations expressed in this material are those of the author and do not necessarily reflect the views of the National Science Foundation.

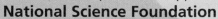

Cover Illustration: © Josh Brill

Printed in the U.S.A.

ISBN 978-0-544-91974-7

8 9 10 11 12 13 0029 25 24 23 22 21 20

4500809974 D E F G

Unit 1 | Addition and Subtraction Within 20

BIG IDEA 1 - Strategies for Addition and Subtraction

BIG IDEA 2 - Addition and Subtraction Situations

Unit 2 | Addition Within 200

BIG IDEA 1 - Use Place Value

BIG IDEA 2 - Add 2-Digit Numbers

BIG IDEA 3 - Money and Fluency for Addition Within 100

Unit 3 | Length and Shapes

BIG IDEA 1 - Length and Shapes

BIG IDEA 2 - Estimate, Measure, and Make Line Plots

Student Resources

addend	doubles minus 2
addition doubles	doubles plus 1
doubles minus 1	doubles plus 2

$7 + 7 = 14$, so
$7 + 5 = 12$, 2 less than 14.

$$5 + 6 = 11$$

addends

$6 + 6 = 12$, so
$6 + 7 = 13$, 1 more than 12.

Both addends (or partners) are the same.

$$4 + 4 = 8$$

$6 + 6 = 12$, so
$6 + 8 = 14$, 2 more than 12.

$7 + 7 = 14$, so
$7 + 6 = 13$, 1 less than 14.

equation	extra information
equation chain	fewer
even	hidden information

Franny has 8 kittens and 2 dogs. 4 kittens are asleep. How many kittens are awake?

$8 - 4 = \boxed{4}$

The number of dogs is extra information. It is not needed to solve the problem.

$4 + 3 = 7$
$7 = 4 + 3$
$9 - 5 = 4$
$4 + 5 = 8 + 1$

An equation must have an = sign.

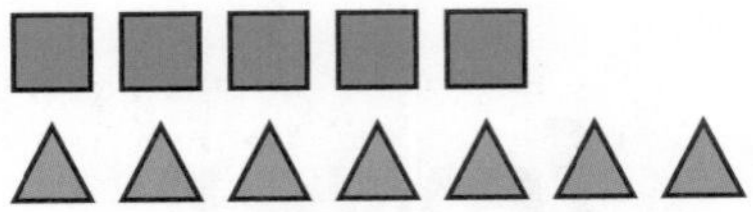

There are fewer ■ than ▲.

$3 + 4 = 5 + 2 = 8 - 1 = 7$

Heather bought a dozen eggs. She used 7 of them to make breakfast. How many eggs does she have left?

$12 - 7 = \boxed{5}$

The hidden information is that a dozen means 12.

A number is even if you can make groups of 2 and have none left over.

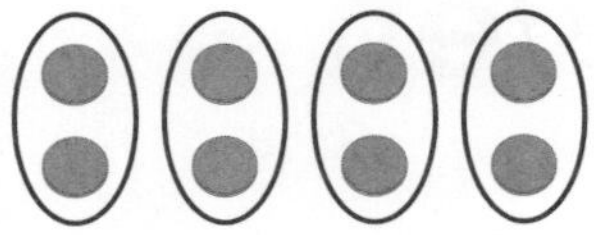

8 is an even number.

more	pattern
odd	subtraction doubles
pairs	total

This pattern shows counting by 2s.

2, 4, 6, 8, 10

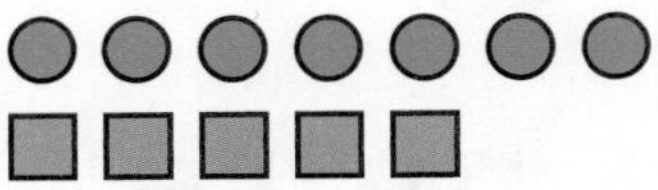

There are more ● than ■.

The subtrahend and the difference, or partners, are the same.

8 – 4 = 4

A number is odd if you can make groups of 2 and have 1 left over.

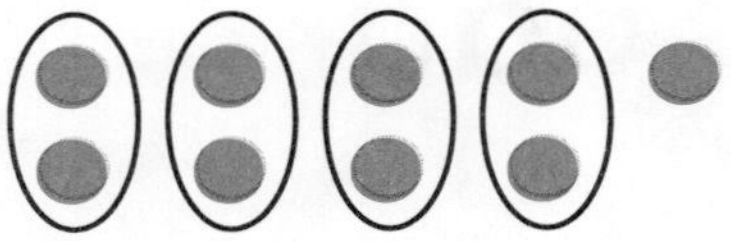

9 is an odd number.

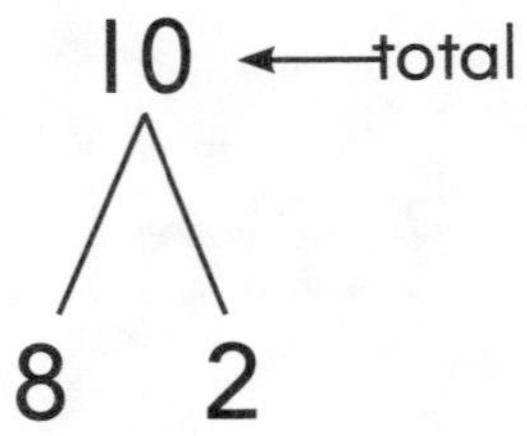

A group of 2 is a pair.

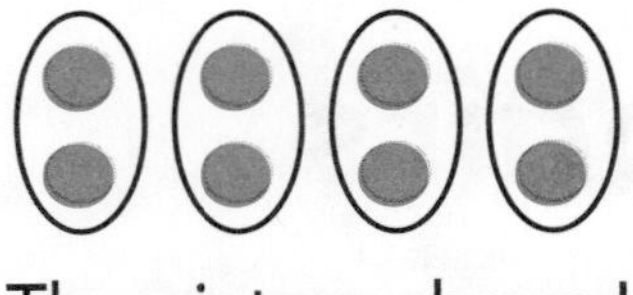

The picture shows 4 pairs of counters.

unknown addend

vertical form

$$3 + \square = 9$$

unknown addend

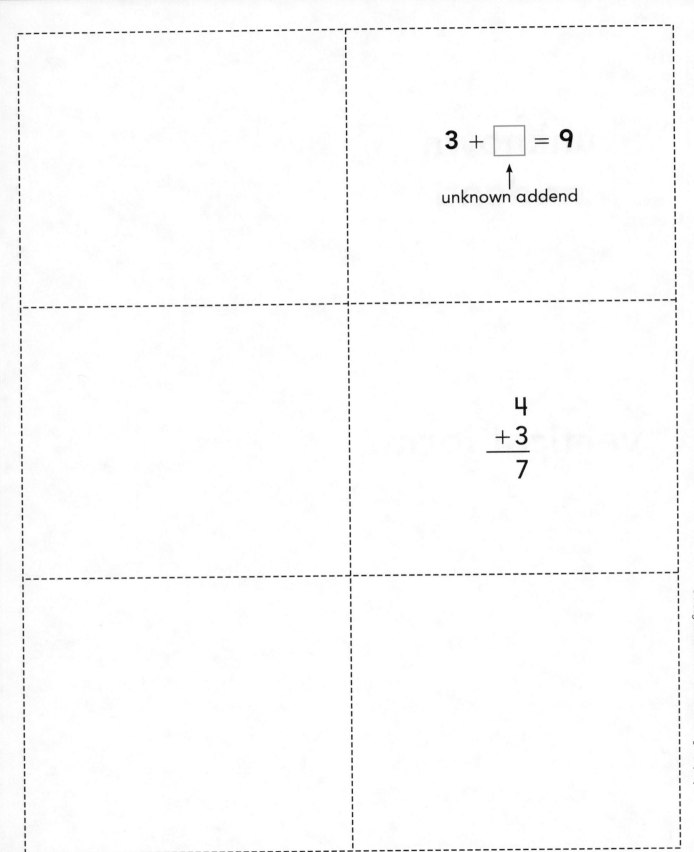

$$\begin{array}{r} 4 \\ +3 \\ \hline 7 \end{array}$$

Name ______________________________

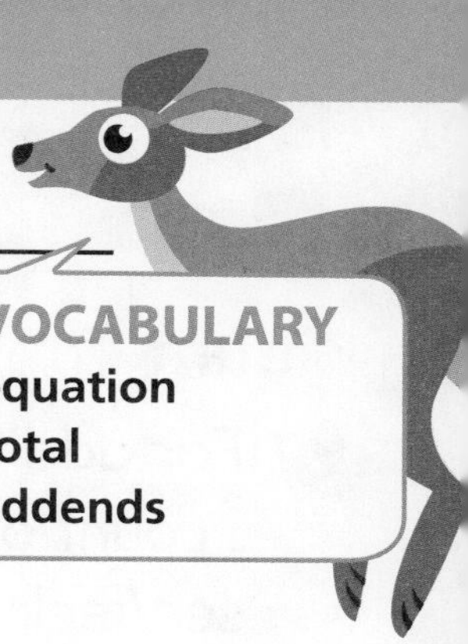

VOCABULARY
equation
total
addends

Relate Math Mountains and Equations for Addition

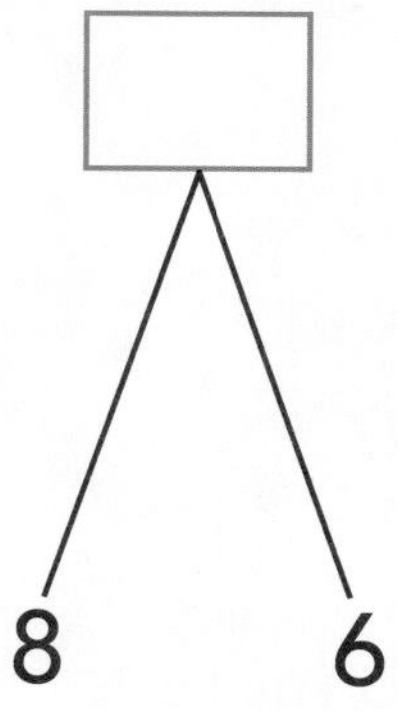

$8 + 6 = \square$

Discuss the Math Mountain and the **equation**.

1. Where is the **total**? Where are the partners or **addends**?
2. Tell word problems for both.
3. Solve both and compare your strategies.

Relate Math Mountains and Equations for Subtraction

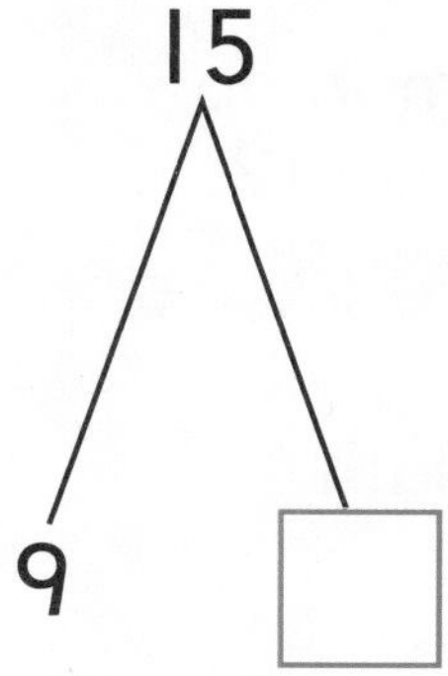

$9 + \square = 15$

$15 - 9 = \square$

Discuss this Math Mountain and the equations.

4. Where is the total? Where are the partners or addends?
5. Tell word problems for all.
6. Solve all and compare your strategies.

CC SS Content Standards **2.OA.A.1, 2.OA.B.2, 2.NBT.B.9**
Mathematical Practices **MP3, MP6**

Count On for Addition or Subtraction

7 For addition, I pretend I already counted 9. Then I count on 3 more to get the total. I stop when I see/feel 3. I hear 12, the unknown total.

$9 + 3 = \boxed{12}$

Already 9 ● ● ● 10 11 12 ← Stop when I see/feel 3 more.

$9 + 3 = \mathbf{12}$

Already 9 10 11 12

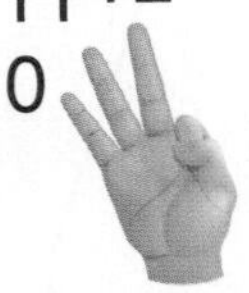

3 more to make 12.

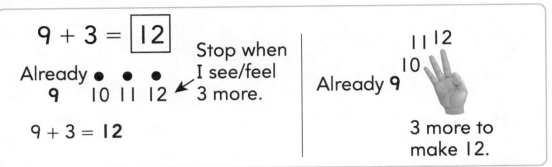

8 For subtraction, I pretend I already counted 9. I count on until I get to 12. I stop when I hear 12. I see/feel 3, the unknown partner.

$12 - 9 = \boxed{3}$

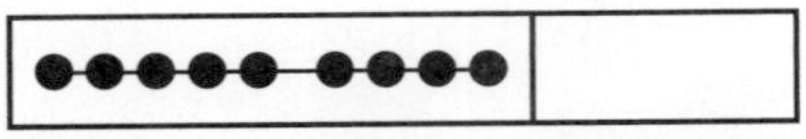

I took 9 away.

● ● ● 10 11 12

3 more to make 12.

$12 - 9 = \mathbf{3}$

I took 9 away. 10 11 12

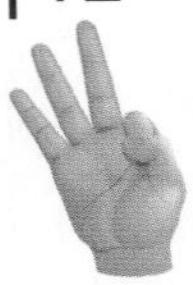

3 more to make 12.

Patterns in Equations

9 Discuss patterns in the eight equations for a Math Mountain with total 12 and partners 9 and 3.

$9 + 3 = 12$ 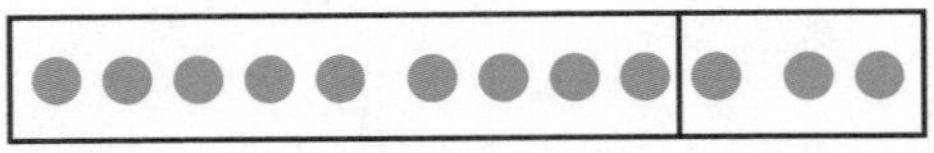 $12 = 9 + 3$

$3 + 9 = 12$ 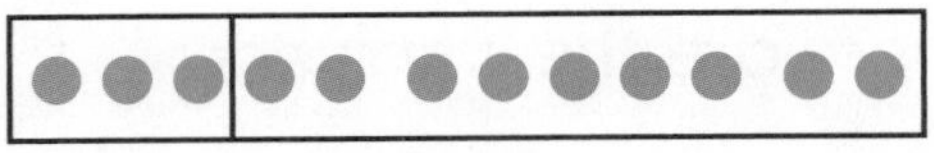 $12 = 3 + 9$

$12 - 9 = 3$ 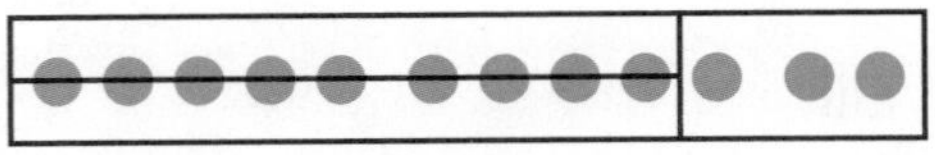 $3 = 12 - 9$

$12 - 3 = 9$ 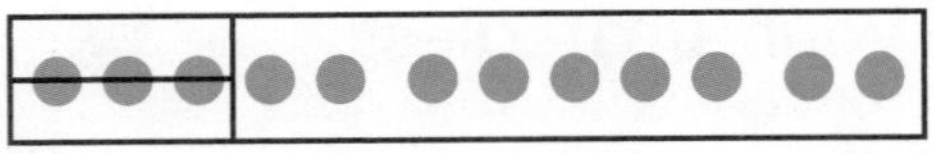 $9 = 12 - 3$

Name ______________________

Write Equations for Math Mountains

Write two equations for each Math Mountain.
Use a □ for the unknown number.

10
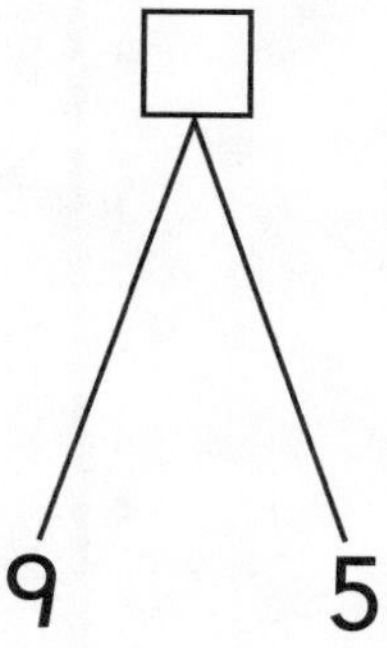

$9 + 5 = \square$

____

____

11
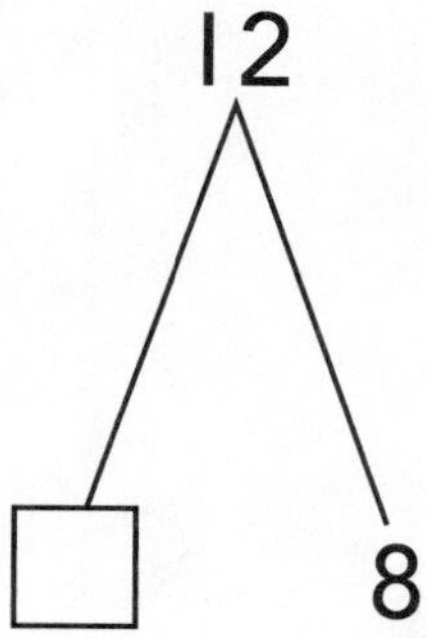

____

____

12
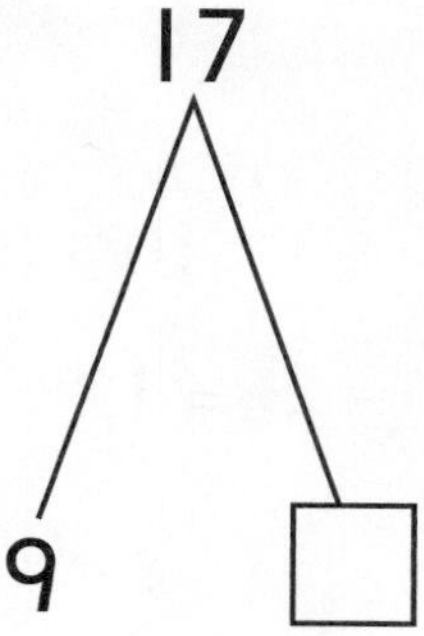

____

____

13
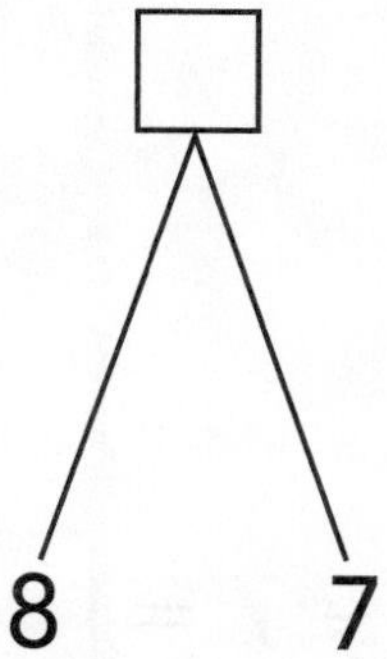

____

____

14
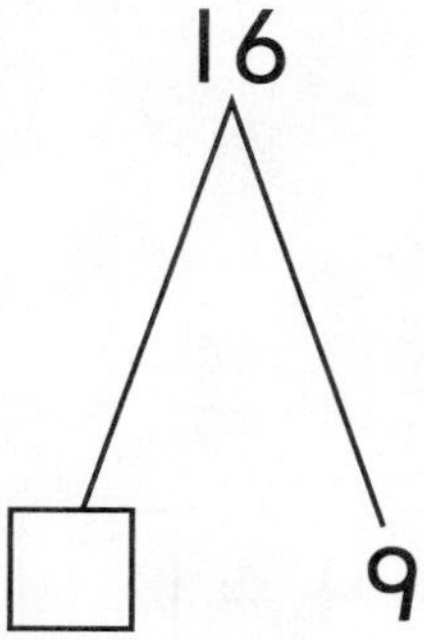

____

____

15
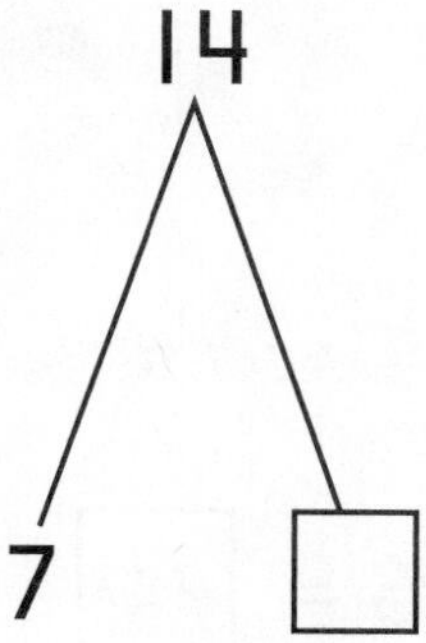

____

____

Draw Math Mountains

Draw a Math Mountain and write one more equation. Use a ☐ for the unknown number.

16

$9 + 6 = \square$

17

$9 + \square = 12$

18

$8 + \square = 16$

19

$5 + 6 = \square$

20

$13 - 4 = \square$

21

$15 - 7 = \square$

Check Understanding

Draw one Math Mountain with all three numbers in place.

Dear Family:

Your child is exploring addition and subtraction equations with Math Mountain Cards. The cards have a large number at the top and two smaller numbers at the bottom. From the cards, children can see that two smaller numbers can be added together to make a larger number. They can also see that a large number can be broken apart into two smaller numbers.

Children will write addition and subtraction equations that they can make from the cards, as shown in the example. The two partners, 9 and 6, can be added to make the total, 15. They can be switched (6 and 9) and still make 15.

$9 + 6 = 15$

$6 + 9 = 15$

$15 - 9 = 6$

$15 - 6 = 9$

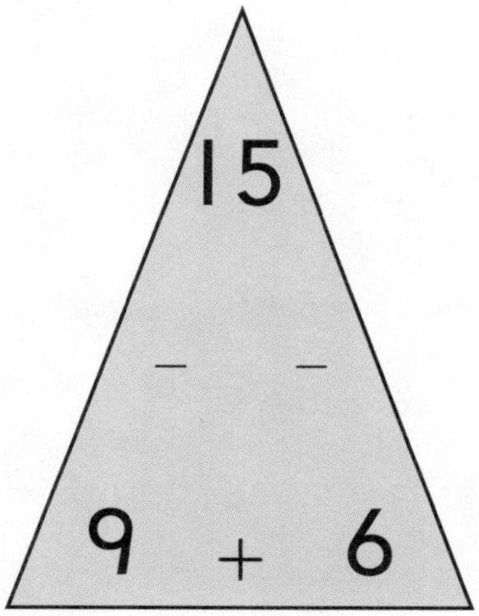

$15 = 9 + 6$

$15 = 6 + 9$

$6 = 15 - 9$

$9 = 15 - 6$

Children see and write all eight equations. It is important for understanding algebra that they sometimes see equations with only one number on the left.

Please contact me if you need practice materials. Thank you for helping your child learn about the relationship between addition and subtraction.

Sincerely,
Your child's teacher

CCSS **Unit 1 addresses the following standards from the** Common Core State Standards for Mathematics: **2.OA.A.1, 2.OA.B.2, 2.OA.C.3, 2.NBT.A.2, 2.NBT.B.6, 2.NBT.B.9, and all** Mathematical Practices.

Estimada familia:

Su niño está aprendiendo ecuaciones de suma y resta usando las tarjetas *Math Mountain*. Las tarjetas tienen un número grande en la parte superior y dos números más pequeños en la parte inferior. En las tarjetas los niños pueden ver que se pueden sumar dos números más pequeños para obtener un número más grande. También pueden ver que un número grande se puede separar en dos números más pequeños.

Los niños escribirán ecuaciones de suma y resta que puedan hacer a partir de las tarjetas, según se muestra en el ejemplo. Se pueden sumar las dos partes, 9 y 6, para obtener el total, 15. También se pueden intercambiar (6 y 9) y todavía obtener 15.

$9 + 6 = 15$

$6 + 9 = 15$

$15 - 9 = 6$

$15 - 6 = 9$

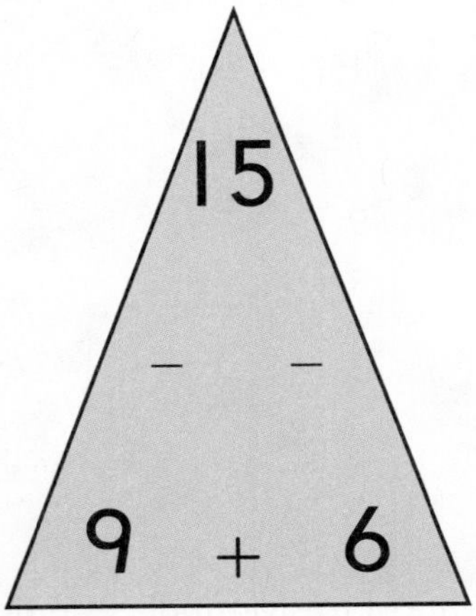

$15 = 9 + 6$

$15 = 6 + 9$

$6 = 15 - 9$

$9 = 15 - 6$

Los niños ven y escriben las ocho ecuaciones. Para comprender álgebra es importante que vean ecuaciones con un solo número a la izquierda.

Por favor comuníquese conmigo si necesita materiales para practicar. Gracias por ayudar a su niño a aprender la relación entre suma y resta.

Atentamente,
El maestro de su niño

En la Unidad 1 se aplican los siguientes estándares de los Estándares estatales comunes de matemáticas: **2.OA.A.1, 2.OA.B.2, 2.OA.C.3, 2.NBT.A.2, 2.NBT.B.6, 2.NBT.B.9 y todos los de** Prácticas matemáticas.

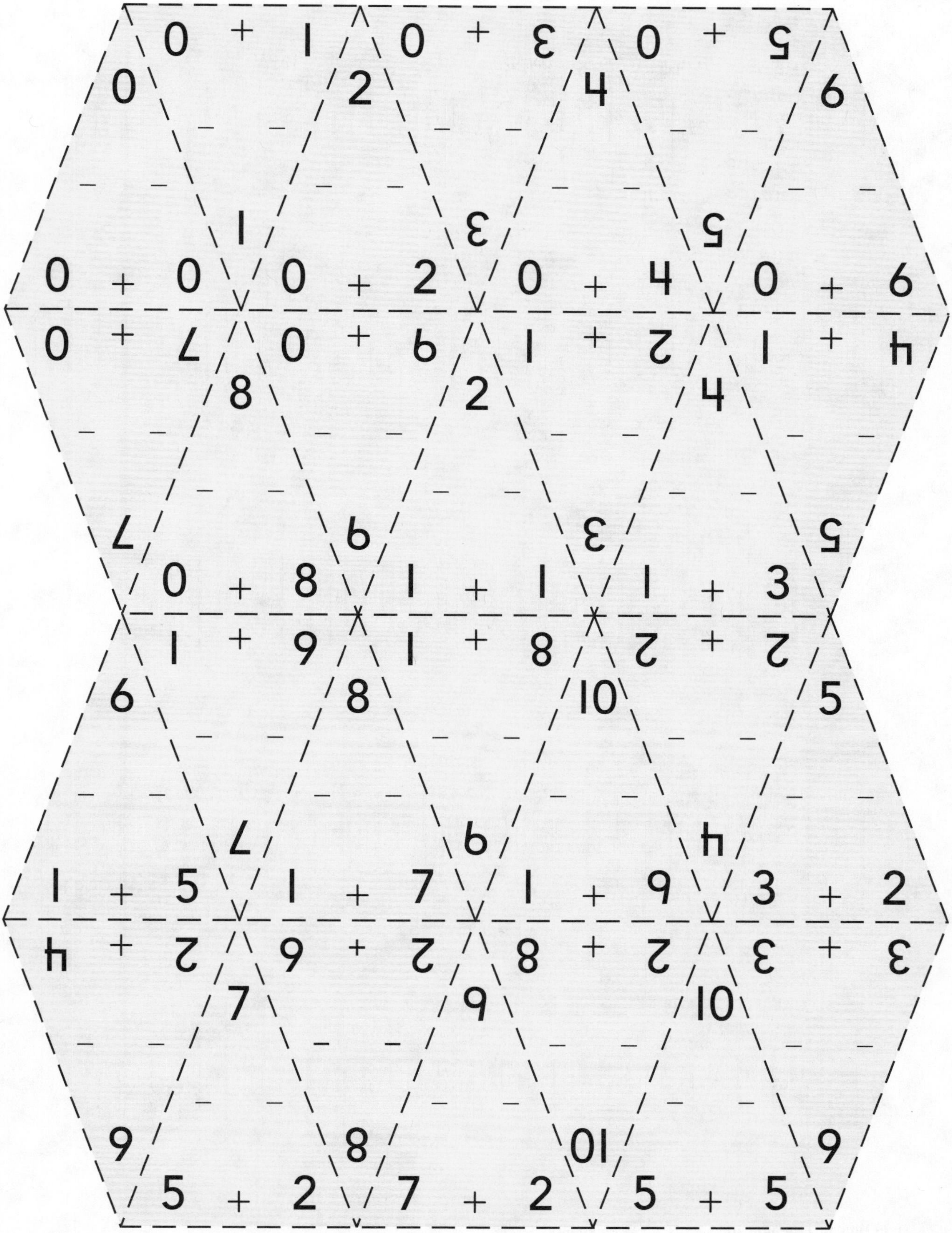

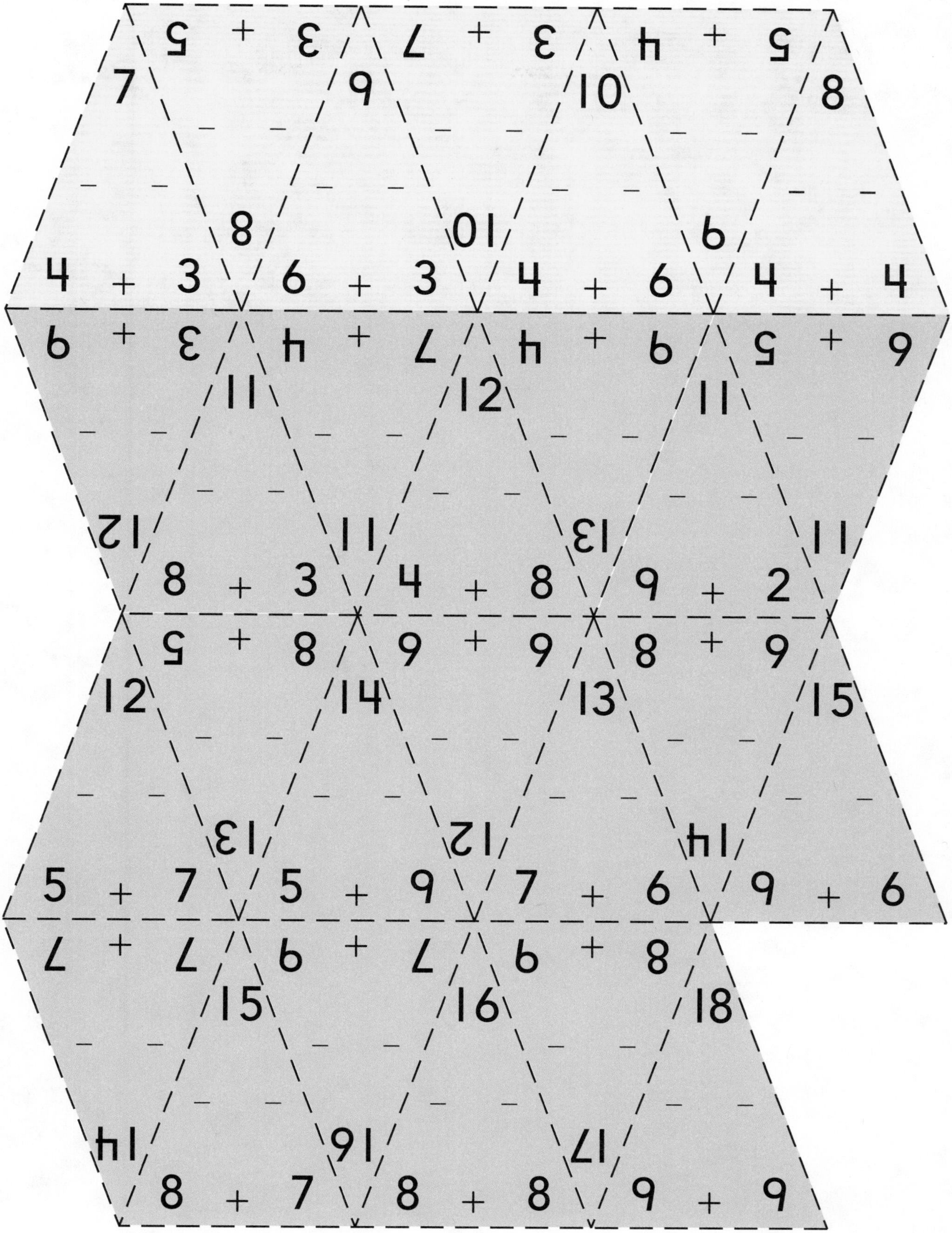
5 + 3
7 + 3
4 + 5
7
9
10
8
8
10
9
4 + 3
6 + 3
4 + 6
4 + 4
9 + 3
4 + 7
4 + 9
5 + 6
11
12
11
12
11
13
11
8 + 3
4 + 8
9 + 2
5 + 8
6 + 9
8 + 9
12
14
13
15
13
12
14
5 + 7
5 + 9
7 + 6
9 + 6
7 + 7
9 + 7
9 + 8
15
16
18
14
16
17
8 + 7
8 + 8
9 + 9

Name ______________________________

Add and Subtract with Math Mountains

Complete the Math Mountain to solve the problem. Complete the equation.

1 Vicki has 8 stickers.
She gives 2 stickers to Judy.
How many stickers does
Vicki have now?

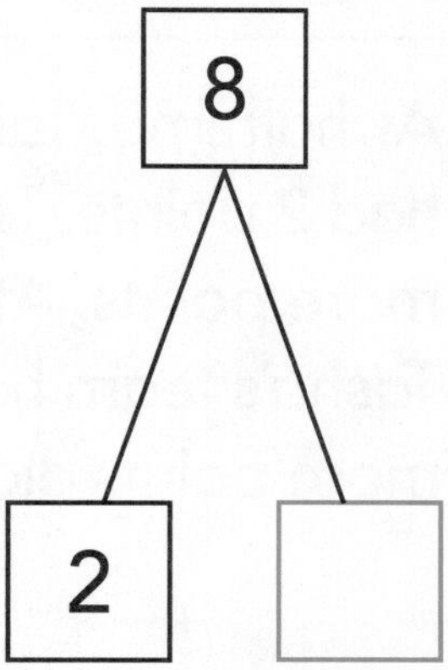

$8 - 2 = \square$ stickers

2 At the park, Rashad counts
4 birds. His sister counts
5 birds. How many birds do
they count together?

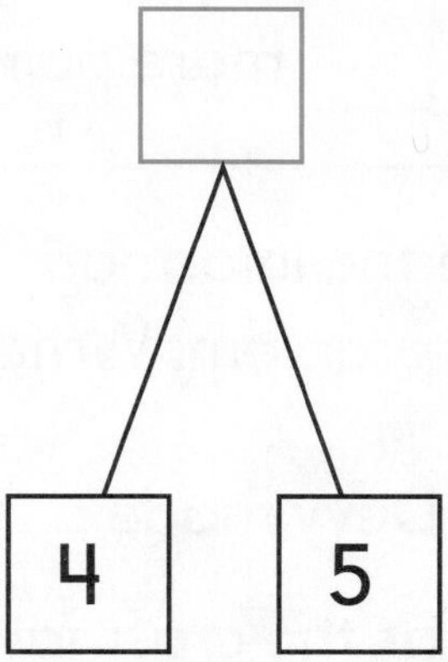

$4 + 5 = \square$ birds

3 Odalis played on the computer
for 10 minutes. Liam played on
the computer for 3 fewer minutes
than Odalis. How many minutes
did Liam play on the computer?

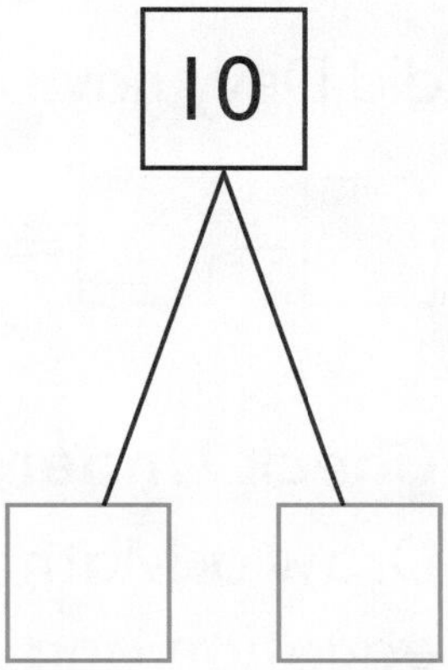

$\square - \square = \square$ minutes

Add and Subtract with Math Mountains (continued)

Complete the Math Mountain to solve the problem. Complete the equation.

---

4 At halftime, Tasha's soccer team had 2 points. Then they scored some more points. At the end of the game, Tasha's team had 5 points. How many more points did Tasha's team score?

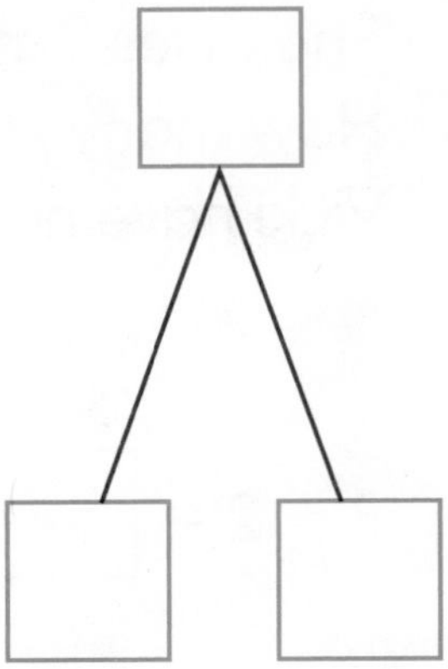

$\square + \square = \square$

$\square$ more points

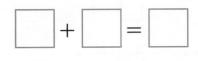

Use the information in the Math Mountain to complete the problem. Write the equation.

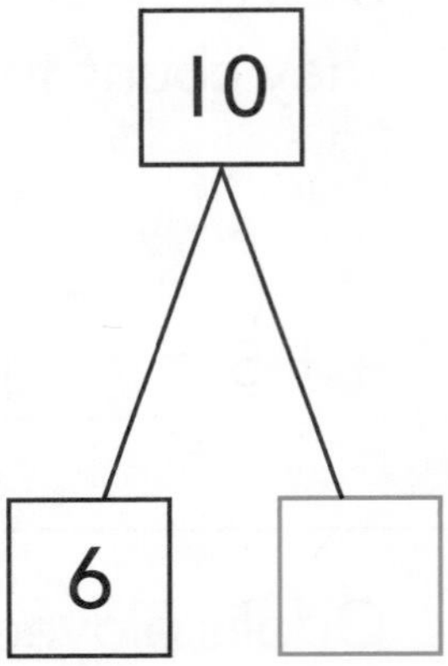

5 Devy made ______ bookmarks to sell at the craft fair last weekend. He sold ______ bookmarks on Saturday. How many bookmarks did Devy have left to sell on Sunday?

$\square - \square = \square$ bookmarks

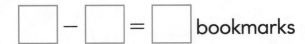

Check Understanding

Draw a Math Mountain. Write one addition equation and one subtraction equation for that Math Mountain.

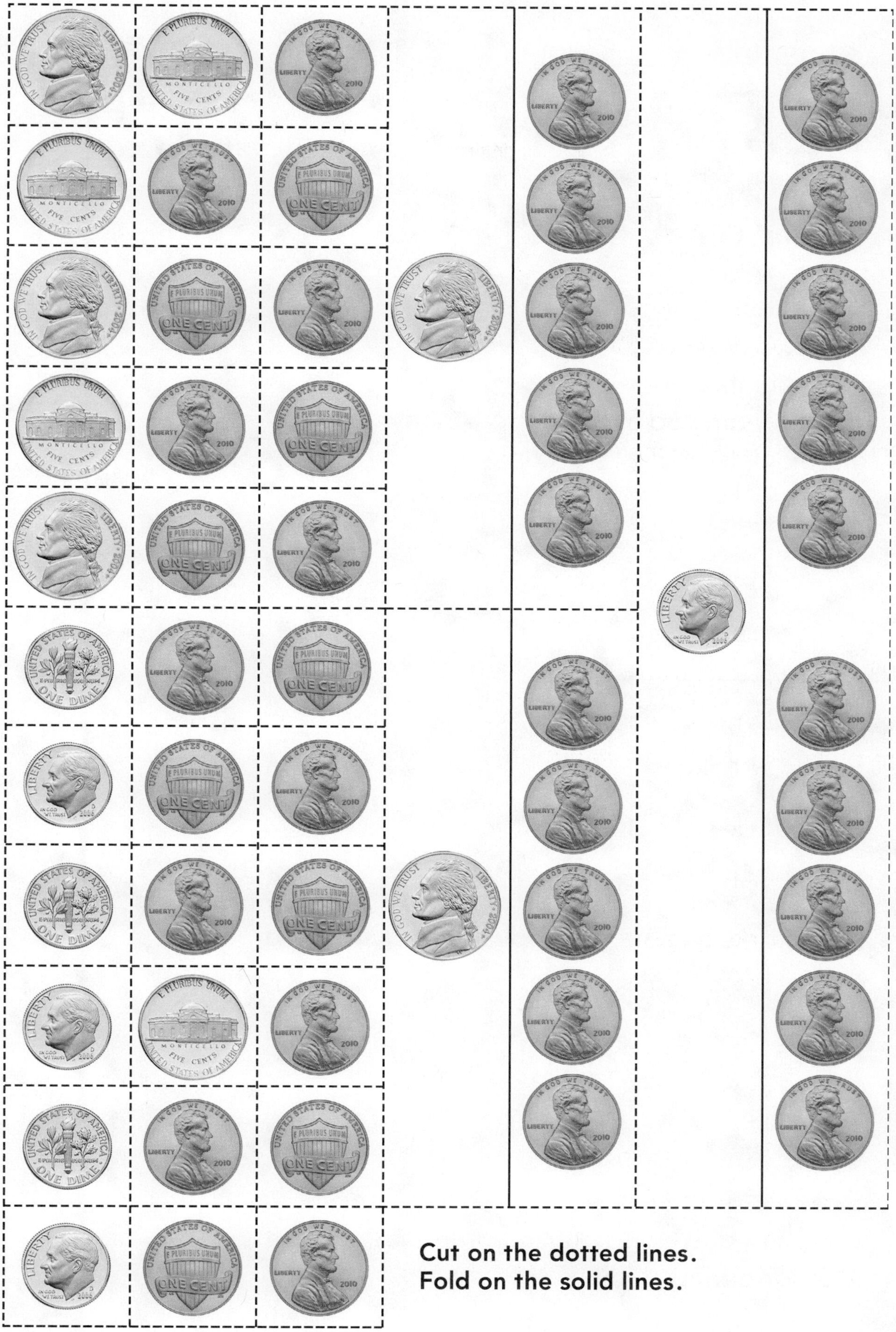

Cut on the dotted lines.
Fold on the solid lines.

Name ______________________________

Make a Ten to Solve

Make a ten to solve. Draw to show your work.
Complete the make-a-ten equation.

1. 7 + 4 = ☐　　10 + ☐ = ☐

2. 5 + 8 = ☐　　☐ + ☐ = ☐

3. 3 + 9 = ☐　　☐ + ☐ = ☐

4. 7 + 6 = ☐　　☐ + ☐ = ☐

5. 6 + 8 = ☐　　☐ + ☐ = ☐

6. 9 + 7 = ☐　　☐ + ☐ = ☐

CC SS Content Standards 2.OA.B.2, 2.NBT.B.9
Mathematical Practices MP1, MP7

Make a Ten with Math Mountains

Complete the Math Mountain.
Write the make-a-ten Math Mountain.

7

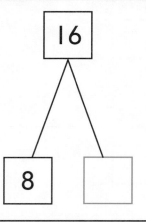

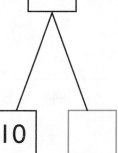

8

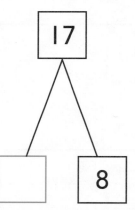

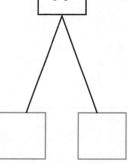

9

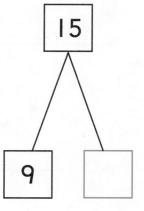

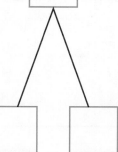

Check Understanding

Show and explain how to use the Make-a-Ten strategy to solve $7 + 5$.

Name ____________________

VOCABULARY
unknown addend

Find the Unknown Addend

$7 + \boxed{5} = 12$

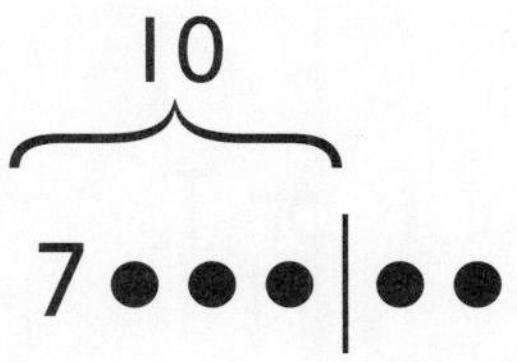

$3 + 2 = 5$

$12 - 7 = \boxed{5}$

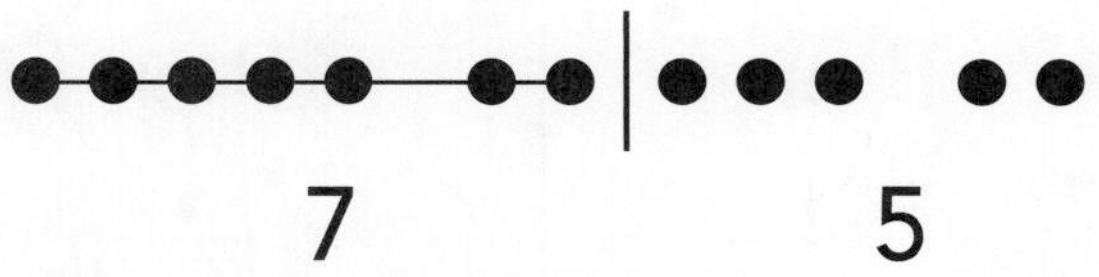

Find the **unknown addend** (unknown partner).

1. $8 + \square = 11$ $15 - 6 = \square$ $8 + \square = 14$

2. $7 + \square = 13$ $12 - 8 = \square$ $3 + \square = 12$

3. $5 + \square = 14$ $16 - 9 = \square$ $9 + \square = 17$

4. $9 + \square = 14$ $18 - 9 = \square$ $7 + \square = 11$

5. $8 + \square = 13$ $13 - 9 = \square$ $15 - \square = 8$

13: 8, $\square$ 13: 9, $\square$ 15: $\square$, 8

6. Find the partner for $11 - 6 = \square$.

Make a math drawing to show what you did.

CC SS Content Standards 2.OA.B.2, 2.NBT.B.9
Mathematical Practices MP1

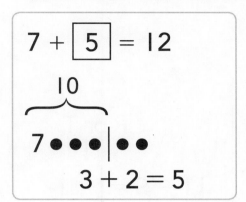

Practice Finding Teen Totals and Unknown Addends

Are we looking for a partner or total?
Circle the P or the T for each column.

Then write each partner or total.

	P or T	P or T	P or T
7	5 + 8 = ☐	7 + ☐ = 11	11 − 9 = ☐
8	4 + 8 = ☐	9 + ☐ = 17	16 − 8 = ☐
9	7 + 9 = ☐	7 + ☐ = 12	13 − 7 = ☐
10	5 + 6 = ☐	8 + ☐ = 16	14 − 7 = ☐
11	8 + 3 = ☐	9 + ☐ = 18	14 − 9 = ☐
12	8 + 4 = ☐	6 + ☐ = 15	12 − 5 = ☐

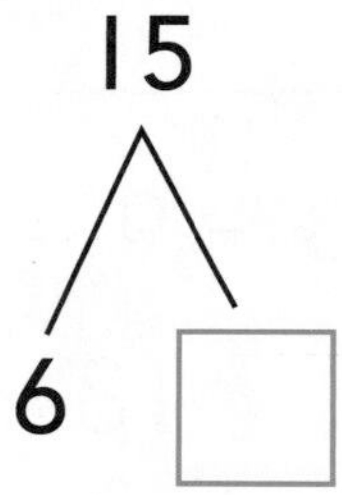

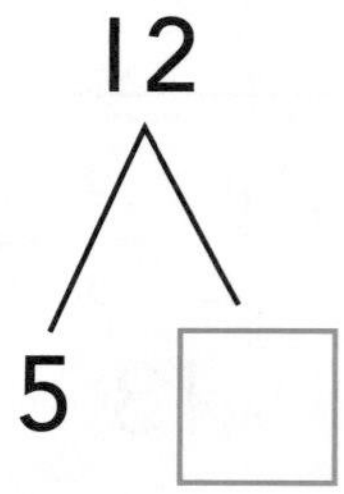

Check Understanding

Explain how to use the Make-a-Ten strategy to find the unknown addend below.

8 + ☐ = 13

Name ______________________________

Equation Pairs and Math Mountains

Find the unknown addend. Draw to show your work.
Complete the Math Mountain.

1 $8 + \square = 15$

$15 - 8 = \square$

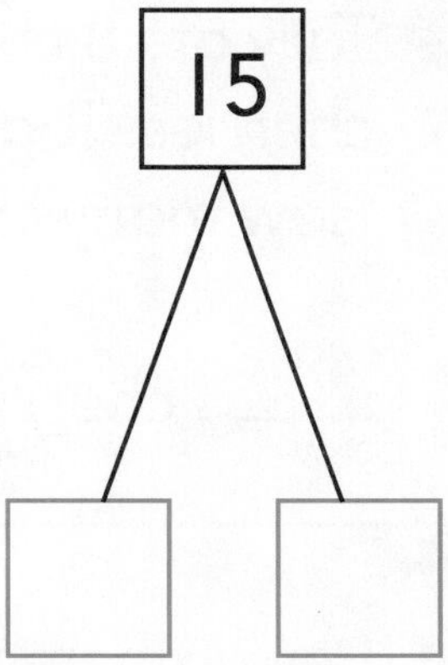

2 $6 + \square = 15$

$15 - 6 = \square$

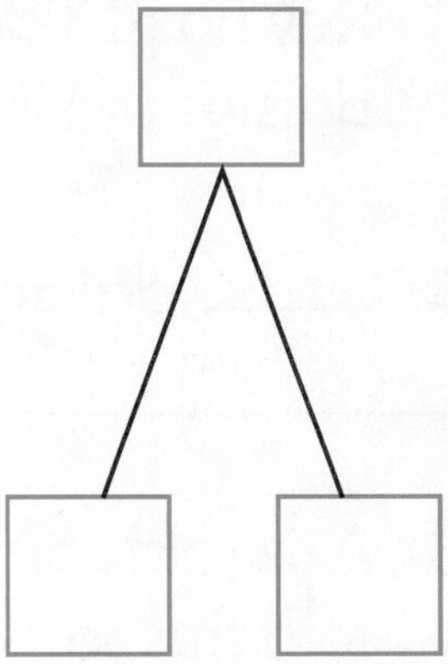

3 $7 + \square = 12$

$12 - 7 = \square$

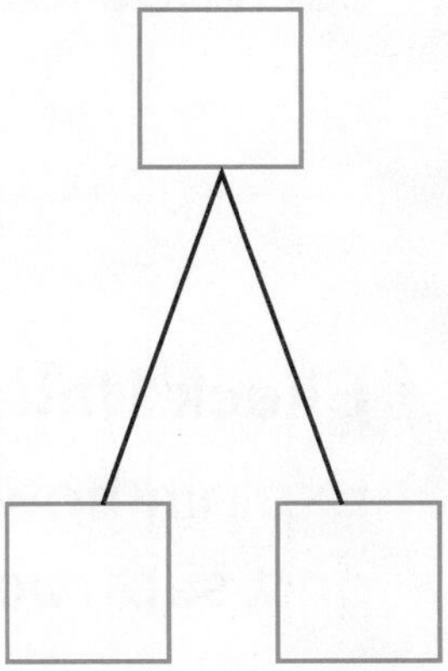

Unknown Addends and Equation Pairs

Read the problem. Write an unknown addend equation and a subtraction equation to solve.

4. Tally ate 8 cherries. Rita ate some cherries. Together, they ate 12 cherries. How many cherries did Rita eat?

$8 + \square = 12$

$12 - \square = 8$

_____ cherries

---

5. Rey gathered some daisies. Ben gave Rey 6 more daisies. Now Rey has 13 daisies. How many daisies did Rey gather?

$\square + 6 = 13$

$13 - \square = 6$

_____ daisies

---

6. Aziz told some jokes. His cousin Harris told the same number of jokes. In all, they told 18 jokes. How many jokes did each boy tell?

$9 + \square = 18$

$18 - \square = 9$

_____ jokes

Check Understanding

Explain how unknown addend equations and subtraction equations are the same.

Name ______________________________

VOCABULARY
pairs

Count by 2s

1 Loop **pairs** of jars.

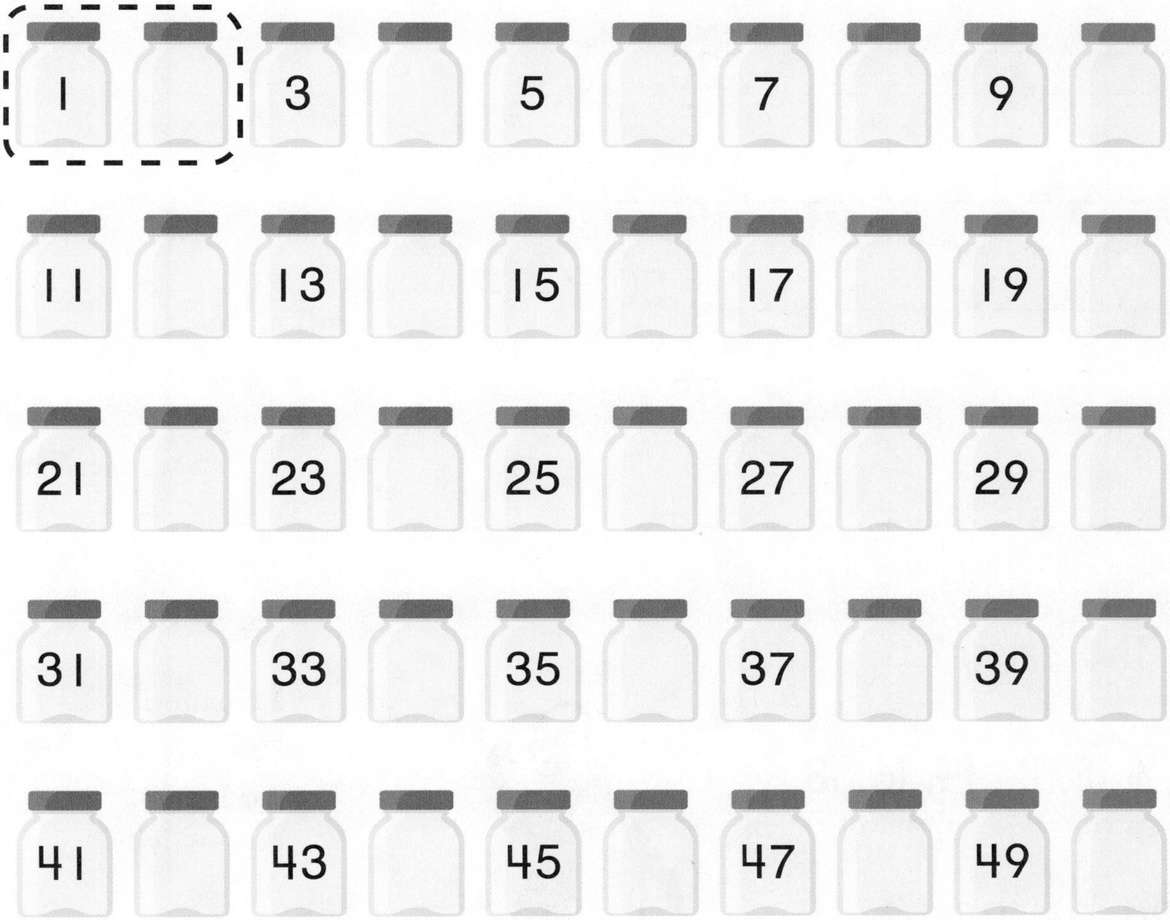

2 Number the jars from 1 to 50.

3 Count by 2s from 2 to 50.

2, ____, 6, ____, 10, ____, ____, 16, ____, ____,

____, 24, ____, ____, ____, ____, ____, 36, ____,

____, ____, ____, ____, ____, 50

Patterns

VOCABULARY
pattern

Count by 2s to complete each **pattern**.

4. 6, 8, ____, ____, 14

5. 12, ____, ____, ____, 20

6. 26, ____, ____, ____, ____

7. ____, ____, ____, ____, 50

8. 50, ____, ____, ____, 58

9. 76, ____, ____, ____, ____

What's the Error?

2, 4, 6, 8, 12, 14, 16, 18,

22, 24, 26, 28

I counted
by 2s to 28.
Did I count
correctly?

10. Show how to count by 2s from 2 to 28.

2, ____, ____, ____, ____,

____, ____, ____, ____, ____,

____, ____, ____, 28

Name ________________________________

VOCABULARY
odd
even

Make Pairs

Draw lines to make pairs.
Circle **odd** or **even**.

11 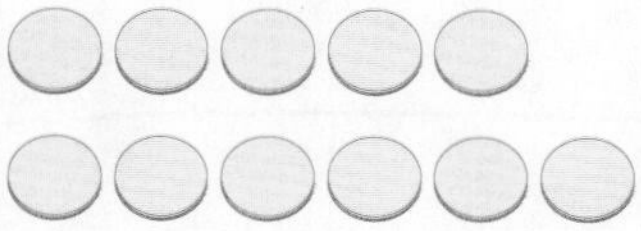

odd even

12 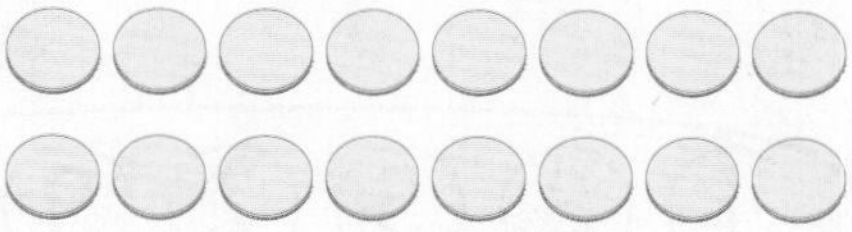

odd even

13 

odd even

14 

odd even

15 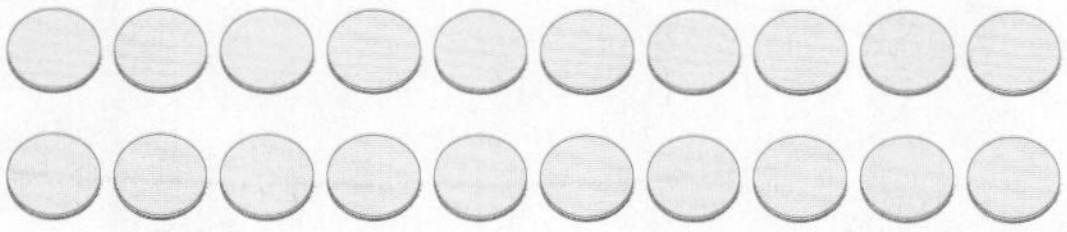

odd even

16 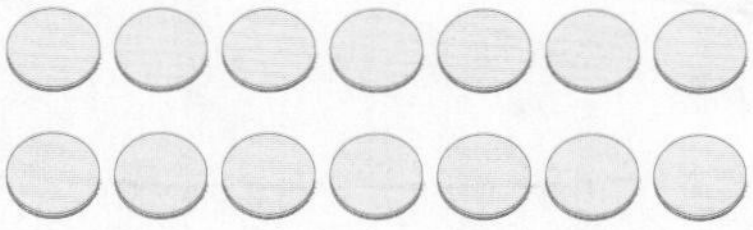

odd even

17 

odd even

18 

odd even

19 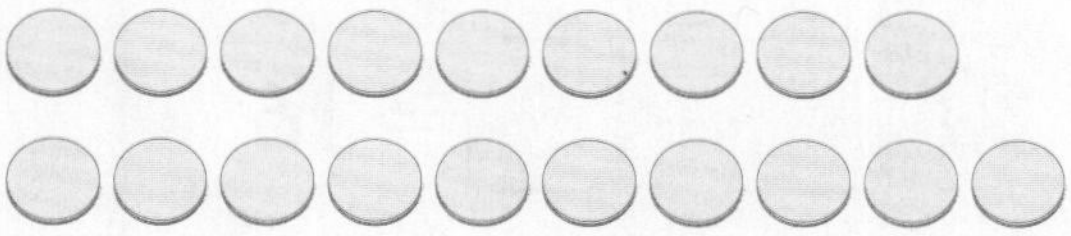

odd even

20 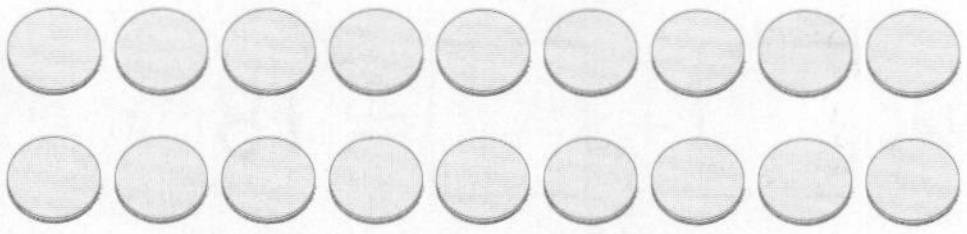

odd even

Make Equal Groups

VOCABULARY
addition doubles

Try to make equal groups.
Circle odd or even.

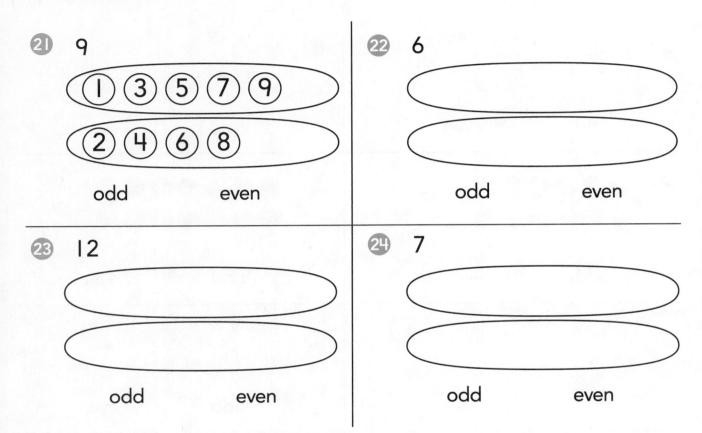

21. 9

(1) (3) (5) (7) (9)

(2) (4) (6) (8)

odd even

22. 6

odd even

23. 12

odd even

24. 7

odd even

Write Addition Doubles

Complete the **addition doubles** equation.

25. ☐ + ☐ = 8

26. ☐ + ☐ = 10

27. ☐ + ☐ = 18

28. ☐ + ☐ = 16

Check Understanding

Show or write two ways to decide if 6 is *even* or *odd*.

Name ____________________

Use Doubles

VOCABULARY

addition doubles	subtraction doubles
doubles plus 1	doubles minus 1
doubles plus 2	doubles minus 2

	Addition Doubles and Subtraction Doubles	Doubles Plus 1 and Doubles Minus 1	Doubles Plus 2 and Doubles Minus 2
1	5 + 5 = ☐	5 + 6 = ☐	5 + 7 = ☐
	10 − 5 = ☐	5 + 4 = ☐	5 + 3 = ☐
2	6 + 6 = ☐	6 + 7 = ☐	6 + 8 = ☐
	12 − 6 = ☐	6 + 5 = ☐	6 + 4 = ☐
3	7 + 7 = ☐	7 + 8 = ☐	7 + 9 = ☐
	14 − 7 = ☐	7 + 6 = ☐	7 + 5 = ☐
4	8 + 8 = ☐	8 + 9 = ☐	8 + 10 = ☐
	16 − 8 = ☐	8 + 7 = ☐	8 + 6 = ☐
5	9 + 9 = ☐	9 + 10 = ☐	9 + 11 = ☐
	18 − 9 = ☐	9 + 8 = ☐	9 + 7 = ☐

CC SS Content Standards **2.OA.B.2, 2.OA.C.3**
Mathematical Practices **MP8**

Use Doubles (continued)

Add. Use doubles.

6. $9 + 9 = \square$ $8 + 6 = \square$ $6 + 5 = \square$

7. $7 + 7 = \square$ $7 + 6 = \square$ $9 + 11 = \square$

8. $11 + 9 = \square$ $6 + 8 = \square$ $6 + 6 = \square$

9. $7 + 9 = \square$ $5 + 5 = \square$ $8 + 7 = \square$

10. $9 + 8 = \square$ $5 + 7 = \square$ $6 + 4 = \square$

11. $8 + 8 = \square$ $8 + 10 = \square$ $9 + 7 = \square$

12. $5 + 4 = \square$ $6 + 7 = \square$ $5 + 6 = \square$

13. $7 + 8 = \square$ $8 + 9 = \square$ $7 + 5 = \square$

Check Understanding

Describe two ways of using doubles to add $8 + 6$.

Name ______________________________

VOCABULARY
equation chain

What's the Error?

1 Help Puzzled Penguin.

$6 + 3 = \boxed{9} - 5$

Use Equations to Make an Equation Chain

2 Solve the equations.
If the answer is 8, color the block  .

$8 + 9 = \square$	$12 - 6 = \square$	$7 + 5 = \square$
$5 + 3 = \square$	$17 - 9 = \square$	$13 - 5 = \square$
$5 + 4 = \square$	$1 + 7 = \square$	$15 - 8 = \square$
$11 - 3 = \square$	$4 + 4 = \square$	$3 + 8 = \square$
$16 - 8 = \square$	$6 + 6 = \square$	$5 + 7 = \square$

3 Use the blocks you colored to make an **equation chain**.

____

____

VOCABULARY
vertical form

Show Three Ways

Write the equation, the **vertical form**, and the Math Mountain.
Use a ☐ to show the unknown number.

4. 8 and 5 make how many?

5. 7 and what number make 15?

6. 18 take away 8 equals what number?

7. 17 minus 8 makes what number?

Check Understanding

Write $7 + 5 = \square$ in vertical form. Then find the total.

Dive the Deep

Name ______________________________

11 − 6 = 5	12 − 6 = 6	13 − 8 = 5
12 − 7 = 5	17 − 8 = 9	15 − 6 = 9
12 − 9 = 3	13 − 5 = 8	11 − 9 = 2
13 − 4 = 9	14 − 6 = 8	13 − 9 = 4
11 − 5 = 6	17 − 9 = 8	15 − 7 = 8
14 − 9 = 5	11 − 8 = 3	14 − 8 = 6
14 − 7 = 7	12 − 4 = 8	12 − 5 = 7
16 − 7 = 9	16 − 8 = 8	11 − 3 = 8
11 − 7 = 4	15 − 7 = 8	13 − 6 = 7
12 − 3 = 9	16 − 9 = 7	18 − 9 = 9
13 − 7 = 6	11 − 4 = 7	12 − 8 = 4

Dive the Deep

11 − 5 = [6]
12 − 5 = [7]
12 − 3 = [9]
13 − 9 = [4]
11 − 6 = [5]
14 − 5 = [9]
14 − 7 = [7]
16 − 9 = [7]
11 − 4 = [7]
12 − 9 = [3]
13 − 6 = [7]

12 − [6] = 6
17 − [9] = 8
13 − [8] = 5
14 − [8] = 6
17 − [8] = 9
11 − [3] = 8
12 − [8] = 4
16 − [8] = 8
15 − [8] = 7
16 − [7] = 9
11 − [7] = 4

13 − 5 = [8]
15 − 9 = [6]
11 − 2 = [9]
13 − 4 = [9]
15 − 8 = [7]
14 − 6 = [8]
12 − 7 = [5]
11 − 8 = [3]
13 − 7 = [6]
18 − 9 = [9]
12 − 4 = [8]

Name ______________________________

Find a Sum of 10

Circle the two addends that make ten. Then write the total.

1. 6 + 9 + 1 = □
2. 5 + 7 + 3 = □
3. 5 + 9 + 5 = □
4. 6 + 4 + 7 = □
5. 4 + 1 + 6 = □
6. 1 + 9 + 4 = □
7. 3 + 2 + 8 = □
8. 3 + 2 + 7 = □

Add in Any Order

Write the total.

9. 9 + 3 + 5 = □
10. 9 + 7 + 2 = □
11. 8 + 9 + 2 = □
12. 7 + 8 + 5 = □
13. 7 + 5 + 2 = □
14. 7 + 7 + 2 = □
15. 3 + 9 + 6 = □
16. 3 + 8 + 2 = □

CC SS Content Standards **2.OA.B.2**
Mathematical Practices **MP2, MP3, MP6, MP7**

Add Four Addends

Add in any order. Write the sum.

17 $4 + 4 + 5 + 2 = \square$

18 $8 + 8 + 5 + 2 = \square$

19 $5 + 5 + 3 + 9 = \square$

20 $3 + 6 + 5 + 4 = \square$

21 $4 + 8 + 9 + 3 = \square$

22 $1 + 8 + 8 + 4 = \square$

PATH to FLUENCY Add and Subtract Within 20

Add.

23 $6 + 8 =$ ____

24 $9 + 9 =$ ____

25 $7 + 0 =$ ____

26 $\begin{array}{r} 9 \\ +\ 7 \\ \hline \end{array}$

27 $\begin{array}{r} 8 \\ +\ 5 \\ \hline \end{array}$

28 $\begin{array}{r} 8 \\ +\ 2 \\ \hline \end{array}$

29 $\begin{array}{r} 9 \\ +\ 9 \\ \hline \end{array}$

Subtract.

30 $\begin{array}{r} 15 \\ -\ 8 \\ \hline \end{array}$

31 $\begin{array}{r} 9 \\ -\ 7 \\ \hline \end{array}$

32 $\begin{array}{r} 9 \\ -\ 0 \\ \hline \end{array}$

33 $\begin{array}{r} 12 \\ -\ 4 \\ \hline \end{array}$

Check Understanding

Which two numbers did you add first in Exercise 20?

____

Which two numbers did you add first in Exercise 22?

____

Dear Family:

Your child is learning to solve word problems called *Add To* and *Take From* problems. These problems begin with a quantity that is then modified by change—something is added or subtracted—which results in a new quantity.

Proof drawings show what your child was thinking when solving the problem. It is important that children label their drawings to link them to the problem situation.

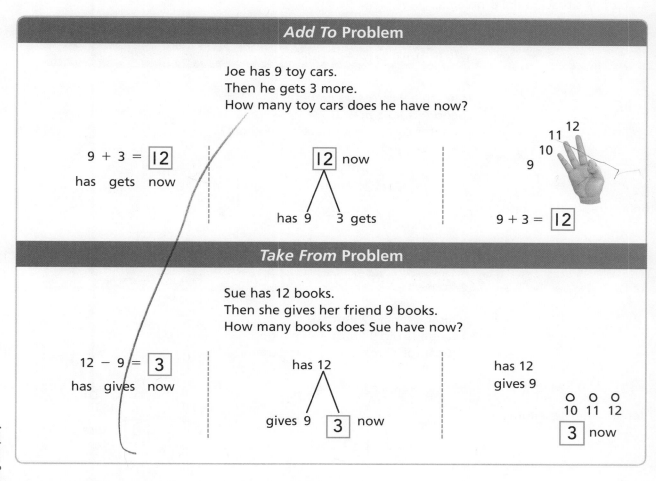

Add To Problem

Joe has 9 toy cars.
Then he gets 3 more.
How many toy cars does he have now?

9 + 3 = [12]
has gets now

[12] now
has 9 3 gets

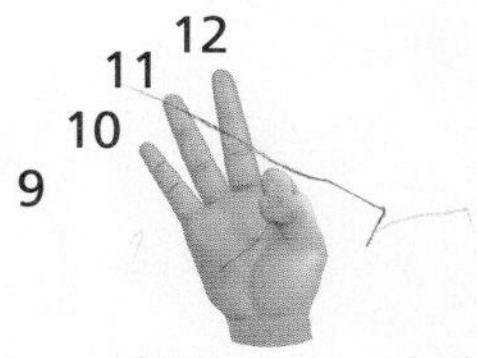

9 + 3 = [12]

Take From Problem

Sue has 12 books.
Then she gives her friend 9 books.
How many books does Sue have now?

12 − 9 = [3]
has gives now

has 12
gives 9 [3] now

has 12
gives 9
○ ○ ○
10 11 12
[3] now

Please contact me if you have any questions or concerns.

Sincerely,
Your child's teacher

CC SS **Unit 1 addresses the following standards from the** Common Core State Standards for Mathematics: **2.OA.A.1, 2.OA.B.2, 2.OA.C.3, 2.NBT.A.2, 2.NBT.B.6, 2.NBT.B.9, and all** Mathematical Practices.

Estimada familia:

Su niño está aprendiendo a resolver problemas conocidos como problemas de *cambio al sumar* o de *cambio al restar*. Estos empiezan con una cantidad que luego es modificada por un cambio (algo que se suma o se resta), lo que resulta en una nueva cantidad.

Los dibujos muestran lo que su niño estaba pensando mientras resolvía el problema. Es importante que los niños rotulen sus dibujos para relacionarlos con la situación del problema.

Problema de *Cambio al sumar*

José tenía 9 carros de juguete.
Luego recibió 3 más.
¿Cuántos carros de juguete tiene ahora?

9 + 3 = 12
tenía recibió ahora

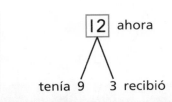

12 ahora
tenía 9 3 recibió

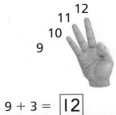

12
11
10
9

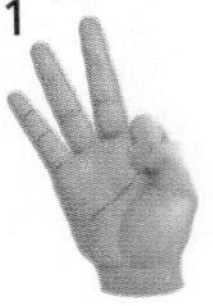

9 + 3 = 12

Problema de *Cambio al restar*

Susana tenía 12 libros.
Luego le dio 9 libros a su amigo.
¿Cuántos libros tiene ahora Susana?

12 − 9 = 3
tenía dio ahora

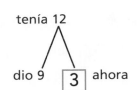

tenía 12
dio 9 3 ahora

tenía 12
dio 9
o o o
10 11 12
3 ahora

Si tiene alguna pregunta o algún comentario, por favor comuníquese conmigo.

Atentamente,
El maestro de su niño

CCSS **En la Unidad 1 se aplican los siguientes estándares de los** Estándares estatales comunes de matemáticas: **2.OA.A.1, 2.OA.B.2, 2.OA.C.3, 2.NBT.A.2, 2.NBT.B.6, 2.NBT.B.9 y todos los de** Prácticas matemáticas.

Name ____________________

Solve and Discuss

Make a drawing. Write an equation.
Solve the problem.

1. The school has 5 computers in the library. They buy some more computers. Now there are 12. How many computers does the school buy?

school

☐ ____________
label

2. Alina has 17 beads. She uses 9 of them to make a bracelet. How many beads does she have left?

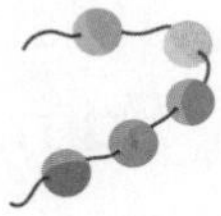

beads

☐ ____________
label

3. Erin buys 6 party favors. She needs to buy 15 favors in all. How many favors does she still need to buy?

party favors

☐ ____________
label

CC SS Content Standards **2.OA.A.1, 2.OA.B.2**
Mathematical Practices **MP1, MP4**

Solve and Discuss (continued)

Make a drawing. Write an equation.
Solve the problem.

4 There are 16 children at the playground. Some children go home. Now there are 7 children at the playground. How many children went home?

children

☐ ______________
label

5 Lila has 6 stickers. Sam gives her some more stickers. Now Lila has 14 stickers. How many stickers does Sam give Lila?

sticker

☐ ______________
label

6 There are 5 deer in the forest. 6 more deer enter the forest. How many deer are in the forest now?

forest

☐ ______________
label

Check Understanding

Choose one of the problems from this page. Write the equation a different way.

____

Name ______________________

Solve and Discuss

Make a drawing. Write an equation.
Solve the problem.

1. Moshe has 5 toy cars. Mary gives him 7 more toy cars. How many toy cars does Moshe have now?

car

☐ ______________
label

2. Heather buys 5 puzzles at a yard sale. Then her brother gives her some more. Now she has a total of 11 puzzles. How many puzzles did Heather's brother give her?

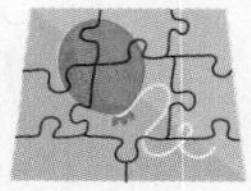

puzzle

☐ ______________
label

3. The cook has 16 bags of potatoes. He uses some to make potato salad. Now he has 7 bags of potatoes left. How many bags did he use?

potatoes

☐ ______________
label

CCSS **Content Standards 2.OA.A.1, 2.OA.B.2, 2.NBT.B.9**
Mathematical Practices MP1, MP3, MP6

Solve and Discuss (continued)

Make a drawing. Write an equation.
Solve the problem.

4. Charisa buys 4 new books. Now she has 13 books. How many books did Charisa have before?

book

☐ ________
label

5. Shahla has 16 dolls. She gives 8 dolls to her sister. How many dolls does Shahla have now?

doll

☐ ________
label

6. Brian has some tomato plants in his garden. 9 of the plants are eaten by worms. 4 plants are left. How many plants did Brian have in the beginning?

worm

☐ ________
label

Check Understanding

Explain how you represented the problem situation in Problem 4.

Name ____________________

Solve and Discuss

Make a drawing. Write an equation.
Solve the problem.

1. There are 13 people in a bike race. 8 people are on top of the hill. The rest are at the bottom of the hill. How many people are at the bottom of the hill?

hill

☐ ____________________
label

2. 4 horses are in the barn. 8 horses are in the field. How many horses are on the farm altogether?

horse

☐ ____________________
label

3. Andrew makes some sandwiches. 6 are turkey sandwiches and 7 are ham sandwiches. How many sandwiches does Andrew make in all?

sandwich

☐ ____________________
label

4. Keisha has 11 cousins. 4 are boys and the rest are girls. How many are girls?

girl

☐ ____________________
label

CCSS Content Standards 2.OA.A.1, 2.OA.B.2
Mathematical Practices MP3, MP6

Solve and Discuss (continued)

Make a drawing. Write an equation.
Solve the problem.

---

5 There are 7 books on the shelf and 5 books on the table. How many books are there?

book

☐ ______________
label

---

6 Mandy sews 8 blue beads and 6 red beads on a ribbon. How many beads are on the ribbon?

ribbon

☐ ______________
label

---

7 Lisa has 5 green pencils and some yellow pencils. She has 13 pencils in all. How many yellow pencils does Lisa have?

pencil

☐ ______________
label

✓ Check Understanding

Circle the correct answer for each exercise.

In problem 5, the unknown is the total. / part.

In problem 6, the unknown is the total. / part.

In problem 7, the unknown is the total. / part.

Name ______________________________

Solve and Discuss

Make a drawing. Write an equation.
Solve the problem.

---

1 Teodor has 12 flowers in a vase. 8 are daisies. The rest are roses. How many flowers are roses?

rose

☐ ____________
label

---

2 There are 13 animals at the animal shelter. 7 of them are dogs. The rest are cats. How many cats are at the shelter?

animal shelter

☐ ____________
label

---

3 Walt saw 4 crows. Then he saw some finches at the feeder. He saw 12 birds in all. How many finches did Walt see?

finch

☐ ____________
label

You Decide

Complete this problem.

4 Juana has 4 ____________ and Bill has 6 ____________. How many ____________ do they have altogether?

☐ ____________
label

Both Addends Unknown

5 Saira wants to put 7 flowers in a vase. She wants to use lilies and tulips. How many of each flower could she use?

☐ and ☐
lilies tulips

$7 = \square + \square$

☐ and ☐
lilies tulips

$7 = \square + \square$

☐ and ☐
lilies tulips

$7 = \square + \square$

☐ and ☐
lilies tulips

$7 = \square + \square$

☐ and ☐
lilies tulips

$7 = \square + \square$

☐ and ☐
lilies tulips

$7 = \square + \square$

Check Understanding

Group some classroom items. Name the group.

Name ____________________

VOCABULARY
more
fewer

Solve and Discuss

Make a matching drawing or draw comparison bars. Write an equation. Solve the problem.

---

1. Ben has 11 library books. If Ben returns 4 books, he will have as many library books as Dale. How many library books does Dale have?

library

☐ ____________________ label

---

2. Shelley washes 14 toy cars. Amir washes 9 toy cars. How many **more** toy cars does Shelley wash than Amir?

toy car

☐ ____________________ label

---

3. Gale has 6 peaches in a basket. If Gale gets 5 more peaches, he will have as many peaches as Carl. How many peaches does Carl have?

basket

☐ ____________________ label

---

4. Rob has 12 markers. Ann has 5 **fewer** markers than Rob. How many markers does Ann have?

marker

☐ ____________________ label

CCSS Content Standards **2.OA.A.1, 2.OA.B.2**
Mathematical Practices **MP1, MP4**

Solve and Discuss (continued)

Make a matching drawing or draw comparison bars.
Write an equation. Solve the problem.

5 Helena has 8 toys. If she gets 3 more, she will have as many toys as Matt. How many toys does Matt have?

toy

☐ ______________
label

6 Martin has 14 plants in his garden.
Jacob has 5 fewer plants than Martin.
How many plants does Jacob have?

garden

☐ ______________
label

PATH to FLUENCY Add and Subtract Within 20

Add.

7 $5 + 6 = \square$ 8 $8 + 7 = \square$ 9 $13 + 0 = \square$

Subtract.

10 $14 - 6 = \square$ 11 $12 - 3 = \square$ 12 $11 - 9 = \square$

Check Understanding

Explain how comparison bars can be used to represent one of the word problems on this page.

Name ______________________________

Solve and Discuss

Make a drawing. Write an equation.
Solve the problem.

1. Bo has 13 books in her bag. Gabrielle has 8 books in her bag. How many fewer books does Gabrielle have in her bag than Bo?

book

☐ ______________
label

2. Alani has 11 stickers. Nat has 3 stickers. How many fewer stickers does Nat have than Alani?

sticker

☐ ______________
label

3. An eraser costs 7 cents. A pencil costs 9 cents more than an eraser. How many cents does a pencil cost?

pencil

☐ ______________
label

4. Linda has 11 cherries. If she eats 4 cherries, she will have the same number as Collis. How many cherries does Collis have?

cherries

☐ ______________
label

CCSS Content Standards **2.OA.A.1, 2.OA.B.2**
Mathematical Practices **MP3, MP6**

Solve and Discuss (continued)

Make a drawing. Write an equation.
Solve the problem.

5 Idris has 8 notebooks. He has to get 6 more notebooks to have as many as Ben.
How many notebooks does Ben have?

notebook

☐ ________________
label

6 Rasha solves 3 more puzzles than Leena. Leena solves 9 puzzles. How many puzzles does Rasha solve?

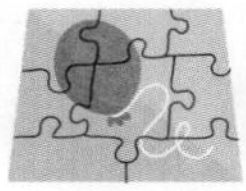
puzzle

☐ ________________
label

What's the Error?

Latoya has 12 buttons. If she gives away 5 buttons, she will have as many as Ron. How many buttons does Ron have?

7 Draw comparison bars to help Puzzled Penguin.

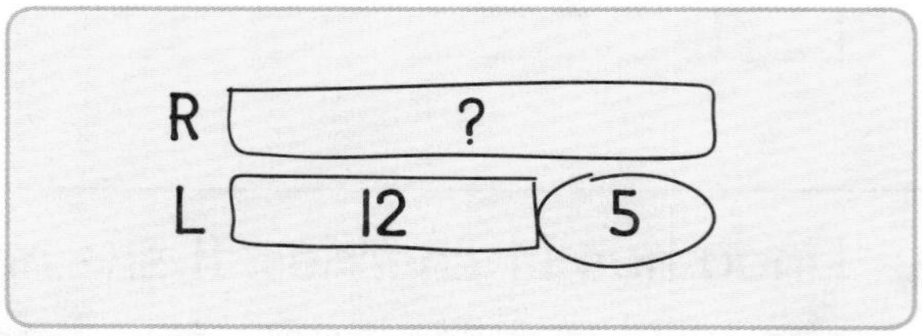

Check Understanding

Choose one problem from this lesson.
Draw comparison bars to show the information in that problem.

Name ______________________________

Solve and Discuss

Make a drawing. Write an equation.
Solve the problem.

---

1. Erica has 13 color pencils. She has 8 at home and some at school. How many are at school?

school

☐ ______________
label

---

2. Joan has 15 toy dinosaurs. Delia has 7 toy dinosaurs. How many fewer toy dinosaurs does Delia have than Joan?

dinosaur

☐ ______________
label

---

3. Ed has 14 puppets. He gives some to his brother. Now Ed has 5 puppets left. How many puppets does Ed give to his brother?

puppet

☐ ______________
label

---

4. Yolanda has a box of tennis balls. Alvin takes 7 of them. Now Yolanda has 5 left. How many tennis balls does Yolanda have in the beginning?

tennis ball

☐ ______________
label

Solve and Discuss (continued)

Make a drawing. Write an equation.
Solve the problem.

5 Meena has 6 cherries. Anika gives her some more cherries. Meena has 13 cherries now. How many cherries does Anika give Meena?

cherries

☐ ________________
label

6 Lisha wants to put 15 apples in a bowl. She wants to use green apples and red apples. How many of each could she use? Show three answers.

bowl

☐ green apples and ☐ red apples

☐ green apples and ☐ red apples

☐ green apples and ☐ red apples

Check Understanding

Complete these statements about Problem 5.

____ is the whole.

____ is a part.

____ is a part.

$5+7=\square$	$6+7=\square$	$9+9=\square$
$8+7=\square$	$9+7=\square$	$3+8=\square$
$4+8=\square$	$5+8=\square$	$6+8=\square$
$7+8=\square$	$8+8=\square$	$9+8=\square$
$3+9=\square$	$4+9=\square$	$5+9=\square$

9 + 9 = 18 9 + 1 + 8	6 + 7 = 13 7 + 3 + 3	5 + 7 = 12 7 + 3 + 2
3 + 8 = 11 8 + 2 + 1	9 + 7 = 16 9 + 1 + 6	8 + 7 = 15 8 + 2 + 5
6 + 8 = 14 8 + 2 + 4	5 + 8 = 13 8 + 2 + 3	4 + 8 = 12 8 + 2 + 2
9 + 8 = 17 9 + 1 + 7	8 + 8 = 16 8 + 2 + 6	7 + 8 = 15 8 + 2 + 5
5 + 9 = 14 9 + 1 + 4	4 + 9 = 13 9 + 1 + 3	3 + 9 = 12 9 + 1 + 2

6 + 9 = ☐	7 + 9 = ☐	7 + 4 = ☐
8 + 4 = ☐	9 + 4 = ☐	6 + 5 = ☐
7 + 5 = ☐	8 + 5 = ☐	9 + 5 = ☐
5 + 6 = ☐	8 + 9 = ☐	7 + 6 = ☐
8 + 6 = ☐	9 + 6 = ☐	4 + 7 = ☐

7 + 4 = 11 7 + 3 + 1	7 + 9 = 16 9 + 1 + 6	6 + 9 = 15 9 + 1 + 5
6 + 5 = 11 6 + 4 + 1	9 + 4 = 13 9 + 1 + 3	8 + 4 = 12 8 + 2 + 2
9 + 5 = 14 9 + 1 + 4	8 + 5 = 13 8 + 2 + 3	7 + 5 = 12 7 + 3 + 2
7 + 6 = 13 7 + 3 + 3	8 + 9 = 17 9 + 1 + 7	5 + 6 = 11 6 + 4 + 1
4 + 7 = 11 7 + 3 + 1	9 + 6 = 15 9 + 1 + 5	8 + 6 = 14 8 + 2 + 4

Unit 1
Quick Quiz 2

Name ____________________ Date ____________

Solve.

Show your work.

1. Jon has some baseball cards. He buys 6 more. Now he has 14 baseball cards. How many baseball cards did Jon have at first?

☐ ____________
label

2. There are 13 children at the park. 7 of the children are girls. The rest are boys. How many boys are at the park?

☐ ____________
label

3. Georgia has 7 fewer books than her sister. Her sister has 15 books. How many books does Georgia have?

☐ ____________
label

4. Jill has 12 stickers. Aspen has 5 stickers. How many fewer stickers does Aspen have than Jill?

☐ ____________
label

5. Timothy had 6 markers. Jake gave him some more. Timothy has 11 markers now. How many markers did Jake give Timothy?

☐ ____________
label

Fluency Check 2

Name ______________________ Date ______________________

PATH to FLUENCY

Add or subtract.

1. $3 + 0 = \square$
2. $5 + 3 = \square$
3. $6 + 1 = \square$
4. $12 - 2 = \square$
5. $8 - 2 = \square$
6. $14 - 7 = \square$
7. $9 + 1 = \square$
8. $6 + 7 = \square$
9. $11 + 9 = \square$
10. $\begin{array}{r} 19 \\ -\ 9 \\ \hline \end{array}$
11. $\begin{array}{r} 20 \\ -\ 18 \\ \hline \end{array}$
12. $\begin{array}{r} 18 \\ -\ 10 \\ \hline \end{array}$
13. $\begin{array}{r} 14 \\ +\ 4 \\ \hline \end{array}$
14. $\begin{array}{r} 12 \\ +\ 6 \\ \hline \end{array}$
15. $\begin{array}{r} 16 \\ +\ 4 \\ \hline \end{array}$

Name ______________________________

Complete and Solve Word Problems

Add information so you can solve the problem.
Then solve the problem.

Show your work.

1. Shannon makes a pitcher of lemonade. She uses 8 lemons. How many lemons does she have left?

pitcher

____

____

☐ ______________
label

2. Sam walks his dog in the morning and again in the afternoon. Altogether Sam and the dog walk 15 blocks. How far do they walk in the morning?

dog

____

____

☐ ______________
label

3. Kari makes a bracelet with blue and purple beads. 6 beads are blue. How many beads are purple?

beads

____

____

☐ ______________
label

CCSS Content Standards 2.OA.A.1, 2.OA.B.2
Mathematical Practices MP1, MP6, MP7

Solve Problems with Extra Information

VOCABULARY
extra information

Cross out the **extra information**. Solve. **Show your work.**

4 The dentist has 8 red toothbrushes and 6 green ones. Then she buys 9 more red ones. How many red toothbrushes does she have now?

toothbrush

____
label

5 Rosa has 5 gold coins and 6 silver coins in her collection. Her brother gives her 7 more gold coins. How many gold coins does Rosa have in all?

coin

____
label

6 Pam has 7 long ribbons and 9 short ribbons. She gives away 5 short ones. How many short ribbons does Pam have now?

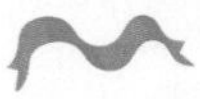
ribbon

____
label

7 Franny has 8 kittens and 2 dogs. 4 kittens are asleep. How many kittens are awake?

kitten

____
label

Name ______________________________

Find Information in a Story

The Zoo

Today my class went to the zoo. I saw 4 elephants and 5 tigers. The giraffes were tall. There were 8 monkeys playing. I counted 13 penguins. I had fun at the zoo.

By Robbie

Use the story to solve the problems.

Show your work.

8 How many more monkeys than tigers did Robbie see?

☐ ______________
label

9 How many more penguins than elephants did Robbie see?

☐ ______________
label

10 How many fewer tigers than penguins did Robbie see?

☐ ______________
label

Practice Solving Word Problems

VOCABULARY
hidden information

Cross out extra information or write missing or **hidden information**. Solve the problem.

Show your work.

11 Mr. Chris and Mrs. Kelly wash 16 cars at the car wash. How many cars did Mrs. Kelly wash?

car wash

☐ ________ label

12 Kat puts 13 markers and 6 crayons in her book bag. When she gets to school, she gives 4 of the markers to her friend. How many markers does Kat have left?

marker

☐ ________ label

13 There are 9 children and a set of triplets in the library. How many children are in the library?

library

☐ ________ label

Check Understanding

Will everyone get the same answer to a problem with extra information? How about a problem with missing information? Hidden information?

Name ______________________________

Solve and Discuss

Draw comparison bars. Write an equation.
Solve the problem.

1. Darnell has 6 pens. That is 5 fewer pens than Natasha. How many pens does Natasha have?

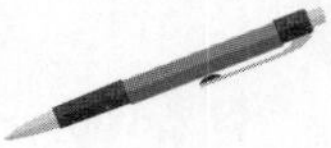

pen

☐ ____________________
label

2. There are 7 tigers at the Smithfield Zoo. The zoo has 9 more lions than tigers. How many lions does the zoo have?

lion

☐ ____________________
label

3. Sherean saves \$7 more in May than in April. She saves \$15 in May. How many dollars does she save in April?

dollar

☐ ____________________
label

4. There are 8 fewer airplane models than boat models at the craft store. If there are 9 airplane models, how many boat models are there?

airplane model

☐ ____________________
label

CCSS Content Standards **2.OA.A.1, 2.OA.B.2**
Mathematical Practices **MP1**

Solve and Discuss (continued)

Draw comparison bars. Write an equation. Solve the problem.

5 Chris catches 15 fish. Sean catches 9 fewer fish than Chris. How many fish does Sean catch?

fish

☐ ________________
label

6 There are 9 more apples in the basket than bananas. There are 17 apples in the basket. How many bananas are in the basket?

basket

☐ ________________
label

7 There are 5 more horses in the barn than the field. There are 12 horses in the barn. How many horses are in the field?

barn

☐ ________________
label

✓ Check Understanding

Look at Problem 5. What is another way to say the comparison?

____

____

Name ____________________

Model Two-Step Word Problems

Solve the two-step word problem. **Show your work.**

1. Lindsay brings in 5 cans for the school food drive. Olivia brings in 4 more cans than Lindsay. Matt brings in 6 more cans than Olivia. How many cans does Matt bring?

a. How many cans does Olivia bring?

☐ ____________________
label

b. How many cans does Matt bring?

☐ ____________________
label

Model Two-Step Word Problems (continued)

Solve the two-step word problem. **Show your work.**

2 There are 14 computers in the school library. 5 girls and 3 boys are each using a computer right now. How many more children can use a computer?

a. How many children are using computers right now?

☐ ______
label

b. How many more children can use a computer?

☐ ______
label

Name ______________________

Solve Two-Step Word Problems

Think about the first-step question.
Then solve the problem.

Show your work.

---

3. Mrs. Hadid has 17 tomatoes. She uses 9 tomatoes to make a sauce. Then she makes a salad with 4 tomatoes. How many tomatoes does she have left?

tomato

☐ ______________
label

---

4. There are 16 robins in a tree. 9 robins fly away. Then 4 blue jays fly into the tree. How many birds are in the tree now?

robin

☐ ______________
label

---

5. Julie has 6 red pencils. She has 2 more blue pencils than red pencils. How many pencils does she have in all?

pencil

☐ ______________
label

Solve Two-Step Word Problems (continued)

Think about the first-step question.
Then solve the problem.

Show your work.

6 Lana had 9 sheep and some horses on her farm. Altogether there were 17 animals. Her grandmother gives her 3 more horses. How many horses does she have on the farm now?

sheep

☐ ____________ label

7 Rafa has 13 marbles. He has 6 red marbles and the rest are green. Mia gives him some more green marbles. Now Rafa has 12 green marbles. How many green marbles does Mia give Rafa?

marbles

☐ ____________ label

Check Understanding

What is the first-step question for Problem 7?

____

____

____

Name ____________________________

Solve and Discuss

Make a drawing. Write an equation.
Solve the problem.

Show your work.

1. Mina buys some new shirts. She returns 4 shirts to the store. Now she has 8 new shirts. How many shirts does Mina buy at first?

store

☐ ____________
label

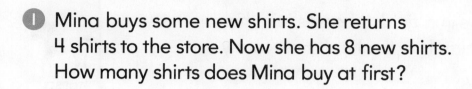

2. Marie buys 8 peaches and a dozen apples. That is 6 fewer peaches than Rubin buys. How many peaches does Rubin buy?

peach

☐ ____________
label

3. There are 15 children in the class play. 9 are boys and the rest are girls. Then 3 more girls join the play. How many girls are in the play?

children

☐ ____________
label

4. Ed buys 9 books at one store and 3 books at another. He buys 8 more books than Brenda. How many books does Brenda buy?

book

☐ ____________
label

CCSS Content Standards **2.OA.A.1, 2.OA.B.2**
Mathematical Practices **MP1, MP3, MP4, MP6**

Solve and Discuss (continued)

Make a drawing. Write an equation.
Solve the problem.

Show your work.

5. There are some cows in a field. 4 horses join them. Now there are 12 animals in the field. How many cows are in the field?

horse

☐ ______ label

6. Rob visits the skate park. He sees 6 skateboards on Friday, 3 skateboards on Saturday, and 2 skateboards on Sunday. How many skateboards does Rob see in all?

skateboard

☐ ______ label

What's the Error?

Felix has 7 white potatoes, 8 purple potatoes, and 5 green apples. He uses all the potatoes to make a soup. How many potatoes does Felix use?

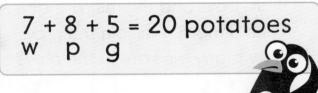

7 + 8 + 5 = 20 potatoes
w p g

7. Help Puzzled Penguin.

Check Understanding

Choose one of the problems from this activity and retell it in your own words. ______

______

15 − 6 = ☐	16 − 7 = ☐	11 − 7 = ☐
12 − 8 = ☐	13 − 9 = ☐	11 − 6 = ☐
12 − 7 = ☐	13 − 8 = ☐	14 − 9 = ☐
11 − 5 = ☐	17 − 8 = ☐	13 − 7 = ☐
14 − 8 = ☐	15 − 9 = ☐	11 − 4 = ☐

11 − 7 = 4 3 1	16 − 7 = 9 3 6	15 − 6 = 9 4 5
11 − 6 = 5 4 1	13 − 9 = 4 1 3	12 − 8 = 4 2 2
14 − 9 = 5 1 4	13 − 8 = 5 2 3	12 − 7 = 5 3 2
13 − 7 = 6 3 3	17 − 8 = 9 2 7	11 − 5 = 6 5 1
11 − 4 = 7 6 1	15 − 9 = 6 1 5	14 − 8 = 6 2 4

12 − 5 = ☐	13 − 6 = ☐	18 − 9 = ☐
15 − 8 = ☐	16 − 9 = ☐	11 − 3 = ☐
12 − 4 = ☐	13 − 5 = ☐	14 − 6 = ☐
15 − 7 = ☐	16 − 8 = ☐	17 − 9 = ☐
12 − 3 = ☐	13 − 4 = ☐	14 − 5 = ☐

$18 - 9 = 9$ 1 8	$13 - 6 = 7$ 4 3	$12 - 5 = 7$ 5 2
$11 - 3 = 8$ 7 1	$16 - 9 = 7$ 1 6	$15 - 8 = 7$ 2 5
$14 - 6 = 8$ 4 4	$13 - 5 = 8$ 5 3	$12 - 4 = 8$ 6 2
$17 - 9 = 8$ 1 7	$16 - 8 = 8$ 2 6	$15 - 7 = 8$ 3 5
$14 - 5 = 9$ 5 4	$13 - 4 = 9$ 6 3	$12 - 3 = 9$ 7 2

Name ________________________________

Solve Problems and Compare Methods

Beren and her friends are making funny face pizzas.

1. Darryl uses 2 green olives for eyes and 9 black olives to make a big smile. How many olives does he use?

   ☐ ____________________
   label

---

2. Sarah uses 6 fewer mushroom slices than Darryl. Sarah uses 8 slices. How many slices of mushroom does Darryl use?

   ☐ ____________________
   label

---

3. When they start making the pizzas, there are a dozen small tomatoes. Darryl uses 2 tomatoes. Beren and Dawn each use 1 tomato. No one else uses any. How many tomatoes are left?

   ☐ ____________________
   label

CCSS Content Standards 2.OA.A.1, 2.OA.B.2
Mathematical Practices MP1, MP3, MP4, MP5, MP6

Problems with Extra Information

Solve. Cross out the information you do not need. **Show your work.**

4. Beren makes a fruit salad. She uses 2 strawberries, 8 blueberries, 7 raspberries, and 3 apples. How many berries does she use?

☐ ____________
label

5. Darryl makes a snack mix. He uses 2 cups of cereal, 4 cups of raisins, 3 cups of dried cherries, and 2 cups of walnuts. How many more cups of dried fruit does he use than cups of nuts?

☐ ____________
label

Write and Solve a Problem

"Ants on a Log" is a snack made with celery, peanut butter, and raisins.

Beren's Snack

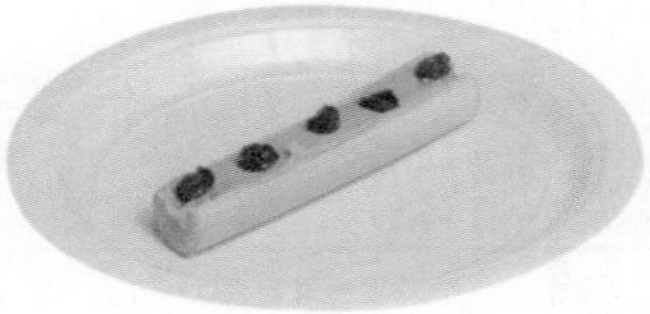

Darryl's Snack

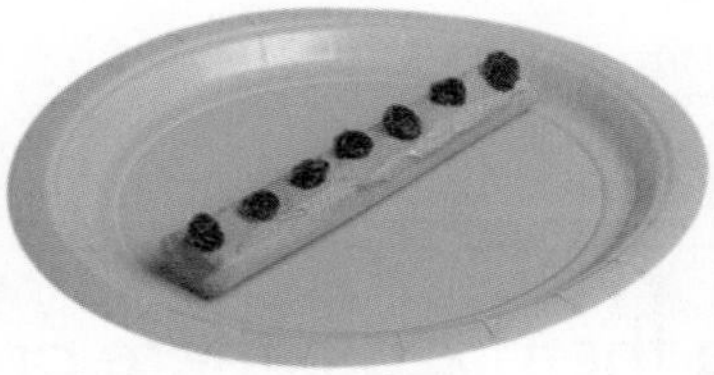

Sarah's Snack

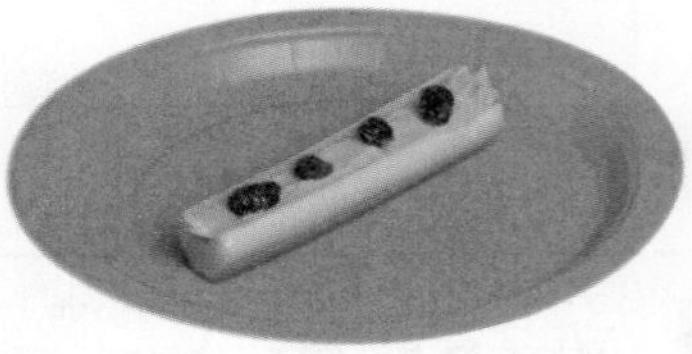

6. Use the pictures. On a separate sheet of paper, write a problem.

   Exchange with a classmate. Solve each other's problem.

Unit 1
Quick Quiz 3

Name ______________________________ Date ______________

1. Add more information so you can solve the problem. Solve.

Kelly makes banana bread. She uses 2 bananas. How many bananas does she have left?

____

2. Write the hidden information. Then solve.

There are 8 children and a set of young twins at the park. How many children are at the park?

____

Solve. **Show your work.**

3. Mrs. Green had 7 science books and 5 history books. Then she bought 8 more science books. How many science books does she have now?

☐ ________________
label

4. Nancy picks 17 apples. Pete picks 9 fewer apples than Nancy. How many apples does Pete pick?

☐ ________________
label

5. Abdul had 14 cards. He had 8 baseball cards and the rest were football cards. Jason gives Abdul some more football cards. Now Abdul has 13 football cards. How many football cards does Jason give Abdul?

☐ ________________
label

Name ______________________ Date ______

PATH to FLUENCY

Add or subtract.

1. $16 - 8 = \square$
2. $11 - 2 = \square$
3. $5 - 2 = \square$
4. $6 + 5 = \square$
5. $2 + 0 = \square$
6. $7 + 4 = \square$
7. $\begin{array}{r} 13 \\ -\ 6 \\ \hline \end{array}$
8. $\begin{array}{r} 16 \\ -\ 9 \\ \hline \end{array}$
9. $\begin{array}{r} 13 \\ -\ 5 \\ \hline \end{array}$
10. $\begin{array}{r} 14 \\ +\ 6 \\ \hline \end{array}$
11. $\begin{array}{r} 10 \\ +\ 8 \\ \hline \end{array}$
12. $\begin{array}{r} 12 \\ +\ 7 \\ \hline \end{array}$
13. $\begin{array}{r} 17 \\ -\ 16 \\ \hline \end{array}$
14. $\begin{array}{r} 19 \\ -\ 15 \\ \hline \end{array}$
15. $\begin{array}{r} 20 \\ -\ 16 \\ \hline \end{array}$

Name ______________________ Date ______________

Write each addition or subtraction in the box below the correct answer.

1 0 + 7   7 + 7   12 − 5   20 − 6   13 − 1

7	12	14

Write the partner or total in the box.

2 5 + 0 = ☐

3 15 − 6 = ☐

4 ☐ = 3 + 8

5 3 + 4 + 6 = ☐

6 7 + 9 = ☐

7 15 − 8 = ☐

8 Is the total 12? Choose Yes or No.

5 + 6	○ Yes	○ No
7 + 5	○ Yes	○ No
12 + 0	○ Yes	○ No
4 + 9	○ Yes	○ No
2 + 10	○ Yes	○ No

Name ______________________ Date ______________

9 Complete the Math Mountain.

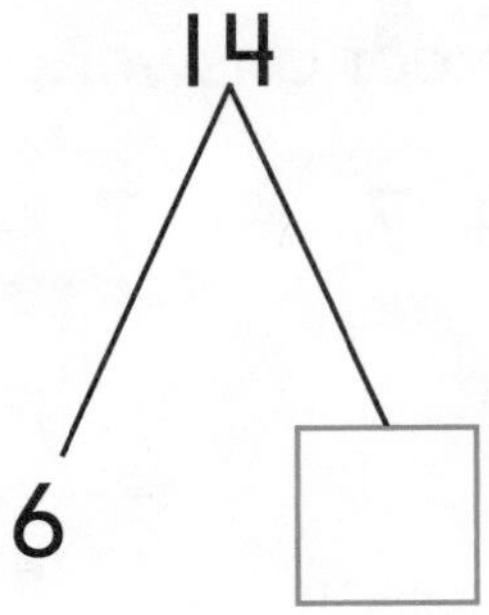

Write an addition and a subtraction equation to go with it.

____

____

How are the equations related?

____

____

Solve.

10 Beth has a bag of apples. She gives 3 apples to Natasha. Now she has 15 apples left. How many apples were in the bag at first?

☐ ______________
label

---

11 Evan finds 12 shells. Aaron finds 5 fewer shells than Evan. How many shells does Aaron find?

☐ ______________
label

Name ______________________ Date ____________

12 Make a drawing. Write an equation.
Solve the problem.

Linda sees 18 cows and 12 horses in a field.
There are 8 brown cows. The rest are white.
How many cows are white?

☐ ______________
label

13 Choose an even number. Write a doubles addition equation with your number. Explain how you know the total is even.

____

____

14 Match each addition or subtraction to the correct answer.

2 + 4 + 6 •	• 9
16 − 8 •	• 12
13 + 7 •	• 20
14 − 5 •	• 8

Name ______________________ Date ______

Solve. Circle the correct answer.

15 There are some frogs on a rock.
Then 9 more frogs jump on the rock.
Now there are 14 frogs.
How many frogs were on the rock at first?

There were [5 / 6 / 13] frogs on the rock at first.

---

16 There are 6 basketballs, 3 footballs, and 9 baseballs on the playground. How many balls are on the playground?

There are [16 / 18 / 19] balls on the playground.

Draw comparison bars. Write an equation.
Solve the problem.

17 Madison has 11 grapes in a bowl.
Hailey has 5 more grapes than Madison.
How many grapes does Hailey have?

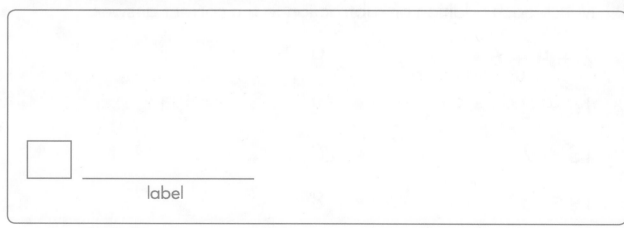

☐ ______________
label

Name ______________________

At the Pond

Choose any method to solve the problem. **Show your work.**

1. 3 ducks are in the pond. Then 6 more ducks jump in the pond. Later, 7 more ducks jump in. How many ducks are in the pond now?

☐ ______________
label

2. Choose one of these numbers for each ◯.

3 7

There are 16 turtles sitting near the pond.

◯ turtles went away.

How many turtles are left?

☐ ______________
label

◯ more turtles went away.

How many turtles are left?

☐ ______________
label

3. Did you use a different method when you subtracted 7 than when you subtracted 3? Explain.

____

____

____

Name ______________________________

4 Sonia and Amy each collected leaves at the pond.
Together they collected 19 leaves.

How many leaves did each girl collect?
Write 3 different possible answers.

__________ and __________
Sonia Amy

OR

__________ and __________
Sonia Amy

OR

__________ and __________
Sonia Amy

5 Pick one of the ways you showed above.
Complete the equation to show how many more leaves one girl collected than the other girl.

__________ – __________ = __________

Make a drawing to show your equation is correct.

expanded form

is less than (<)

is equal to (=)

number name

is greater than (>)

45 $<$ **46**

45 is less than 46.

283 = 200 + 80 + 3

12

twelve ⟵ number name

5 + 3 = 8

5 plus 3 is equal to 8.

34 $>$ **25**

34 is greater than 25.

Unit 2 • **Lesson 1**

Name ______________________________

Write the Numbers 101 to 200

1 Write the numbers going down to see the tens.

101	111								
102	112	122			152				
103	113					163			193
104	114			144					
105	115							185	
106	116				156				
107	117								
108	118	128							
109	119							189	
110	120			150		170			200

CC SS Content Standards **2.OA.A.1, 2.NBT.A.1, 2.NBT.A.2, 2.NBT.A.3**
Mathematical Practices **MP1, MP4, MP7**

Word Problem Practice: Addition and Subtraction Within 20

Solve. **Show your work.**

---

2 Sara has some marbles. Shane gives her 8 more marbles. Now Sara has 17 marbles. How many marbles did Sara have at first?

marbles

☐ marbols
label

---

3 There are 14 children on the soccer field. There are 8 boys, and the rest are girls. Then 2 girls leave the soccer field. How many girls are on the soccer field now?

soccer field

☐ ______
label

---

4 In the lunchroom, 16 children have apples. 9 of these children have red apples, and the rest have green apples. Then 5 more children come with green apples. How many children have green apples now?

apple

☐ ______
label

✓ Check Understanding

Describe the number 106 in two different ways.

Name Lucas Stryker

Add Tens or Ones

Add.

1 10 + 20 = 30	70 + 20 = 90	60 + 30 = 80
1 + 2 = 3	7 + 2 = 9	6 + 3 = 8
2 20 + 70 = 90	30 + 50 = 80	40 + 50 = 90
2 + 7 = 9	3 + 5 = 8	4 + 5 = 9
3 30 + 60 = 80	20 + 80 = 100	50 + 40 = 90
3 + 6 = 8	2 + 8 = 10	5 + 4 = 9
4 50 + 50 = 100	80 + 20 = 100	40 + 60 = 100
5 + 5 = 10	8 + 2 = 10	4 + 6 = 10
5 90 + 10 = 100	90 + 20 = 110	40 + 30 = 70
9 + 1 = 10	9 + 2 = 11	4 + 3 = 7
6 50 + 20 = 70	20 + 30 = 50	60 + 70 = 300
5 + 2 = 7	2 + 3 = 5	6 + 7 = 13

Word Problem Practice: Addition and Subtraction Within 20

Solve. **Show your work.**

7 Some crayons are on the table.
Mrs. Spain takes 5 of the crayons.
Now there are 8 crayons on the table.
How many crayons were on the table before?

crayon

12 crayons
label

8 The jewelry store has 8 red bracelets and some blue bracelets. There are 15 bracelets in all. Then 3 blue bracelets are sold. How many blue bracelets are still in the store?

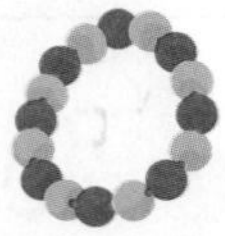
bracelet

4 bracelets
label

9 Mr. Rivera bakes 7 banana muffins and 9 orange muffins. He gives some muffins to his friends. Now he has 8 muffins. How many muffins does he give to his friends?

muffin

8 muffins
label

Check Understanding
Draw Quick Tens and circles to represent 79.

Name ______________________

VOCABULARY
expanded form

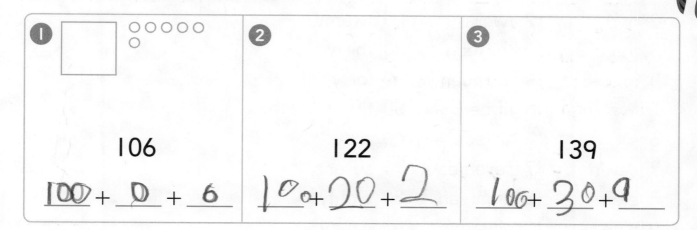

Hundreds, Tens, and Ones

Draw the number using boxes, 10-sticks, and circles.
Then write the expanded form.

1

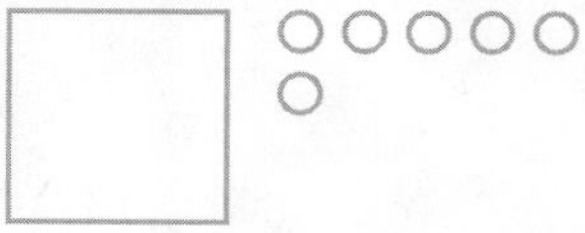

106

100 + 0 + 6

2

122

100 + 20 + 2

3

139

100 + 30 + 9

What number is shown? H = Hundreds, T = Tens, O = Ones

4

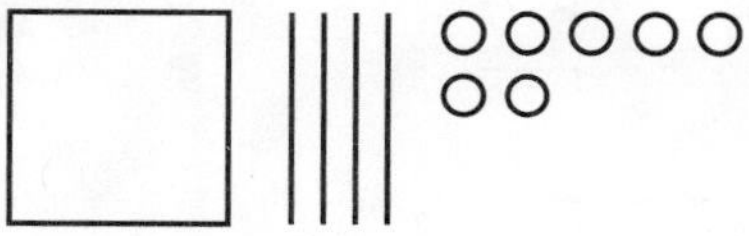

1 H 4 T 7 O

147 = 100 + 40 + 7

5

1 H 7 T 1 O

171 = 1 + 7 + 1

6

1 H 6 T 0 O

160 = 1 + 6 + 0

7

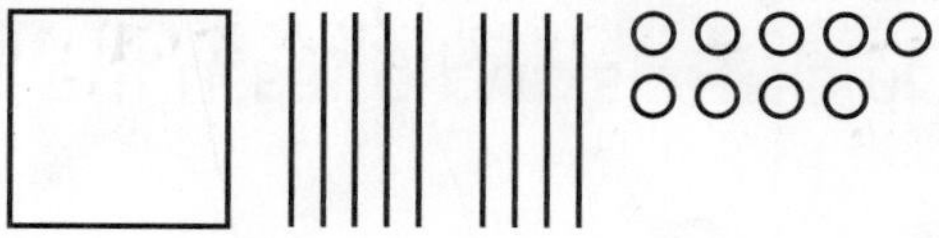

1 H 9 T 9 O

199 = 1 + 9 + 9

Content Standards 2.NBT.A.1, 2.NBT.A.2, 2.NBT.A.3
Mathematical Practices MP7

Read and Write Number Names

VOCABULARY
number name

1 one	11 eleven	10 ten	100 one hundred
2 two	12 twelve	20 twenty	
3 three	13 thirteen	30 thirty	
4 four	14 fourteen	40 forty	
5 five	15 fifteen	50 fifty	
6 six	16 sixteen	60 sixty	
7 seven	17 seventeen	70 seventy	
8 eight	18 eighteen	80 eighty	
9 nine	19 nineteen	90 ninety	

Write the number.

8 thirty-five 35

9 seventy-two 72

10 fifty-four 54

11 eighty-nine 89

Write the **number name**.

12 47 47

13 62 62

14 85 85

15 94 94

Represent Write the number name, then draw Quick Tens and ones in the box.

16 60 60

17 72 72

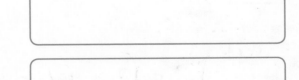

Check Understanding

Explain how to represent 132 in expanded form.

Name ______________________________

Word Problems with Groups of Ten

Solve. Make a proof drawing.

1. Remah has 34 stickers. Only 10 stickers fit on a page in her sticker book. How many pages can she fill with stickers? How many stickers will be left over?

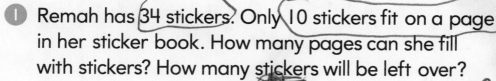

   [3] pages   [4] stickers left over

2. David has 42 beads. He wants to make some necklaces that use 10 beads each. How many necklaces can he make? How many beads will be left over?

   [4] necklaces   [2] beads left over

3. The team wants to buy T-shirts that cost 10 dollars each. They have 57 dollars. How many T-shirts can they buy? How many dollars will be left over?

   [5] T-shirts   [7] dollars left over

4. There are 163 apples at the fruit stand. Each basket can hold 10 apples. How many baskets can be filled with apples? How many apples will be left over?

   [16] baskets   [3] apples left over

CC SS Content Standards **2.NBT.A.1, 2.NBT.A.1.a, 2.NBT.A.3, 2.NBT.B.5, 2.NBT.B.7, 2.NBT.B.8** Mathematical Practices **MP1, MP4, MP7**

Add 1, 10, or 100

Add.

5. 38 + 1 = 39
6. 9 + 10 = 0
7. 24 + 100 = 200
8. 150 + 1 = 0
9. 7 + 100 = 107
10. 92 + 10 = ______
11. 59 + 1 = 20
12. 166 + 10 = ______
13. 10 + 10 = 20
14. 143 + 1 = ______
15. 98 + 100 = 900
16. 46 + 10 = ______
17. 11 + 100 = 1091
18. 195 + 1 = 1000
19. 104 + 10 = 1000
20. 30 + 100 = 300

Check Understanding

Draw to show how to find the total for 58 + 10.

Name ______________________________

VOCABULARY
is less than (<)
is greater than (>)
is equal to (=)

Use Drawings to Compare Numbers

Use these symbols to compare numbers.

< is less than   > is greater than   = is equal to

Make a drawing for each number. Write <, >, or =.

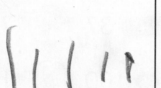

1. 56 (<) 81
2. 123 (>) 109
3. 101 (=) 101
4. 98 (<) 150
5. 67 (<) 76
6. 120 (>) 102

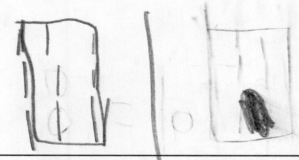

Compare Numbers

Write $<$, $>$, or $=$.

7. 135 ($<$) 137
8. 83 ($=$) 83
9. 119 ($>$) 87
10. 127 ($<$) 172
11. 62 ($>$) 57
12. 51 ($>$) 15
13. 111 ($=$) 111
14. 37 ($<$) 74
15. 192 ($>$) 191
16. 100 ($>$) 10

What's the Error?

149 ($>$) 176

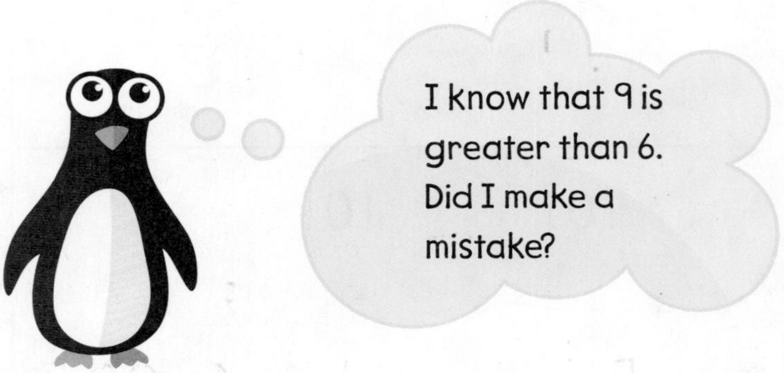
I know that 9 is greater than 6. Did I make a mistake?

17. Make a proof drawing to help Puzzled Penguin. Write $<$, $>$, or $=$.

149 ($<$) 176

Check Understanding

When comparing two 3-digit numbers, which place value position should be compared first? Circle your answer.

hundreds tens ones

Dear Family:

Your child is now learning how to add 2-digit numbers. The "big mystery" in adding is making a new ten or a new hundred. Children can write this new group in several ways.

Show All Totals	New Groups Below
45 + 28 Add tens. → 60 Add ones. → 13 73 Find total tens. Find total ones. 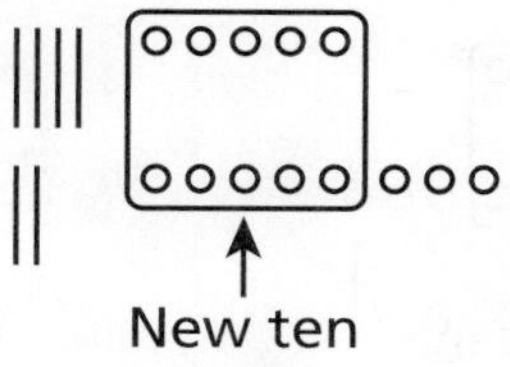	45 + 28 1 73 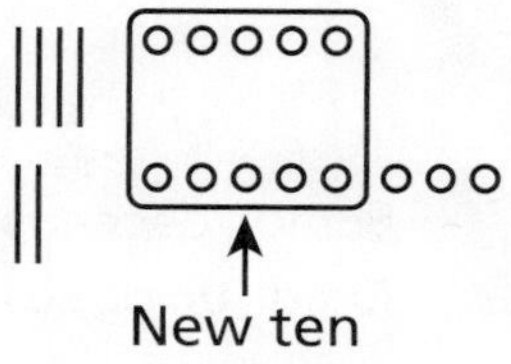 Find total ones. (13) Write 3 and put the new ten in the tens column, ready to add. Add the tens. $(4 + 2 = 6, 6 + 1 = 7)$

New Groups Above

```
  1
  45
+ 28
  73
```

Children usually find it easier to write the new ten below because then they add the new ten last. They add $4 + 2 = 6$ and then $6 + 1 = 7$.

Traditionally, most children have learned to write the new ten above. With this method, you add $1 + 4 = 5$ and then $5 + 2 = 7$. This is more difficult for many children, but some children may still choose this method, particularly if they have been taught to do so previously.

Thank you for helping your child learn mathematics.

Sincerely,
Your child's teacher

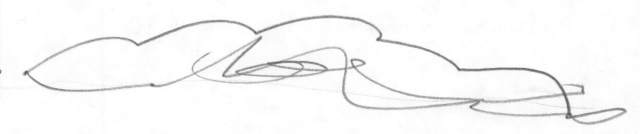

CC SS **Unit 2 addresses the following standards from the** Common Core State Standards for Mathematics: **2.OA.A.1, 2.OA.B.2, 2.NBT.A.1, 2.NBT.A.1.a, 2.NBT.A.2, 2.NBT.A.3, 2.NBT.A.4, 2.NBT.B.5, 2.NBT.B.6, 2.NBT.B.7, 2.NBT.B.8, 2.NBT.B.9, 2.MD.C.8, and all** Mathematical Practices.

Estimada familia:

Su niño está aprendiendo a sumar números de 2 dígitos. El "gran misterio" en la suma de números de 2 dígitos consiste en formar una nueva decena o una nueva centena. Los niños pueden anotar este nuevo grupo de varias maneras.

Mostrar todos los totales

```
                       45
                     + 28
Sumar decenas.  -->    60
Sumar unidades. -->    13
                       73
```

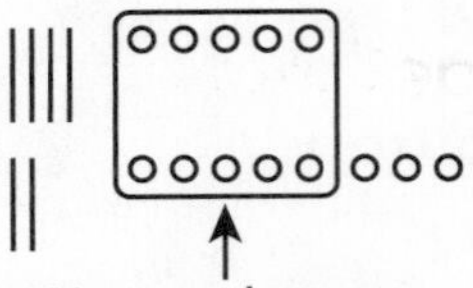

Nueva decena

Hallar el total de decenas. Hallar el total de unidades.

Grupos nuevos abajo

```
  45
+ 28
  1
  73
```

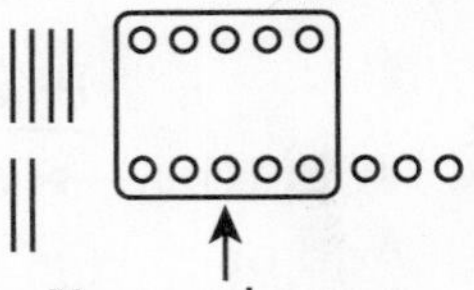

Nueva decena

Hallar el total de unidades. (13) Escribir 3 y poner la nueva decena en la columna de las decenas, lista para sumar.

Sumar las decenas. ($4 + 2 = 6$, $6 + 1 = 7$)

Grupos nuevos arriba

```
   1
  45
+ 28
  73
```

Por lo general a los niños les resulta más fácil escribir la nueva decena abajo, porque entonces suman la nueva decena al final. Suman $4 + 2 = 6$ y luego $6 + 1 = 7$.

Tradicionalmente, la mayoría de los estudiantes han aprendido a escribir la nueva decena arriba. Con ese método, se suma $1 + 4 = 5$ y luego $5 + 2 = 7$. Para muchos niños ese método resulta más difícil pero algunos siguen escogiéndolo, en especial si ya lo han aprendido.

Gracias por ayudar a su niño a aprender matemáticas.

Atentamente,
El maestro de su niño

CC SS **En la Unidad 2 se aplican los siguientes estándares de los** Estándares estatales comunes de matemáticas: **2.OA.A.1, 2.OA.B.2, 2.NBT.A.1, 2.NBT.A.1.a, 2.NBT.A.2, 2.NBT.A.3, 2.NBT.A.4, 2.NBT.B.5, 2.NBT.B.6, 2.NBT.B.7, 2.NBT.B.8, 2.NBT.B.9, 2.MD.C.8 y todos los de** Prácticas matemáticas.

Name ______________________

The New Ten

Solve each word problem.

Show your work.

1. Mr. Green puts 56 red peppers in the vegetable bin. Mrs. Green puts 28 yellow peppers in the bin. How many peppers do they put in the bin altogether?

   [ ] 54 ______ label

2. Mrs. Green stacks 43 tomatoes. Mr. Green adds 39 more. How many tomatoes do they stack in all?

   [82] ______ label

The New Hundred

3. Mr. Green counts 65 cans. Mrs. Green counts 82 cans. How many cans do they count in all?

   [207] ______ label

4. Mrs. Green counts 57 bags of beans. Mr. Green counts 71 bags of beans. How many bags of beans do they count in all?

   [128] ______ label

Make a Ten or Hundred

Solve each word problem. **Show your work.**

5. Mrs. Green stacks 37 boxes of mushrooms.
Mr. Green stacks 29 boxes of mushrooms.
How many boxes do they stack altogether?

[ ] ______
label

6. Mr. Green sells 65 bananas.
Mrs. Green sells 54 bananas.
How many bananas do they sell in all?

[ ] ______
label

PATH to FLUENCY Add and Subtract Within 20

Add or subtract.

7. 6 + 8 = ____
8. 9 + 7 = ____
9. 6 + 10 = ____
10. 9 + 4 = ____
11. 10 + 1 = ____
12. 7 + 6 = ____
13. 15 − 7 = ____
14. 20 − 10 = ____
15. 18 − 9 = ____
16. 11 − 6 = ____
17. 15 − 8 = ____
18. 16 − 7 = ____

Check Understanding

Make a proof drawing to represent how you would add 67 + 41.

Name ______________________________

Show All Totals Method

Solve. Make a proof drawing. **Show your work.**

1. Mr. Green orders 25 jars of grape jelly and 48 jars of strawberry jelly. How many jars of jelly does he order?

   [ ] ________________ label

2. On Monday, Mrs. Green orders 65 pounds of bananas. On Thursday, she orders 29 more pounds of bananas. How many pounds of bananas does she order altogether?

   [ ] ________________ label

3. Mrs. Green orders 78 pounds of white rice and 57 pounds of brown rice. How many pounds of rice does she order?

   [ ] ________________ label

4. Mr. Green orders 49 jars of plain peanut butter and 86 jars of chunky peanut butter. How many jars of peanut butter does he order in all?

   [ ] ________________ label

Word Problem Practice: Two-Step Word Problems

Solve. **Show your work.**

5 There were 17 plums on the table. Nine plums were sold. Mr. Green puts some more plums on the table. Now there are 13 plums. How many plums did Mr. Green put on the table?

plum

☐ ______________
label

6 Some carrots are in a basket. Fran adds 5 more carrots to the basket. James places 4 more carrots there. Now there are 13 carrots. How many carrots were in the basket in the beginning?

carrots

☐ ______________
label

7 Jane buys 8 bananas. Damon buys 4 fewer bananas than Jane. How many bananas do they buy in all?

bananas

☐ ______________
label

Check Understanding

Describe how the Show All Totals method could be used to add 82 + 45.

Name ____

Add with New Groups Below

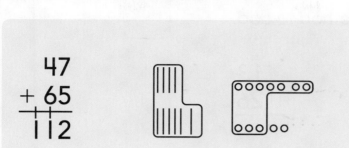

$$\begin{array}{r} 47 \\ +\ 65 \\ \hline 112 \end{array}$$

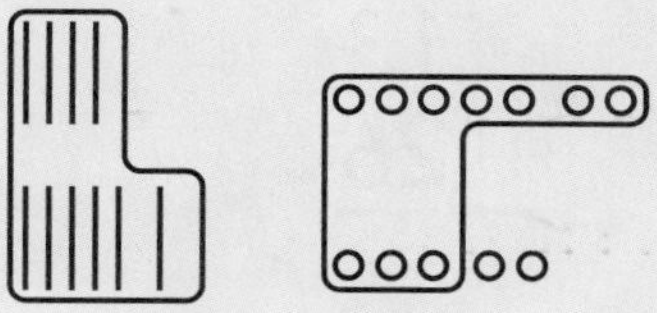

Use the New Groups Below method to add.
Make a proof drawing.

1 $\begin{array}{r} 31 \\ +\ 49 \\ \hline \end{array}$ $\begin{array}{r} 76 \\ +\ 52 \\ \hline \end{array}$

---

2 $\begin{array}{r} 78 \\ +\ 18 \\ \hline \end{array}$ $\begin{array}{r} 67 \\ +\ 69 \\ \hline \end{array}$

---

3 $\begin{array}{r} 26 \\ +\ 78 \\ \hline \end{array}$ $\begin{array}{r} 46 \\ +\ 84 \\ \hline \end{array}$

Add with New Groups Below (continued)

Use the New Groups Below method to add.
Make a proof drawing.

4

$$\begin{array}{r} 72 \\ +\ 54 \\ \hline \end{array} \qquad \begin{array}{r} 13 \\ +\ 26 \\ \hline \end{array}$$

What do you notice about the new groups in these two problems? Explain how the problems are different.

____

____

____

Solve Word Problems with New Groups Below

Read the problem. Write the addition problem in vertical form. Solve it using the New Groups Below method.

5 Kat helped her uncle pull weeds in the garden. Kat pulled 90 weeds. Her uncle pulled 15 weeds. How many weeds did they pull in all?

+ ____

_______ weeds

6 Gia's dress has 17 red polka dots and 34 blue polka dots. How many polka dots are on Gia's dress?

+ ____

_______ polka dots

Check Understanding

Explain how to add 25 + 75 using the New Groups Below method.

Name ____________________

Practice and Share

Add. Use any method.

$$\begin{array}{r} 86 \\ +\ 57 \\ \hline 130 \\ +\ 13 \\ \hline 143 \end{array} \quad \text{or} \quad \begin{array}{r} 86 \\ +\ 57 \\ \hline 143 \end{array}$$

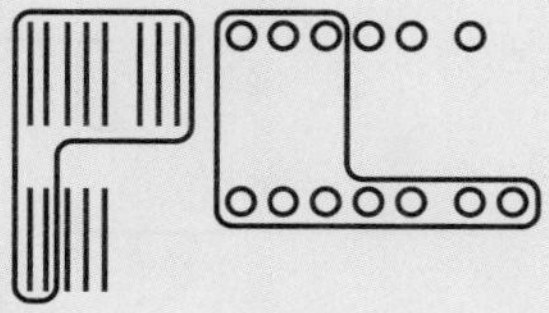

$130 + 13 = 143$

1 $\begin{array}{r} 39 \\ +\ 97 \\ \hline \end{array}$ $\begin{array}{r} 83 \\ +\ 39 \\ \hline \end{array}$

---

2 $\begin{array}{r} 58 \\ +\ 87 \\ \hline \end{array}$ $\begin{array}{r} 72 \\ +\ 37 \\ \hline \end{array}$

---

3 $\begin{array}{r} 49 \\ +\ 85 \\ \hline \end{array}$ $\begin{array}{r} 94 \\ +\ 52 \\ \hline \end{array}$

Predict a New Ten or New Hundred

Add. Use any method.

4

$$\begin{array}{r} 61 \\ +\ 37 \\ \hline \end{array} \qquad \begin{array}{r} 53 \\ +\ 98 \\ \hline \end{array}$$

5

$$\begin{array}{r} 42 \\ +\ 80 \\ \hline \end{array} \qquad \begin{array}{r} 66 \\ +\ 27 \\ \hline \end{array}$$

What's the Error?

$$\begin{array}{r} 38 \\ +\ 46 \\ \hline \end{array}$$

I know that 3 tens
plus 4 tens equals
7 tens. Did I make
a mistake?

6 Show Puzzled Penguin how you would add the numbers. Make a proof drawing to check your work.

$$\begin{array}{r} 38 \\ +\ 46 \\ \hline \end{array}$$

Check Understanding

Find the sum of 76 + 25. Which did you make? Circle your answer.

new ten	both
new hundred	neither

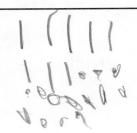

Name ______________________________

What's the Error?

$$\begin{array}{r} 32 \\ +\ 25 \\ \hline 67 \end{array}$$

Did I make a mistake?

1 Add. Make a proof drawing.

$$\begin{array}{r} 32 \\ +\ 25 \\ \hline \end{array}$$

$$\begin{array}{r} 48 \\ +\ 43 \\ \hline 811 \end{array}$$

Is this correct?

2 Add. Make a proof drawing.

$$\begin{array}{r} 48 \\ +\ 43 \\ \hline 91 \end{array}$$

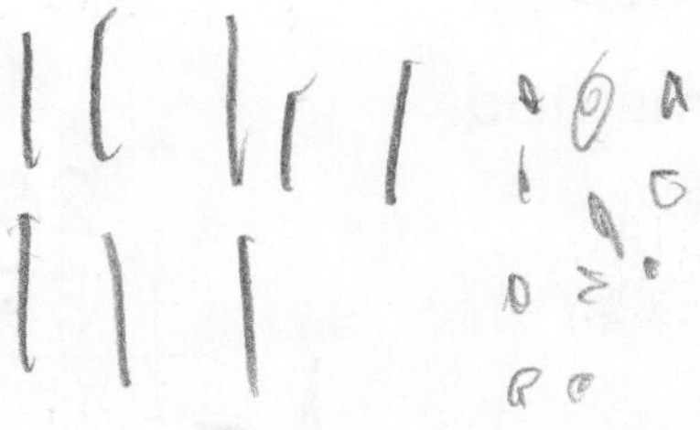

CC SS Content Standards **2.NBT.A.1, 2.NBT.B.6, 2.NBT.B.7, 2.NBT.B.9**
Mathematical Practices **MP3, MP6**

What's the Error? (continued)

$$\begin{array}{r} \scriptstyle 1 \\ 17 \\ +\ 66 \\ \hline 74 \end{array}$$

Is this one correct?

3 Add. Make a proof drawing.

$$\begin{array}{r} 17 \\ +\ 66 \\ \hline 84 \end{array}$$

6+6 = 12
6+7 = 13

$$\begin{array}{r} \scriptstyle 3 \\ 39 \\ +\ 54 \\ \hline 111 \end{array}$$

Did I add correctly this time?

4 Add. Make a proof drawing.

$$\begin{array}{r} 39 \\ +\ 54 \\ \hline 93 \end{array}$$

Choose a Method

Add. Use any method.

5

$$\begin{array}{r} 73 \\ +\ 42 \\ \hline 115 \end{array} \qquad \begin{array}{r} 26 \\ +\ 85 \\ \hline 111 \end{array} \qquad \begin{array}{r} 58 \\ +\ 34 \\ \hline \end{array}$$

✓ Check Understanding

Which method did Puzzled Penguin use in Exercise 4?

Name ____________________

Find the Amount

Write the answer using ¢.
Then write the answer using $.

Show your work.

1. Joe has 11 dimes and 4 pennies.
   How much money does Joe have?

   ________ ________

2. Devin has 1 dollar, 3 dimes, and 8 pennies.
   How much money does Devin have?

   ________ ________

3. Forrest has 14 dimes and 15 pennies.
   How much money does Forrest have?

   ________ ________

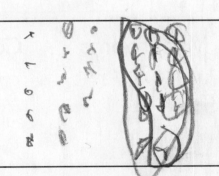

4. Kasey has 2 dimes, 6 pennies, and 1 dollar.
   How much money does Kasey have?

   ________ ________

5. Carlito has 1 dollar, 8 dimes, and 19 pennies.
   How much money does Carlito have?

   ________ ________

CCSS Content Standards 2.NBT.A.1, 2.NBT.A.1.a, 2.NBT.B.6, 2.NBT.B.7, 2.MD.C.8
Mathematical Practices MP1, MP4

The Farm Stand

Potatoes 65¢ 	Corn 56¢ 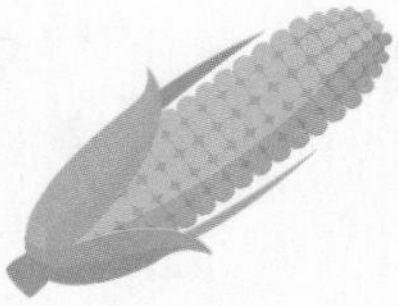	Bananas 89¢ 	Peaches 77¢ 
Radishes 76¢ 	Lemons 88¢ 	Celery 57¢ 	Peppers 78¢ 
Mushrooms 67¢ 	Carrots 86¢ 	Tomatoes 97¢ 	Grapes 98¢ 
Watermelon 59¢ 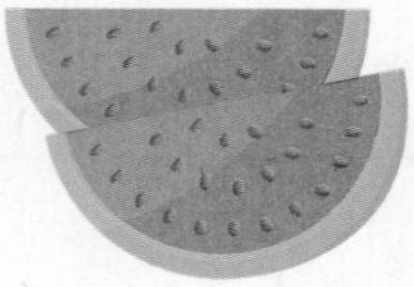	Oranges 85¢ 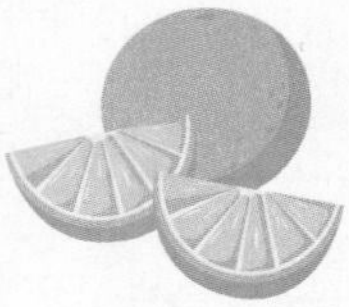	Raspberries 99¢ 	Green Beans 87¢ 

Check Understanding

Explain how to find the sum of 67¢ and 45¢.

Name ______________________________

Practice Counting by 5s

1 Go across. Loop groups of 5 jars. Write the numbers.

1	2	3	4		6	7	8	9	
11	12	13	14		16	17	18	19	
21	22	23	24		26	27	28	29	
31	32	33	34		36	37	38	39	
41	42	43	44		46	47	48	49	
51	52	53	54		56	57	58	59	
61	62	63	64		66	67	68	69	
71	72	73	74		76	77	78	79	
81	82	83	84		86	87	88	89	
91	92	93	94		96	97	98	99	

How Many Cents?

Under the coins, write the total amount of money so far.
Then write the total using $. The first one is done for you.

2 5¢ 5¢ 5¢

5¢ 10¢ 15¢ $ 0 . 1 5 total

---

3 5¢ 5¢ 5¢ 5¢

5 10 15 20 $ ___ . ___ ___ total

---

4 5¢ 5¢ 5¢ 5¢ 5¢

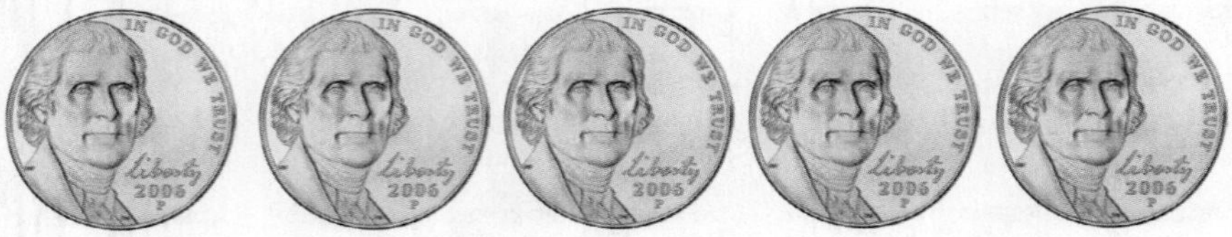

____ ____ ____ ____ ____ $ ___ . ___ ___ total

---

5 Pedro has 9 nickels. Draw (5)s to show his nickels.

Write the total amount of money. $ ___ . ___ ___ total

Name ____________________

Nickels and Pennies

Under the coins, write the total amount of money so far.
Then write the total using $. The first one is done for you.

6 5¢ 5¢ 1¢

5¢ 10¢ 11¢

$ 0.11 total

7 5¢ 5¢ 1¢ 1¢ 1¢

___ ___ ___ ___ ___

$ ___.___ ___ total

8 5¢ 5¢ 5¢ 1¢ 1¢

___ ___ ___ ___ ___

$ ___.___ ___ total

9 Maneka has 3 nickels and 6 pennies.

Draw (5)s and (1)s to show her nickels and pennies.

Write the total amount of money. $ ___.___ ___ total

Dimes, Nickels, and Pennies

Under the coins, write the total amount of money so far.
Then write the total using $. The first one is done for you.

10 10¢ 5¢ 1¢

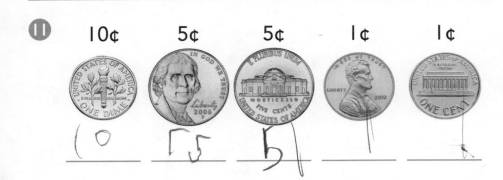

10¢ 15¢ 16¢ $ 0 . 1 6 total

---

11 10¢ 5¢ 5¢ 1¢ 1¢

10 15 5 ___ ___ $ ___ . ___ ___ total

---

12 10¢ 10¢ 10¢ 10¢ 5¢ 1¢

___ ___ ___ ___ ___ ___ $ ___ . ___ ___ total

Check Understanding

Draw a collection of 4 dimes, 4 nickels, and 4 pennies.
Show how to count the value of the collection.

Name ______________________________

PATH to FLUENCY Add Within 100

Add.

36 + 15 = 51	64 + 23 = 81	13 + 22 = 35
47 + 46	60 + 18	11 + 63
28 + 39	76 + 23	33 + 58
63 + 32	44 + 27	45 + 54

CC SS Content Standards **2.NBT.B.5**
Mathematical Practices **MP2, MP5**

PATH to FLUENCY Add Within 100 (continued)

Add.

13. $\begin{array}{r} 49 \\ +\ 51 \\ \hline \end{array}$

14. $\begin{array}{r} 58 \\ +\ 26 \\ \hline \end{array}$

15. $\begin{array}{r} 12 \\ +\ 85 \\ \hline \end{array}$

16. $\begin{array}{r} 28 \\ +\ 31 \\ \hline \end{array}$

17. $\begin{array}{r} 65 \\ +\ 16 \\ \hline \end{array}$

18. $\begin{array}{r} 42 \\ +\ 26 \\ \hline \end{array}$

19. $\begin{array}{r} 77 \\ +\ 19 \\ \hline \end{array}$

20. $\begin{array}{r} 27 \\ +\ 53 \\ \hline \end{array}$

21. $\begin{array}{r} 35 \\ +\ 40 \\ \hline \end{array}$

22. $\begin{array}{r} 33 \\ +\ 67 \\ \hline \end{array}$

23. $\begin{array}{r} 24 \\ +\ 19 \\ \hline \end{array}$

24. $\begin{array}{r} 82 \\ +\ 7 \\ \hline \end{array}$

Check Understanding

Make proof drawings to show how adding 26 + 32 is different from adding 26 + 38.

Name ______________________________

New Ten Challenge

Work in pairs. Lay out Secret Code Cards like this.

10	60	1	6
20	70	2	7
30	80	3	8
40	90	4	9
50		5	

1 Use Secret Code Cards to help you make a 2-digit addition (with a sum less than 100).

40	3
20	9

$$\begin{array}{r} 43 \\ +\ 29 \\ \hline 72 \end{array}$$

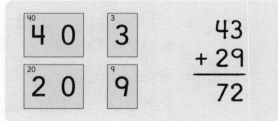

2 Make another 2-digit addition.

- Use the same tens cards.
- If **1** *made a new ten*, use ones cards that *do not make a new ten.*
- If **1** *did not make a new ten*, use ones cards that *make a new ten.*

40	3
20	5

$$\begin{array}{r} 43 \\ +\ 25 \\ \hline 68 \end{array}$$

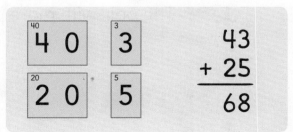

Activity continues on next page.

New Ten Challenge (continued)

2. Work together to check your work. Correct any errors.

3. Put the Secret Code Cards back. Switch roles and repeat. Continue until time is up.

To play the *New Ten Challenge* as a game and compete with another pair, use the **Scoring Rules** below.

Scoring Rules for *New Ten Challenge*

- Each player: Make two 2-digit additions (following the instructions from Step 1 on p. 125). Do not check your work.
- Trade papers with another pair.
- Put a ✓ next to each correct answer. Put an X next to each incorrect answer.
- Give 1 point for each ✓. Subtract 3 points for each X.
- The pair with more points wins.

Name ____________________

Practice Adding Three Addends

Add.

1. 15 + 29 + 36 = 80

2. 24 + 27 + 34 = 85

3. 36 + 33 + 39 = 108

   190
   18
   108

   36
   33
   + 39

4. 35 + 26 + 17 = ____

Practice Adding Four Addends

Add.

5. 18 + 23 + 34 + 17 = ____

6. 38 + 32 + 14 + 25 = ____

7. 20 + 16 + 33 + 27 = ____

8. 26 + 41 + 35 + 12 = ____

Check Understanding

Make two different proof drawings to show two different ways to find the sum of 17 + 49 + 23.

Name ______________________________

Solve Problems and Compare Methods

To recycle means to use again. The second graders at Center School are collecting trash. They will recycle the trash to make musical instruments.

Water Bottle Maracas

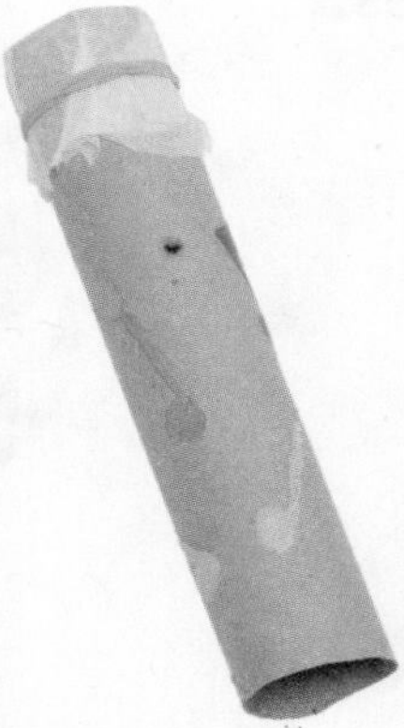

Paper Towel Roll Kazoo

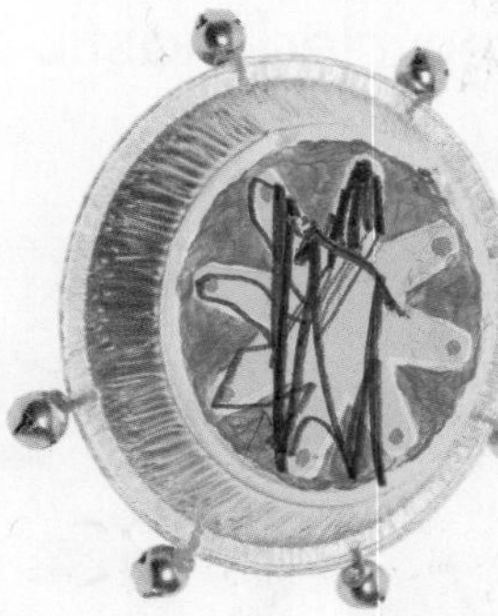

Pie Plate Tambourine

Solve each word problem.

1. There are 48 children that each want to make a tambourine. Each tambourine is made with 2 pie plates. Do they have enough pie plates?

   Circle yes or no. yes no

---

2. If the children collect 10 more water bottles, how many water bottles will they have?

   [ ] ______________ label

---

3. If the children collect 29 more paper towel rolls, will they have enough to make 75 kazoos?

   Circle yes or no. yes no

CCSS Content Standards 2.OA.A.1, 2.NBT.A.2, 2.NBT.A.4, 2.NBT.B.5, 2.NBT.B.6, 2.NBT.B.7, 2.MD.C.8 Mathematical Practices MP1, MP4

Money for Cans and Bottles

Some states help people recycle by giving money back when they return a bottle or can. This fleece jacket, this yo-yo, and this park bench are all made from recycled plastic bottles.

Solve each word problem.

4. Suzanne and Jing get 5 cents for each can or bottle they return. Suzanne returns 29 cans and 18 bottles. Jing returns 15 cans and 34 bottles. Who gets more money back?

____

5. Malia returns 12 bottles. She gets one nickel for each bottle. How much money does she get?

____

6. Roberto gets 5 cents for every can he returns. He gets $1.20. How many cans does he return?

[ ] _______________
label

Unit 2
Performance Task

Name ____________________

Adding Apples

Write a 2-digit number in each ☐.

Use any method to solve each word problem.

Show your work.

1. Martin picks ☐ apples.

   Mindy picks ☐ apples.

   How many apples do they pick in all?

   ☐ ____________
   label

   Explain your method.

   ____

   ____

2. Kelly puts ☐ apples in a box.

   Allie puts ☐ apples in the same box.

   Cory puts in ☐ apples.

   How many apples do they put in the box altogether?

   ☐ ____________
   label

   Explain your method.

   ____

   ____

 Name ____________________

3 Write an addition word problem about apples.
Use 2-digit numbers in your problem.
Then solve.

____

____

____

____

4 Make a proof drawing to show how you solved your word problem.

Dear Family:

Your child is working on a geometry and measurement unit. In this unit, children will use rulers to measure line segments and draw shapes. They will learn about both centimeters and inches.

In Lesson 1, children will work with centimeter units. Through practice, they will learn that when they use a centimeter ruler to measure line segments, they are counting the number of 1-cm length units that comprise the segment.

A ruler shows repeated units of length.

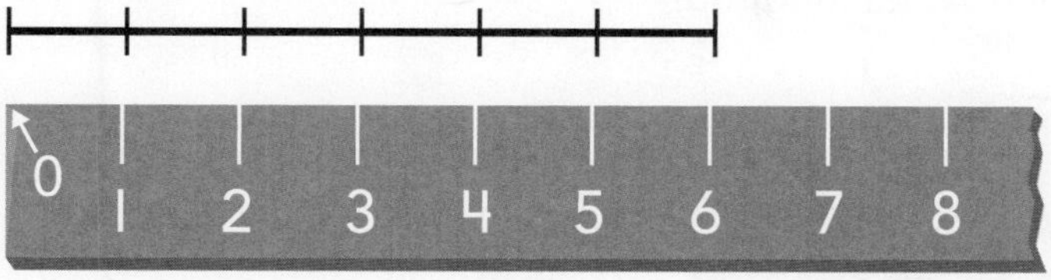

As children measure, compare, and add the lengths of objects, they begin to develop an understanding of the importance of measurement. You can help your child link the measurement and geometry concepts learned in school with the real world. Discuss the lengths of different objects in your home. Talk about objects that are longer or shorter than other objects. Also encourage your child to find examples of different shapes (triangles, quadrilaterals including rectangles and squares, pentagons, and hexagons) in your home or neighborhood. This will help your child enjoy and understand geometry.

If you have any questions or comments, please contact me. Thank you.

Sincerely,
Your child's teacher

CCSS **Unit 3 addresses the following standards from the** Common Core State Standards for Mathematics: **2.OA.B.2, 2.NBT.B.5, 2.NBT.B.7, 2.MD.A.1, 2.MD.A.2, 2.MD.A.3, 2.MD.A.4, 2.MD.D.9, 2.G.A.1, and all** Mathematical Practices.

Estimada familia:

Su niño está trabajando en una unidad que trata sobre geometría y medidas. En esta unidad los niños usarán reglas en centímetros para medir segmentos y trazar figuras. Aprenderán acerca de los centímetros y de las pulgadas.

En la Lección 1, los niños trabajarán con unidades de centímetros. A través de la práctica, aprenderán que cuando usan una regla en centímetros para medir segmentos, están contando el número de unidades de la longitud de 1 cm que componen el segmento.

Una regla muestra las unidades repetidas de longitud.

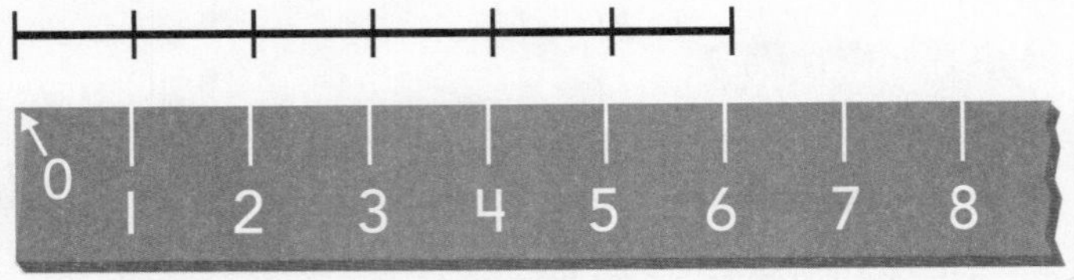

A medida que los niños miden, comparan y agregan las longitudes de los objetos, comienzan a desarrollar la comprensión de la importancia de la medición. Usted puede ayudar a su niño a relacionar los conceptos de medición y geometría aprendidos en la escuela con el mundo real. Comenten sobre las longitudes de los diferentes objetos en su casa. Hablen sobre los objetos que son más largos o más cortos que otros objetos. También anime a su niño a buscar ejemplos de diferentes figuras (triángulos, cuadriláteros incluyendo rectángulos y cuadrados, pentágonos y hexágonos) en su casa o en el vecindario. Esto ayudará a su niño a disfrutar y comprender la geometría.

Si tiene alguna pregunta o algún comentario, por favor comuníquese conmigo. Gracias.

Atentamente,
El maestro de su niño

CCSS **En la Unidad 3 se aplican los siguientes estándares de los** Estándares estatales comunes de matemáticas: **2.OA.B.2, 2.NBT.B.5, 2.NBT.B.7, 2.MD.A.1, 2.MD.A.2, 2.MD.A.3, 2.MD.A.4, 2.MD.D.9, 2.G.A.1 y todos los de** Prácticas matemáticas.

angle	hexagon
centimeter (cm)	inch (in.)
foot (ft)	length

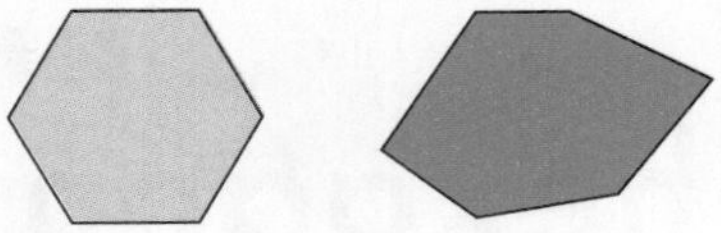

A hexagon has 6 sides and
6 angles.

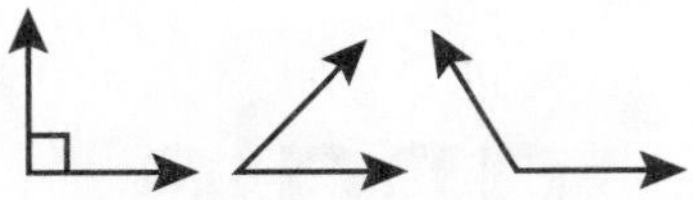

These are angles.

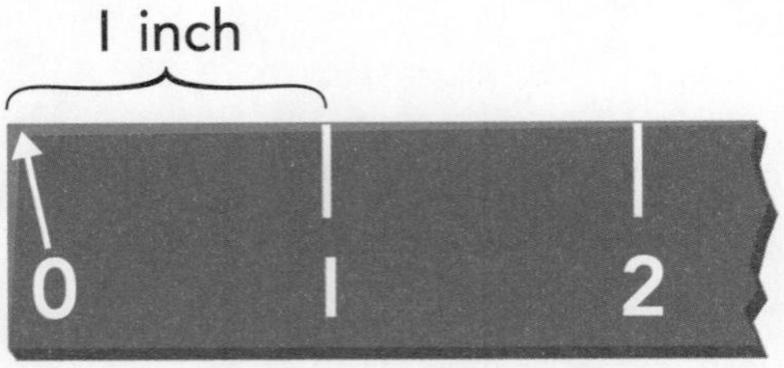

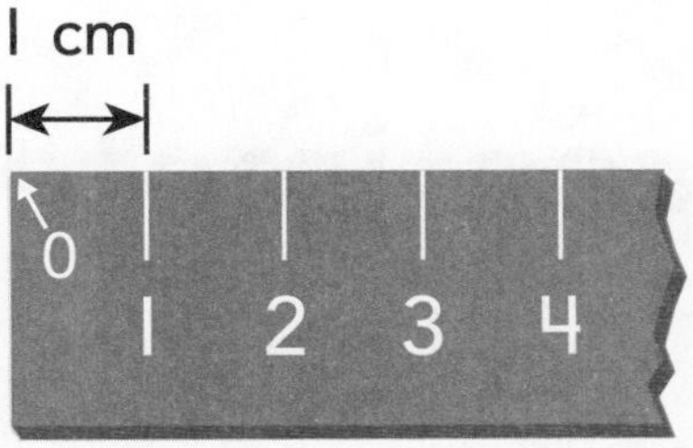

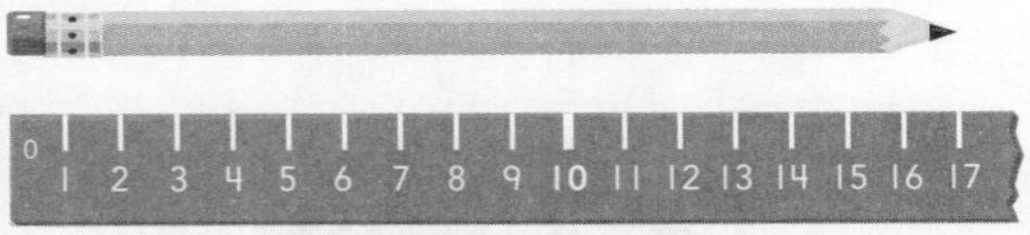

The length of the pencil is
about 17 cm.
(not to scale)

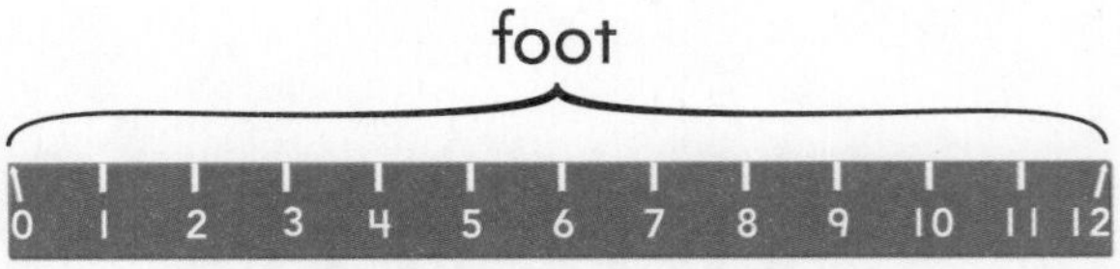

12 inches = 1 foot
(not drawn to scale)

line plot	pentagon
line segment	quadrilateral
opposite sides	rectangle

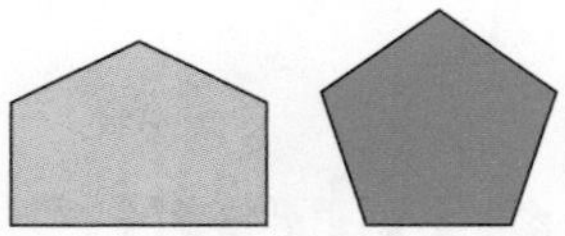

A pentagon has 5 sides and
5 angles.

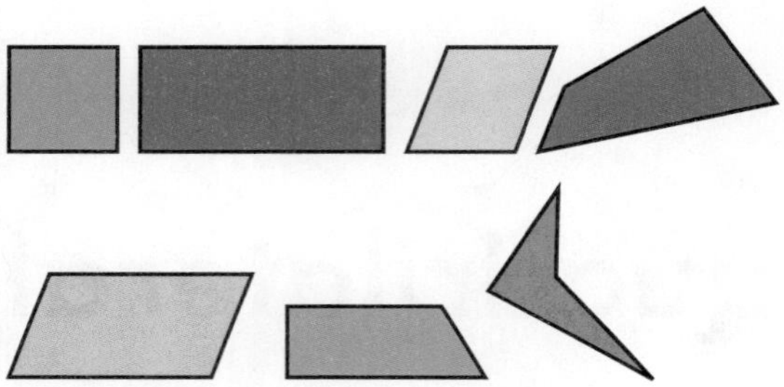

A quadrilateral has 4 sides and
4 angles.

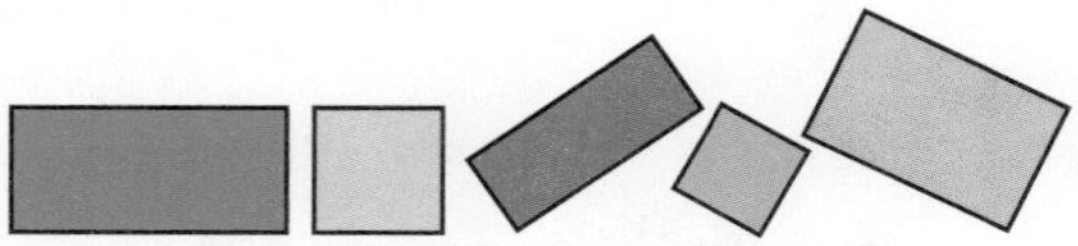

A rectangle has 4 sides and
4 right angles. Opposite sides
have the same length.

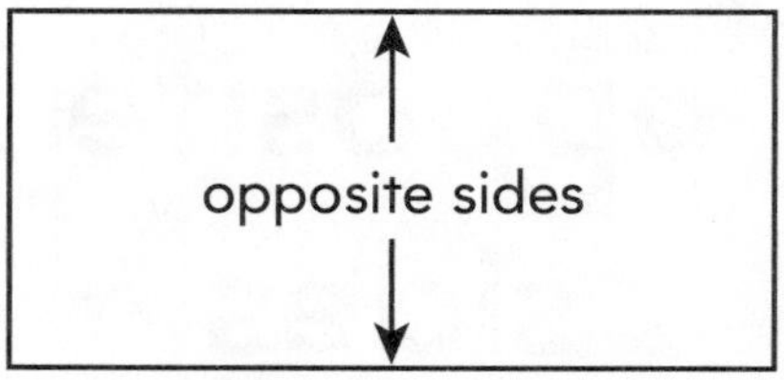

rectangular prism	triangle
right angle	view
square	yard (yd)

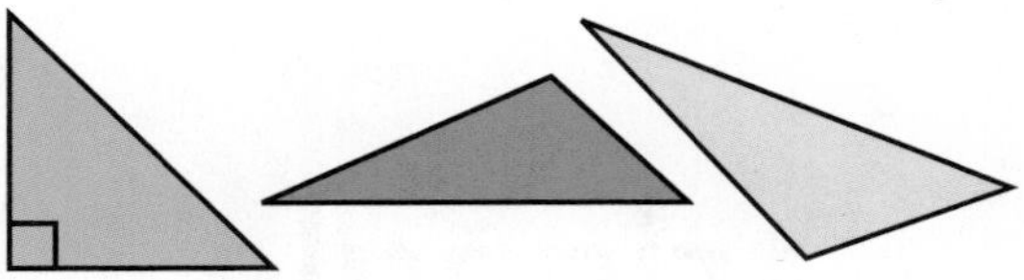

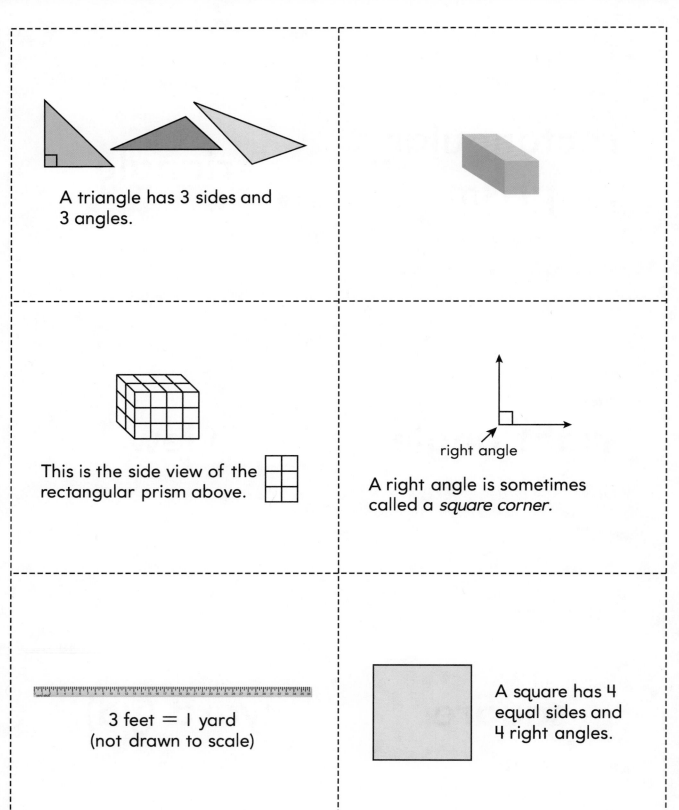

A triangle has 3 sides and 3 angles.

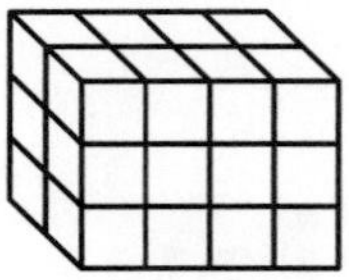

This is the side view of the rectangular prism above.

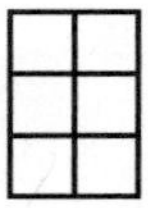

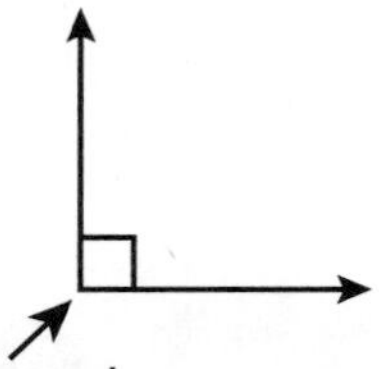

A right angle is sometimes called a *square corner.*

3 feet = 1 yard
(not drawn to scale)

A square has 4 equal sides and 4 right angles.

Name ______________________________

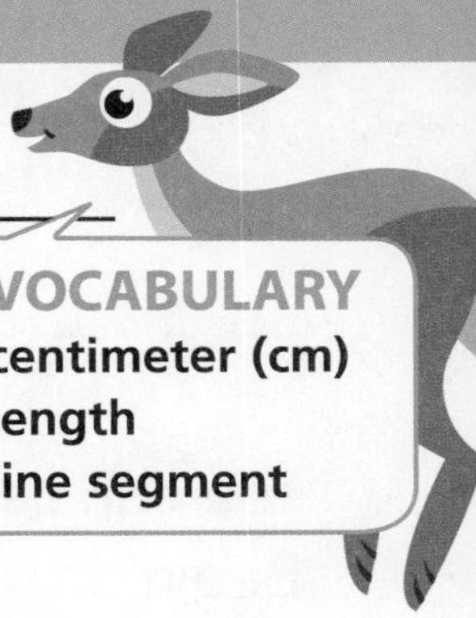

VOCABULARY
centimeter (cm)
length
line segment

Measure and Find Difference in Length

A **centimeter** is a unit of measure for **length**.
The short way to write centimeters is **cm**.

1 cm

To find the measure of the **line segment**, count the 1-cm lengths.

A ruler shows 1-cm lengths.
The 1-cm lengths are marked.

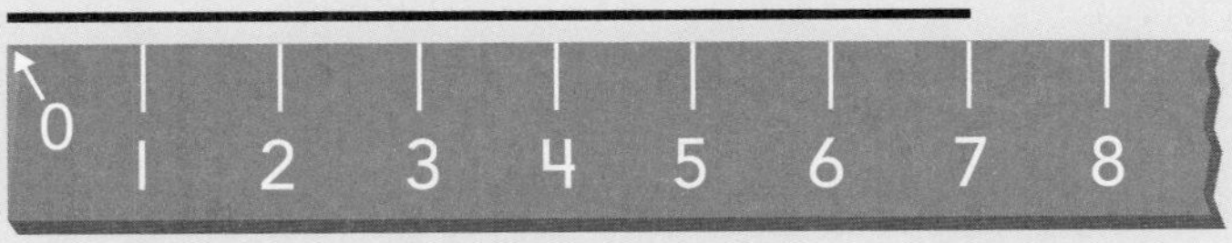

Count the 1-cm lengths. Write the length.

1.  ☐ cm

2.  ☐ cm

Use a centimeter ruler to mark the 1-cm lengths. Write the length.

3. ______________________________ ☐ cm

4. ____ ☐ cm

Use a Ruler to Find Difference in Length

You can use a ruler to draw a line segment 7 cm long.
Begin drawing at the zero edge of your ruler.
Stop when you have counted seven 1-cm lengths.

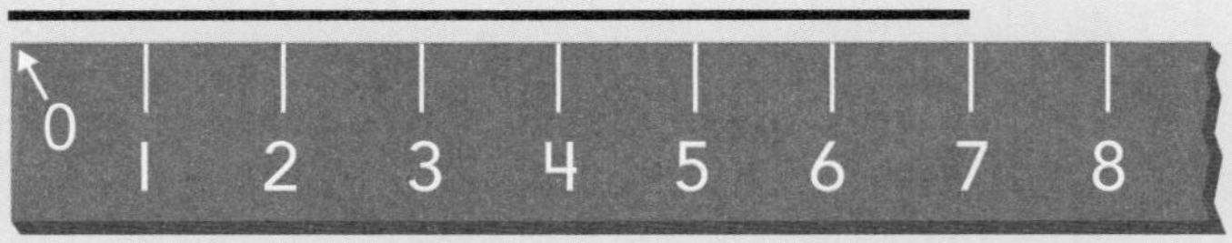

Use your centimeter ruler to draw a line segment with the length given. Mark the 1-cm lengths.

5. 8 cm

6. 5 cm

7. How many centimeters longer is the line segment in Exercise 5 than in Exercise 6? ☐ cm

Draw a line segment with the length given.

8. 6 cm

9. 2 cm

10. How many centimeters longer is the line segment in Exercise 8 than in Exercise 9? ☐ cm

Name ______________________________

Measure Objects and Find Difference in Length

Measure the object. Write the length.
Circle the shorter object.

11

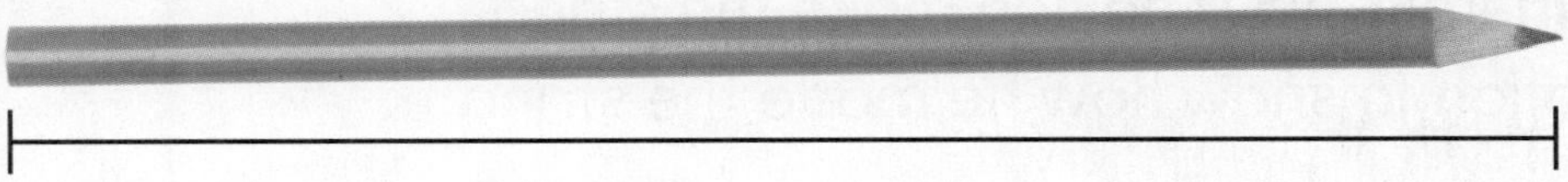

_______ cm

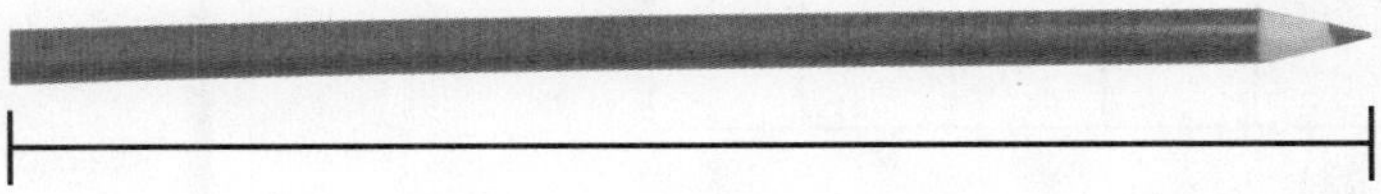

_______ cm

12 The __________ pencil is ☐ cm shorter.

Measure the object. Write the length.
Circle the longer object.

13

_______ cm

_______ cm

14 The __________ straw is ☐ cm longer.

Partners and Adding Lengths

Lee wants to make a string of beads 10 cm long. He has red and blue beads that are each 1 cm long. Color the beads to show 3 different ways he can make the string. Complete the equation to show how he made the string with the two colors.

15 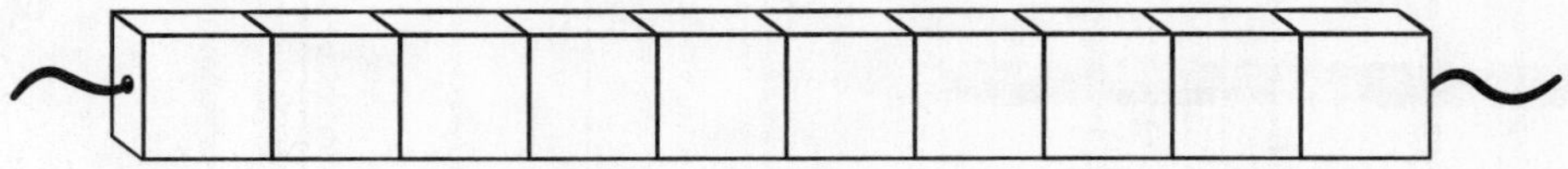

_____ cm + _____ cm = 10 cm

16 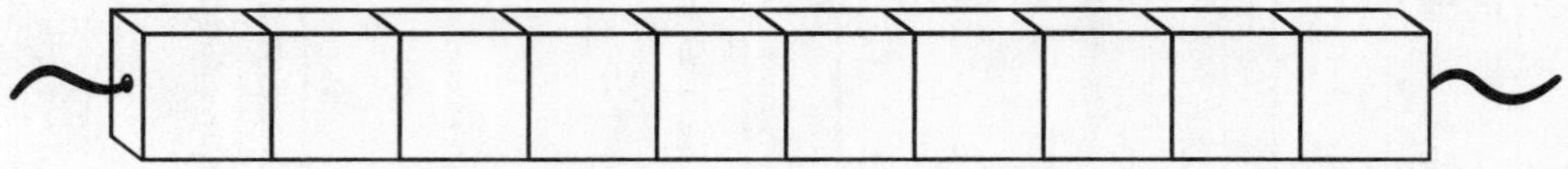

_____ cm + _____ cm = 10 cm

17 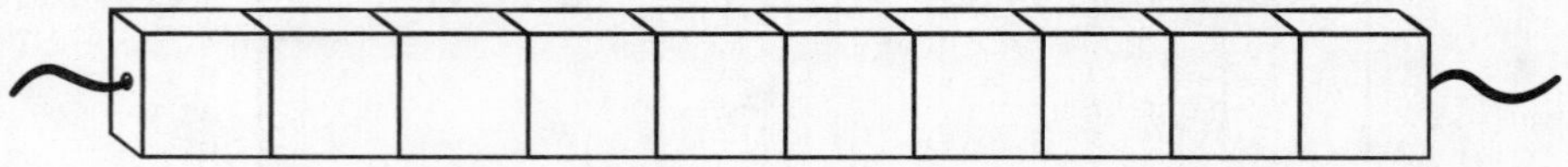

_____ cm + _____ cm = 10 cm

18 Jean has a string of beads that is 14 cm long. She makes it 8 cm shorter. How long is her string now?

_____ cm

Check Understanding

Explain how to find how much longer a 10-cm length is than a 3-cm length.

Name ____________________

Draw and Identify Squares

VOCABULARY
square
right angle
angle

A **square** is a shape with 4 equal sides and 4 **right angles**.

1. Use your centimeter ruler. Draw a square with sides that are each 3 cm long.

Look at these shapes.

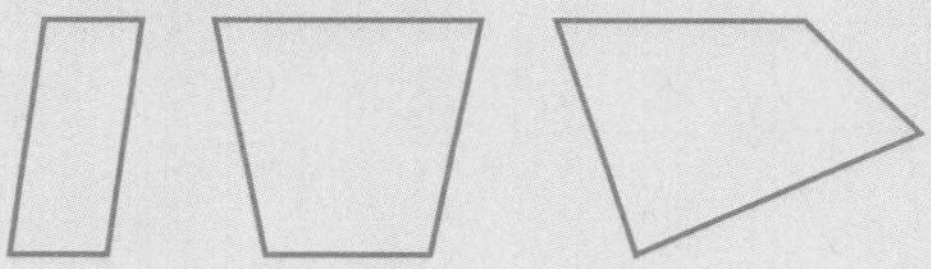

2. Are any of these shapes squares? ____________

3. How are the **angles** of these shapes different from the angles of squares? ____________

____

4. How are the sides of these shapes different from the sides of squares? ____________

____

5. Is this shape a square? Explain why or why not.

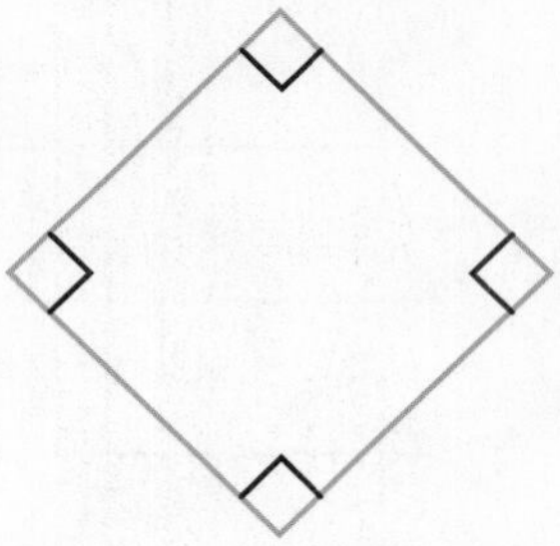

____

____

____

Content Standards 2.MD.A.1, 2.MD.A.4, 2.G.A.1
Mathematical Practices MP2, MP3, MP5, MP6

Draw and Identify Rectangles

VOCABULARY
rectangle
opposite sides

A **rectangle** is a shape with 4 sides and 4 right angles. It has **opposite sides** that are equal in length.

6. Use your centimeter ruler to draw a rectangle that is 6 cm long and 3 cm wide.

Look at these shapes.

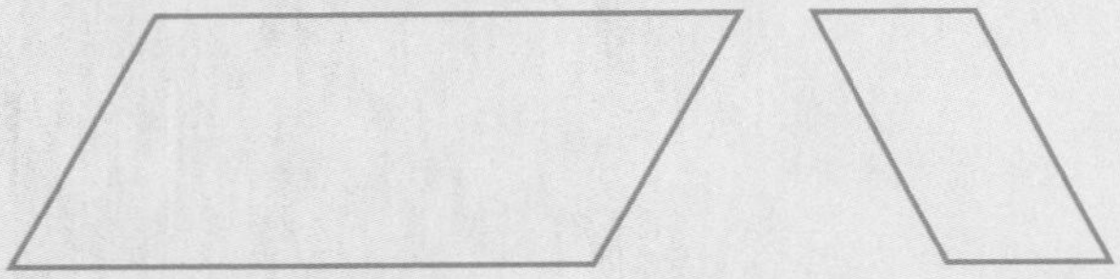

7. Are these shapes rectangles? Explain why or why not.

____

____

8. Is a square a rectangle? Explain why or why not.

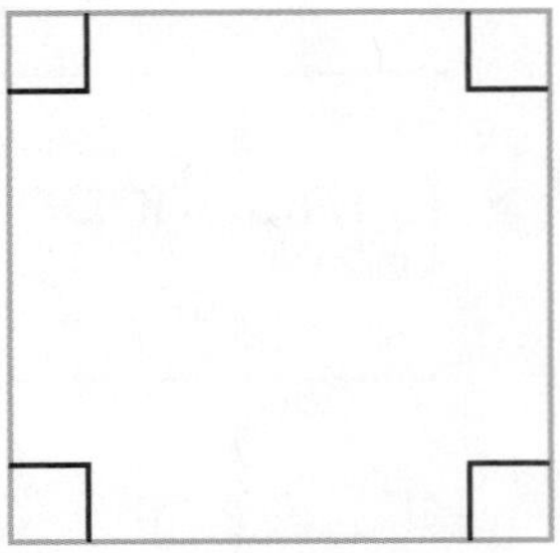

____

____

____

____

Name ____________________

Compare Lengths of Sides of Triangles

VOCABULARY
triangle

A **triangle** is a shape with 3 angles and 3 sides.
All of these shapes are triangles.

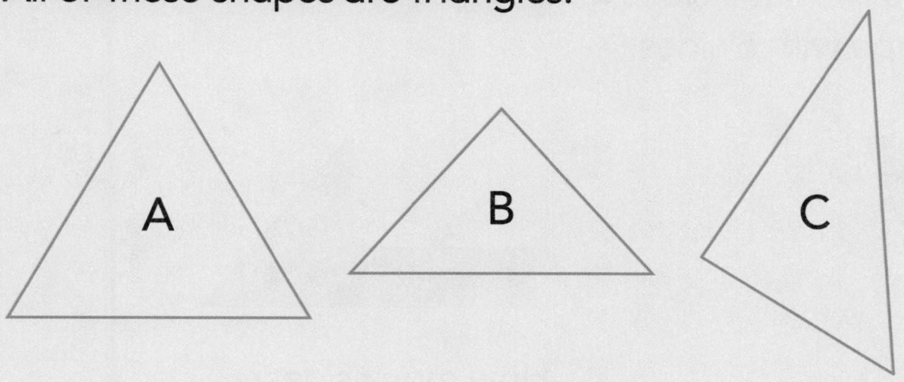

9. Measure each side of Triangle A.
What did you discover about the sides?

____

____

10. Measure each side of Triangle B.
What did you discover about the sides?

____

____

11. Measure each side of Triangle C.
What did you discover about the sides?

____

____

12. Draw a loop to show how much longer the longest side of Triangle C is than the shortest side. The longest side of Triangle C is ☐ cm longer than its shortest side.

Describe Shapes

VOCABULARY
quadrilateral
pentagon
hexagon

A **quadrilateral** is a shape with 4 sides.
A **pentagon** is a shape with 5 sides.
A **hexagon** is a shape with 6 sides.

13 

How many sides? ____
How many angles? ____
Loop the shape.
quadrilateral
square
hexagon

14 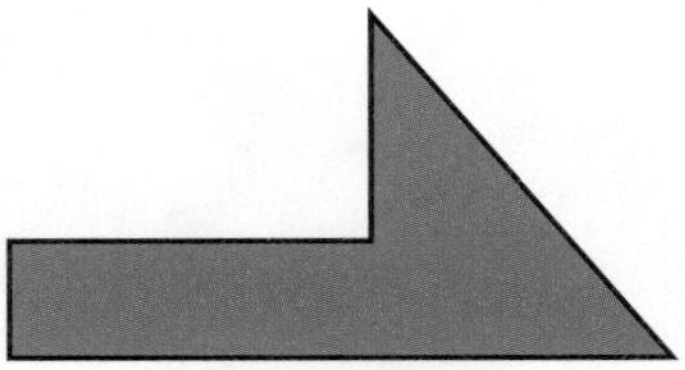

How many sides? ____
How many angles? ____
Loop the shape.
quadrilateral
pentagon
triangle

15 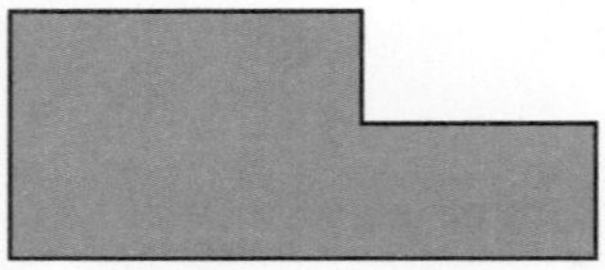

How many sides? ____
How many angles? ____
Loop the shape.
hexagon
triangle
rectangle

16 

How many sides? ____
How many angles? ____
Loop the shape.
rectangle
pentagon
quadrilateral

Check Understanding

Draw a pentagon and a hexagon. How are the shapes alike? How are they different?

Name ______________________________

Estimate and Measure Around a Square

Find the distance around each square.

1

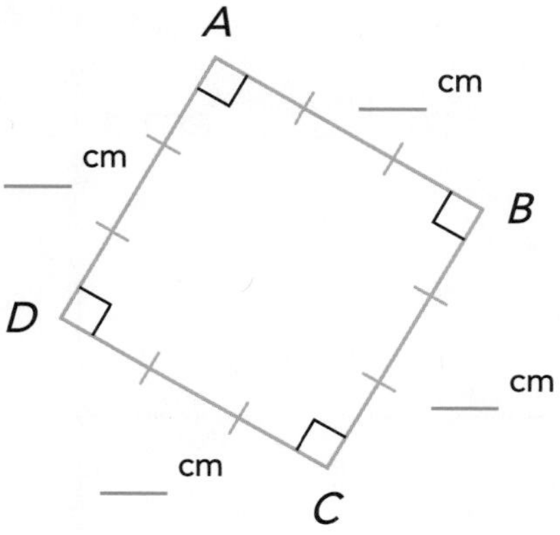

___ cm + ___ cm + ___ cm + ___ cm

= ___ cm

2

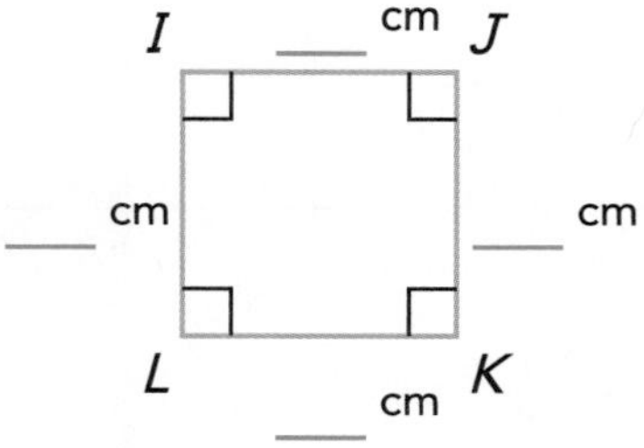

___ cm + ___ cm + ___ cm + ___ cm

= ___ cm

Estimate and then measure each side.
Then find the distance around the square.

3 **a.** Complete the table. Use a centimeter ruler to measure.

Side	Estimate	Measure
EF		
FG		
GH		
HE		

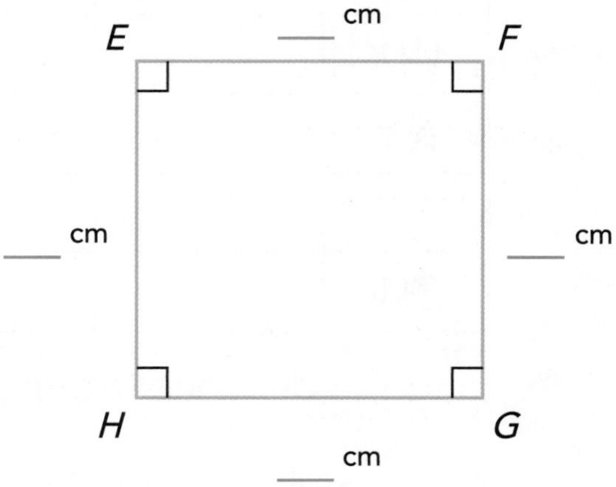

b. Find the distance around the square.

___ cm + ___ cm + ___ cm + ___ cm = ___ cm

Estimate and Measure Around a Rectangle

Find the distance around each rectangle.

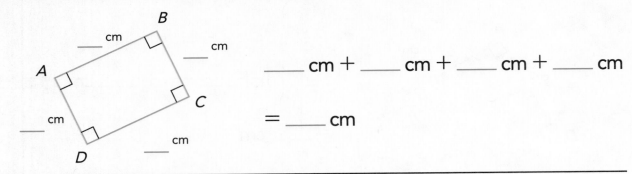

4

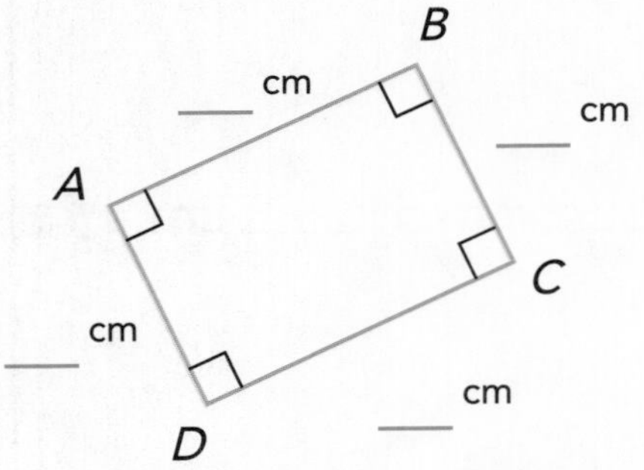

____ cm + ____ cm + ____ cm + ____ cm

= ____ cm

5

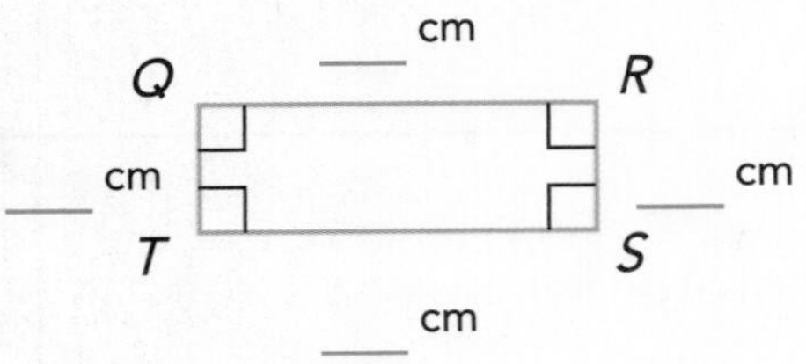

____ cm + ____ cm + ____ cm + ____ cm

= ____ cm

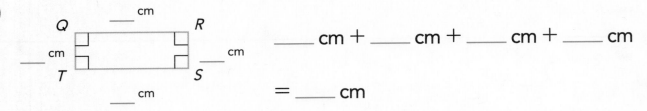

Estimate and then measure each side.

Then find the distance around the rectangle.

6 **a.** Complete the table. Use a centimeter ruler to measure.

Side	Estimate	Measure
WX		
XY		
YZ		
ZW		

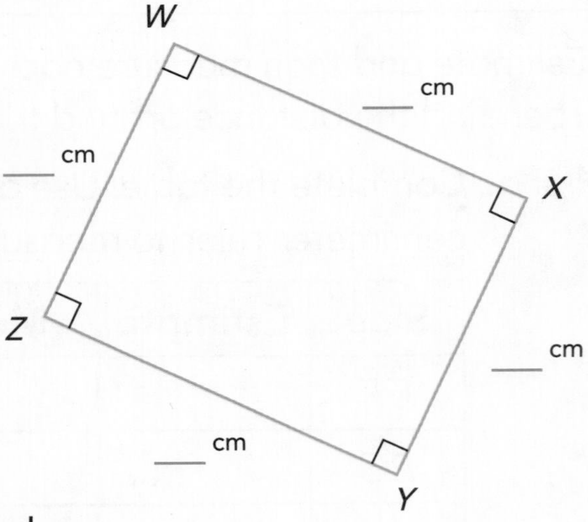

b. Find the distance around the rectangle.

____ cm + ____ cm + ____ cm + ____ cm = ____ cm

Check Understanding

Explain how to estimate the length in centimeters of a side of a square.

Name ______________________________

Estimate and Measure

Find the distance around each triangle.

1

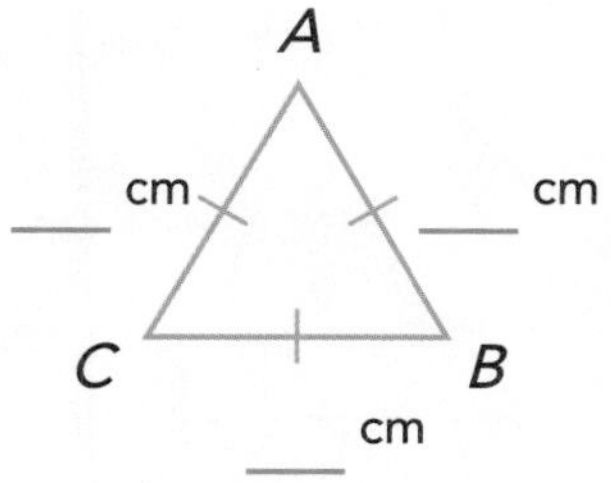

___ cm + ___ cm + ___ cm

= ___ cm

2

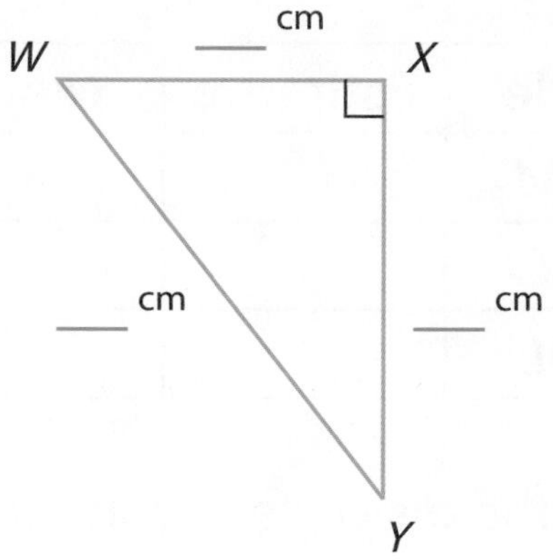

___ cm + ___ cm + ___ cm

= ___ cm

Estimate and then measure each side.
Then find the distance around the triangle.

3 **a.** Complete the table.

Side	Estimate	Measure
HI		
IJ		
JH		

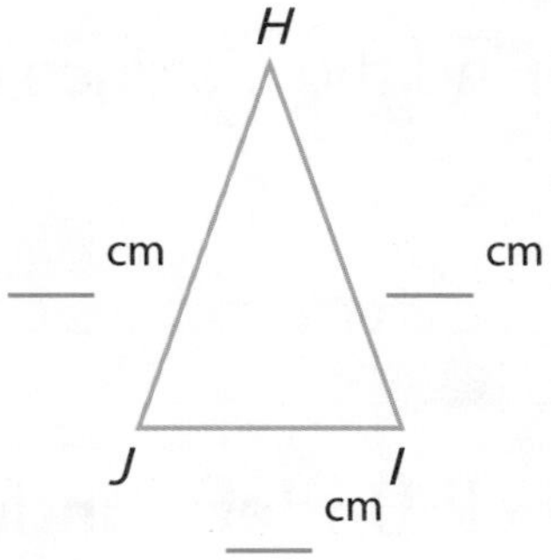

b. Find the distance around the triangle.

___ cm + ___ cm + ___ cm = ___ cm

Estimate and Measure (continued)

4 a. Complete the table.

Side	Estimate	Measure
LM		
MO		
OL		

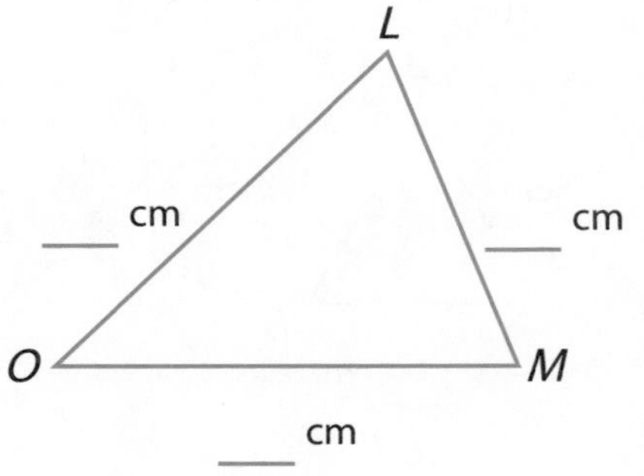

b. Find the distance around the triangle.

____ cm + ____ cm + ____ cm = ____ cm

5 a. Complete the table.

Side	Estimate	Measure
PQ		
QR		
RP		

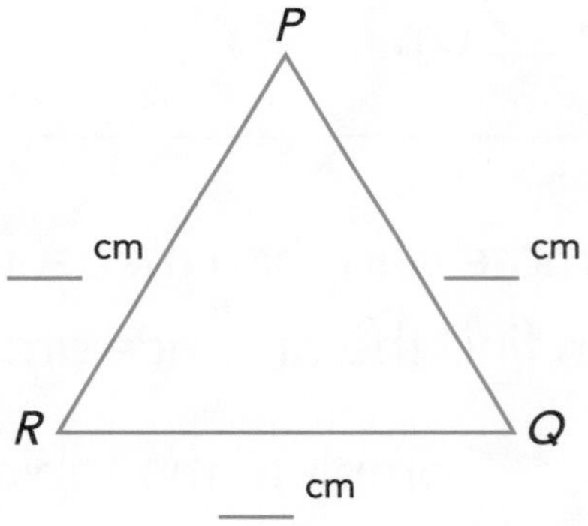

b. Find the distance around the triangle.

____ cm + ____ cm + ____ cm = ____ cm

Check Understanding

Draw two different triangles. Each triangle must have one side 3 cm long and another side 4 cm long.

Name ____________________

Rectangular Prisms

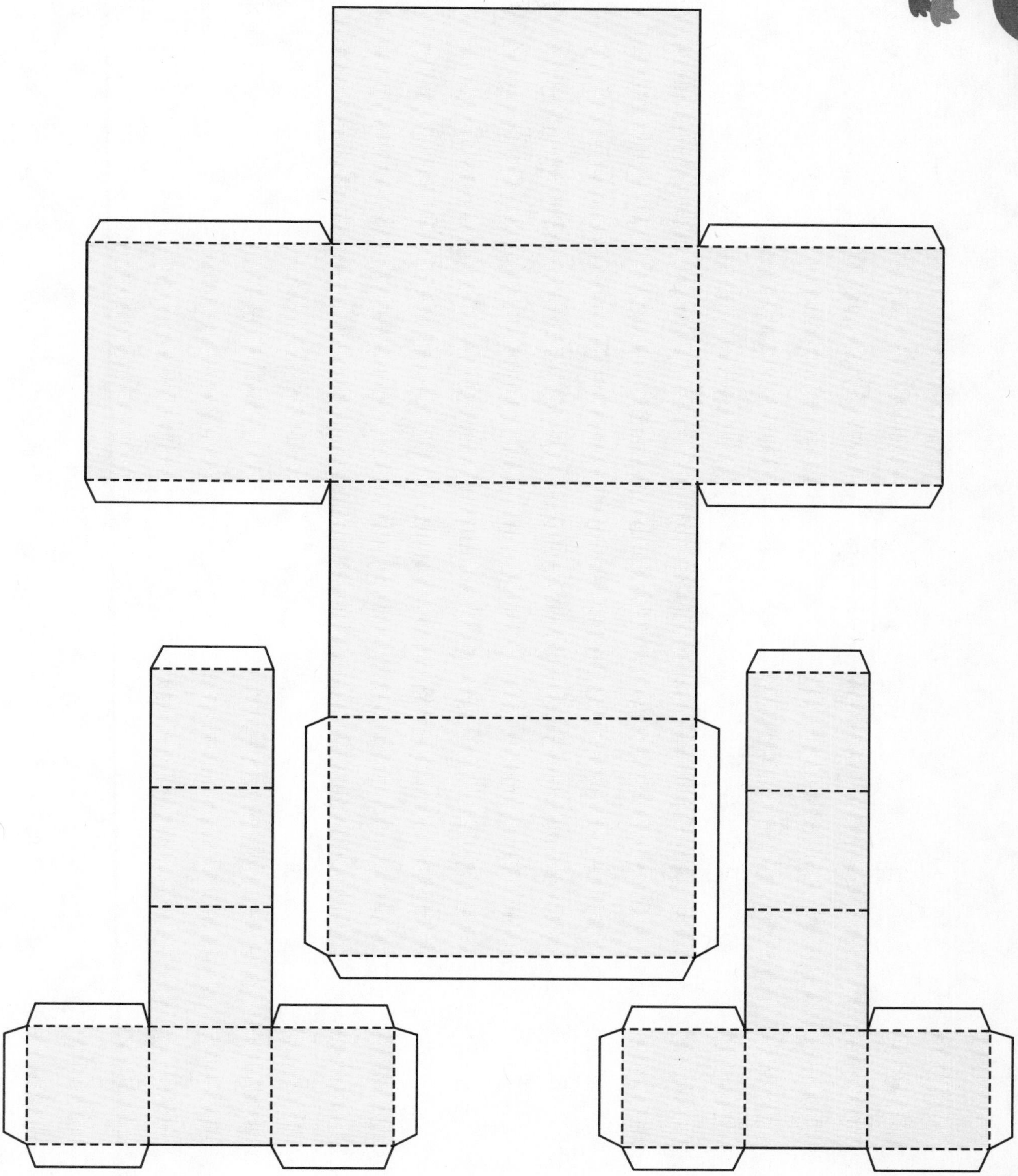

Cut on solid lines.
Fold on dashed lines.

CCSS Content Standards **2.G.A.1**
Mathematical Practices **MP3, MP5, MP6**

Name ____________________

Build and Draw Rectangular Prisms

Using unit cubes, build a **rectangular prism** to match each description. Draw the rectangular prism from the top **view**, front view, and side view.

VOCABULARY
rectangular prism
view

1. two rows of three unit cubes

top view **front view** **side view**

2. one row of two unit cubes stacked on top of another row of two unit cubes

top view **front view** **side view**

Build Rectangular Prisms from Drawings

Build a rectangular prism to match each set of views.

3. **top view**

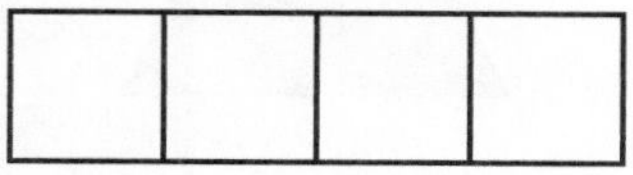

front view

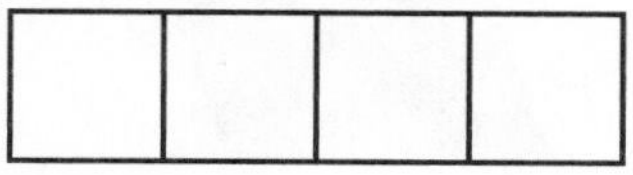

side view

4. **top view**

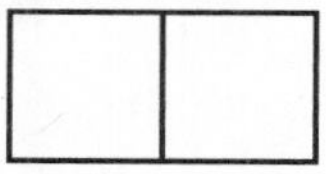

front view

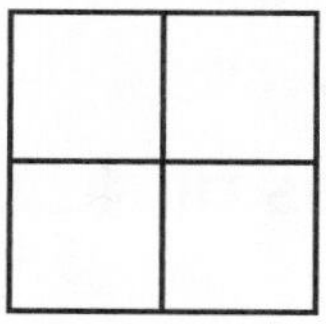

side view

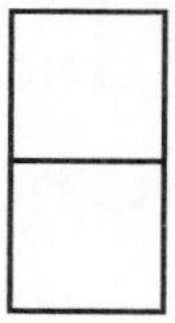

Identify Shapes

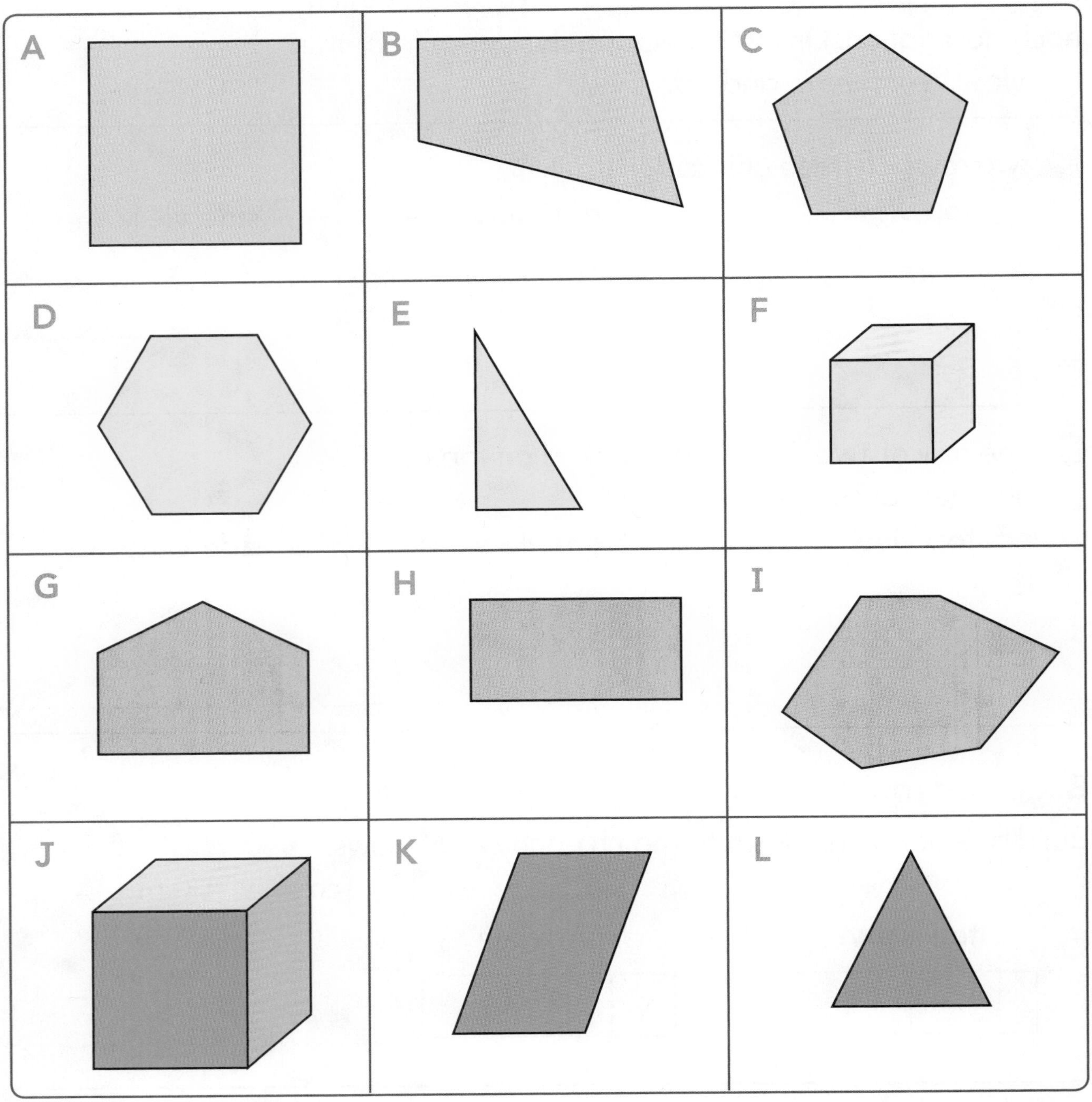

Check Understanding

Shape C has ________ sides and ________ angles.

It is a ______________________.

Unit 3
Quick Quiz 1

Name ______________________ Date ____________

1 Measure each string to the nearest centimeter.

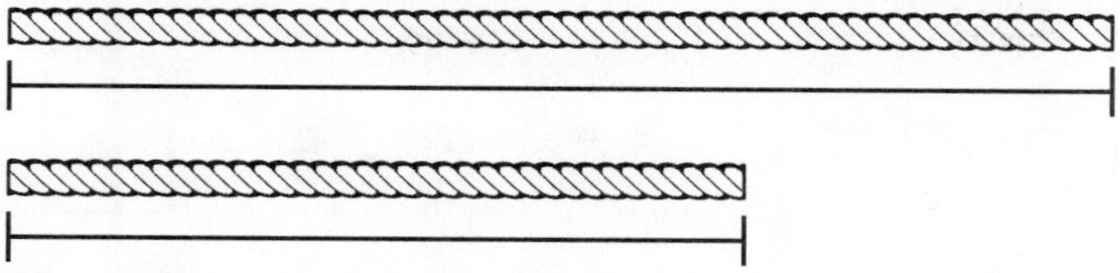

☐ cm

☐ cm

2 Look at Exercise 1. How much longer is the first string than the second string?

☐ cm

3 Name the shape. Choose a word from the box.

cube	hexagon	triangle
pentagon	quadrilateral	

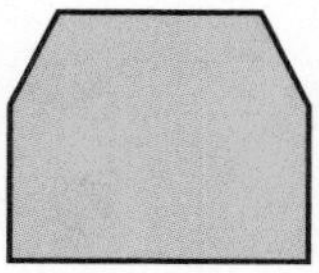

____

4 What is the distance around the triangle?

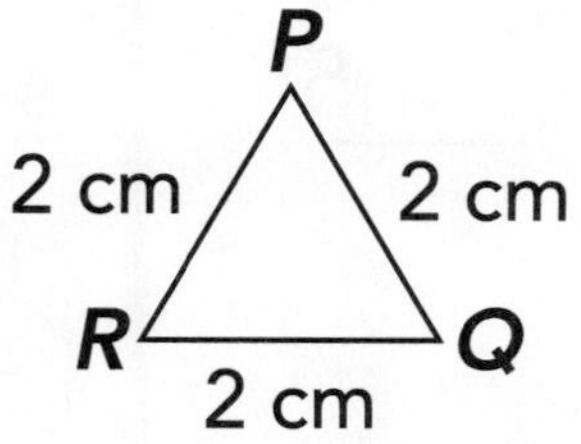

2 cm + ☐ cm + ☐ cm = ☐ cm

5 What shape has this set of views?

top view **front view** **side view**

____

Fluency Check 7

Name ____________________ Date ____________________

PATH to FLUENCY

Add or subtract.

1. $3 + 3 = \square$
2. $9 + 7 = \square$
3. $7 + 5 = \square$
4. $11 - 7 = \square$
5. $10 - 7 = \square$
6. $18 - 9 = \square$
7. $19 - 13$
8. $18 - 16$
9. $20 - 7$
10. $30 + 10$
11. $65 + 17$
12. $33 + 15$
13. $67 + 32$
14. $18 + 16$
15. $58 + 38$

Dear Family:

In this unit, your child will be collecting measurement data and using that data to make line plots. A *line plot* is a display that uses a number line and dots (or other marks) to represent data. For this reason, line plots are sometimes called *dot plots*.

Your child will be asked to bring one or two pencils to school. The length of each pencil should be more than 1 inch and less than 8 inches. Children will work in small groups. They will measure each pencil brought in by the members of their group and then make a line plot similar to the one shown below.

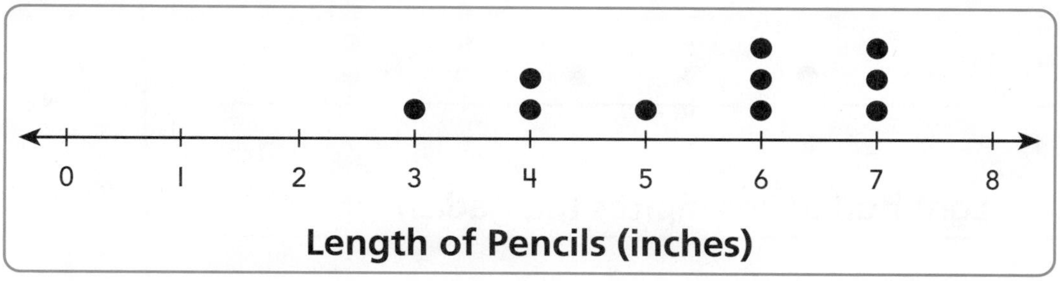

In this unit, your child will also be given several experiences that will help build understanding that the smaller the unit used to measure a given length or distance, the more of those units will be needed.

So, for example, since centimeters are shorter than inches, when the paintbrush below is measured in both centimeters and inches, the number of centimeters is more than the number of inches.

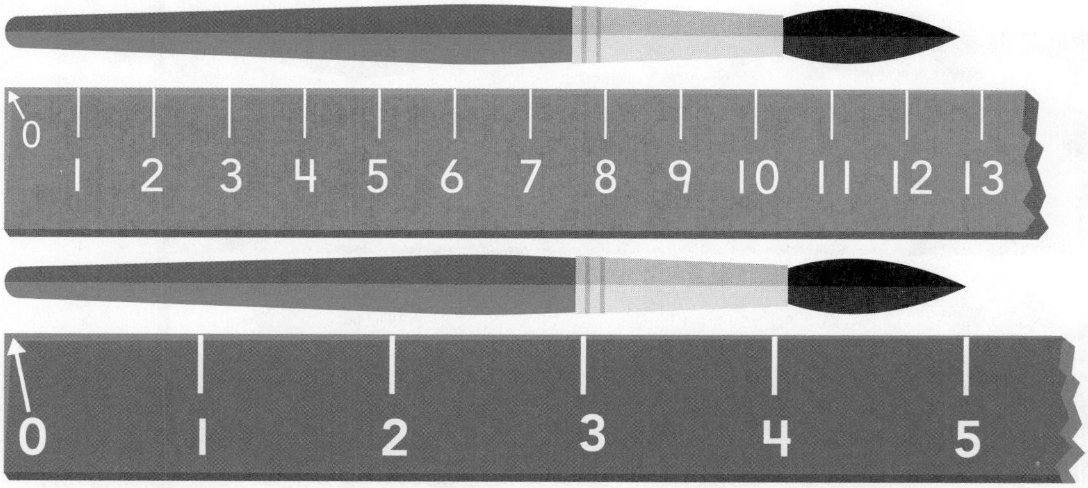

Sincerely,
Your child's teacher

CC SS Unit 3 addresses the following standards from the Common Core State Standards for Mathematics: **2.OA.B.2, 2.NBT.B.5, 2.NBT.B.7, 2.MD.A.1, 2.MD.A.2, 2.MD.A.3, 2.MD.A.4, 2.MD.D.9, 2.G.A.1, and all** Mathematical Practices.

Estimada familia:

En esta unidad, su niño reunirá datos sobre medidas y usará esos datos para hacer diagramas de puntos. Un *diagrama de puntos* es un diagrama que usa una recta numérica y puntos u otras marcas para representar datos.

Se le pedirá a su niño que traiga uno o dos lápices a la escuela. Cada lápiz debe medir más de 1 pulgada de longitud pero menos de 8. Los niños trabajarán en grupos pequeños. Medirán los lápices de cada miembro de su grupo y luego, harán un diagrama de puntos como el que se muestra debajo.

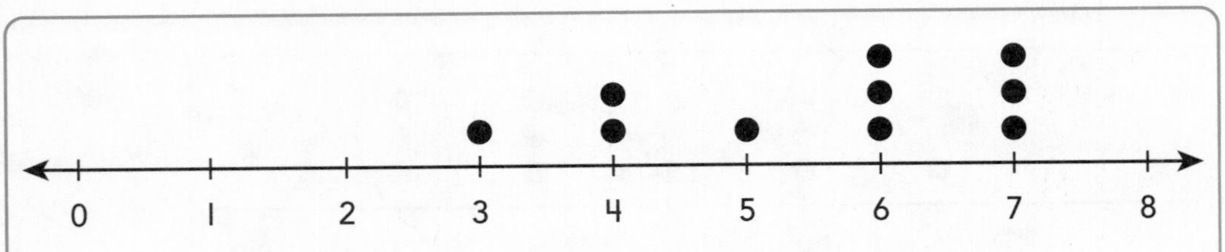

Longitud de los lápices (pulgadas)

También en esta unidad, a su niño se le brindarán diversas experiencias que lo ayudarán a comprender que entre más pequeña sea la unidad que se use para medir una determinada longitud o distancia, más de esas unidades se necesitarán.

Entonces, por ejemplo, como los centímetros son más cortos que las pulgadas, cuando el pincel de abajo se mide en centímetros y en pulgadas, el número de centímetros es mayor que el número de pulgadas.

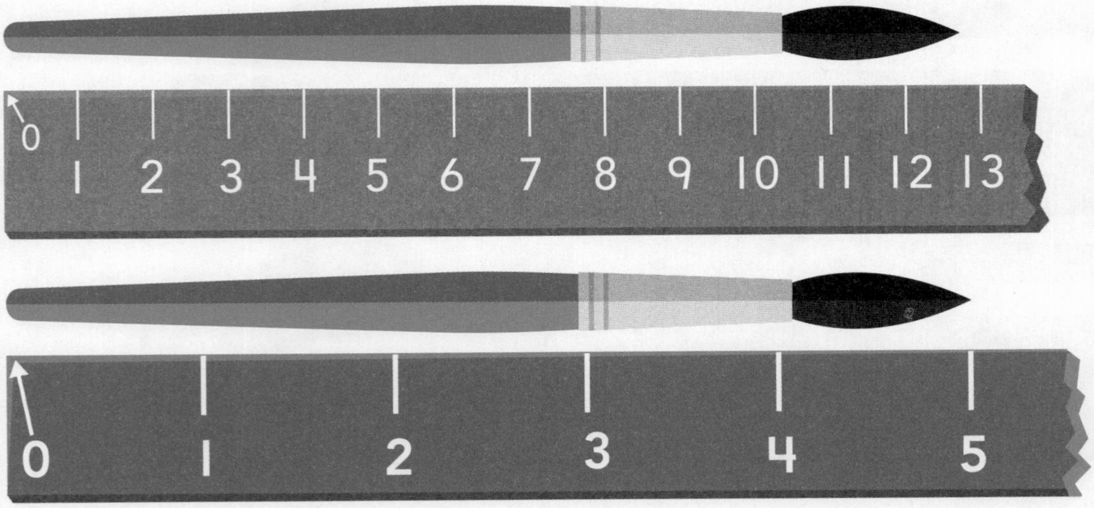

Atentamente,
El maestro de su niño

CC SS **En la Unidad 3 se aplican los siguientes estándares de los** Estándares estatales comunes de matemáticas: **2.OA.B.2, 2.NBT.B.5, 2.NBT.B.7, 2.MD.A.1, 2.MD.A.2, 2.MD.A.3, 2.MD.A.4, 2.MD.D.9, 2.G.A.1 y todos los de** Prácticas matemáticas.

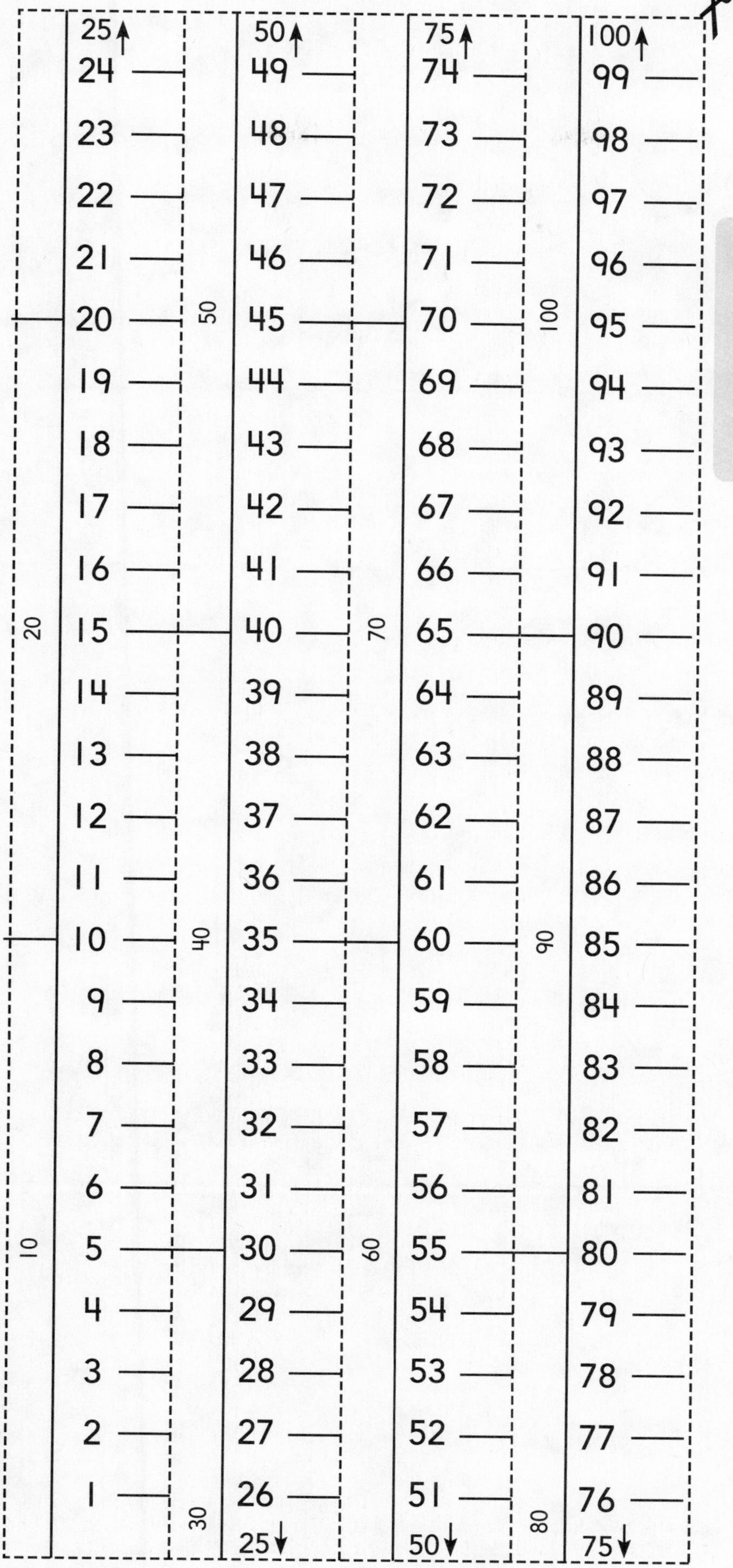

Step 1: Cut out on the dashed lines.

Step 2: Put the sections in order.

Step 3: Tape or paste the sections together.

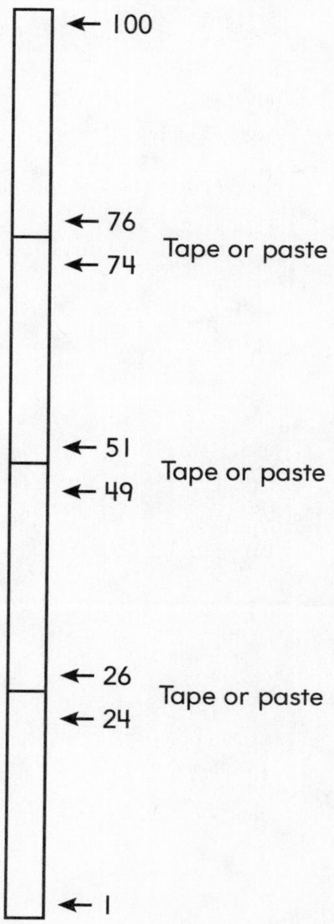

Meter Tape (Vertical)

Name ______________________

Estimate and Measure

Find a part of your hand that is about each length.

1. 1 cm ______________________

2. 10 cm ______________________

Find a part of your body that is about 1 meter long.

3. 1 m ______________________

Find the real object. Circle the name of the tool you will use to measure in centimeters. Measure the object.

4. 

meter stick
centimeter ruler

__________ cm

5. 

meter stick
centimeter ruler

__________ cm

6. 

meter stick
centimeter ruler

__________ cm

7. 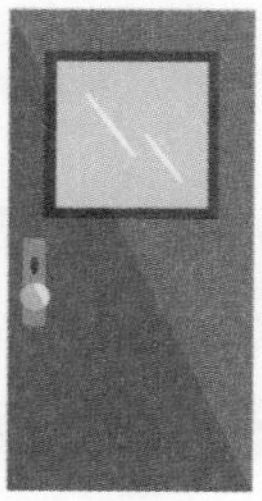

meter stick
centimeter ruler

__________ m

8. Find an object longer than 10 cm and shorter than 30 cm. Draw the object.

CC SS **Content Standards** **2.NBT.B.7, 2.MD.A.1, 2.MD.A.3, 2.MD.D.9**
Mathematical Practices **MP3, MP5, MP6**

Measure Heights

Use the meter sticks at the stations to measure heights.

9 Complete the table for each person in your group.

Person's Name	Estimated Height (cm)	Actual Height (cm)

Use the table to answer these questions.

10 What is the height of the tallest person in your group?

____

11 How much taller is the tallest person than the shortest person? Find the difference by subtracting.

____

What's the Error?

12 Puzzled Penguin measures the height of this bookcase and says it is 38 cm tall. What was Puzzled Penguin's mistake?

____

____

____

Name ________________________________

Introduce Line Plots

VOCABULARY
line plot

Look at this **line plot**.

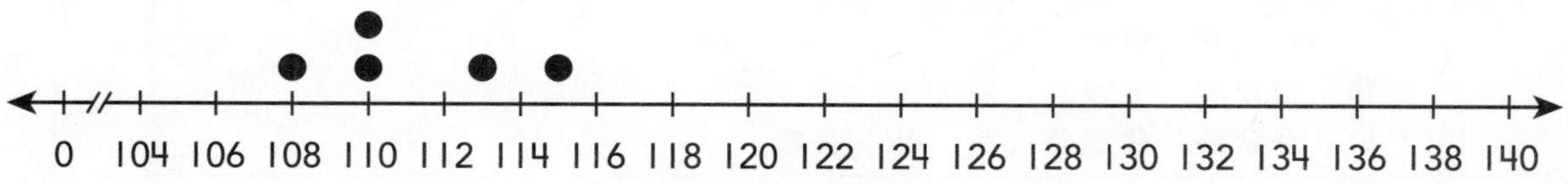

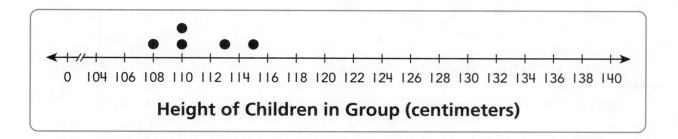

Height of Children in Group (centimeters)

Make a Line Plot

13 Draw dots for the heights of the children in your group. Use data from the table on page 164.

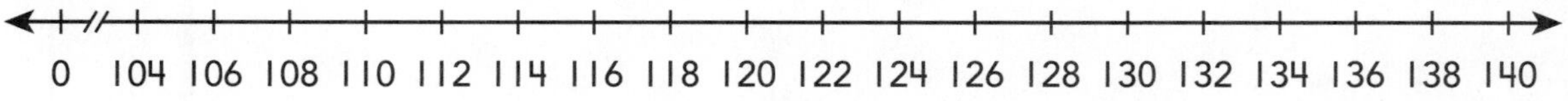

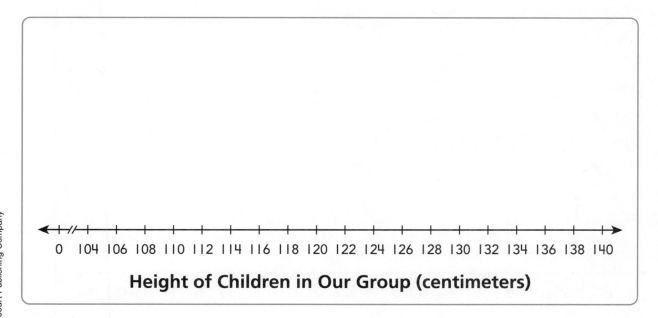

Height of Children in Our Group (centimeters)

14 Which height in your group is the greatest? ________ cm

15 Which height in your group is the least? ________ cm

Discuss a Line Plot

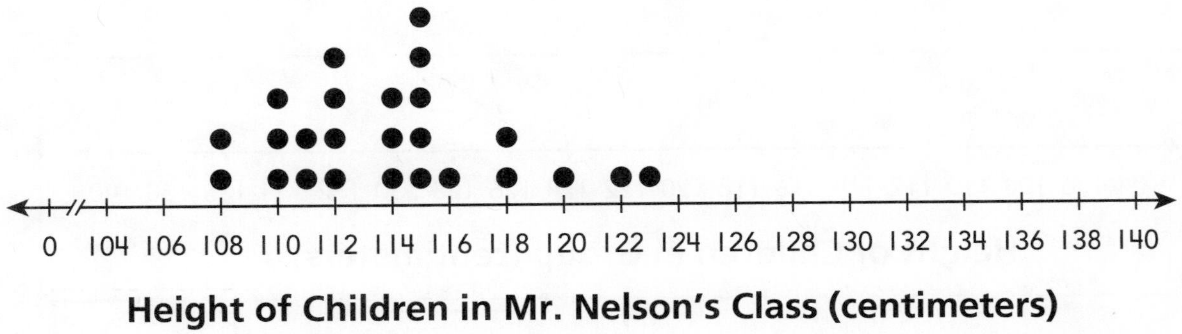

Show Class Data on a Line Plot

16 Draw dots for the heights of the children in your class.

Check Understanding

Write a question about the class line plot. Trade questions with a partner, and answer your partner's question.

Name ______________________________

Make an Inch Ruler

Directions:

Step 1: Cut along the dashed lines.

Step 2: Place the sections in the correct order.

Step 3: Tape or glue together the sections at the tab.

Step 4: Write a ***6*** where the two strips meet.

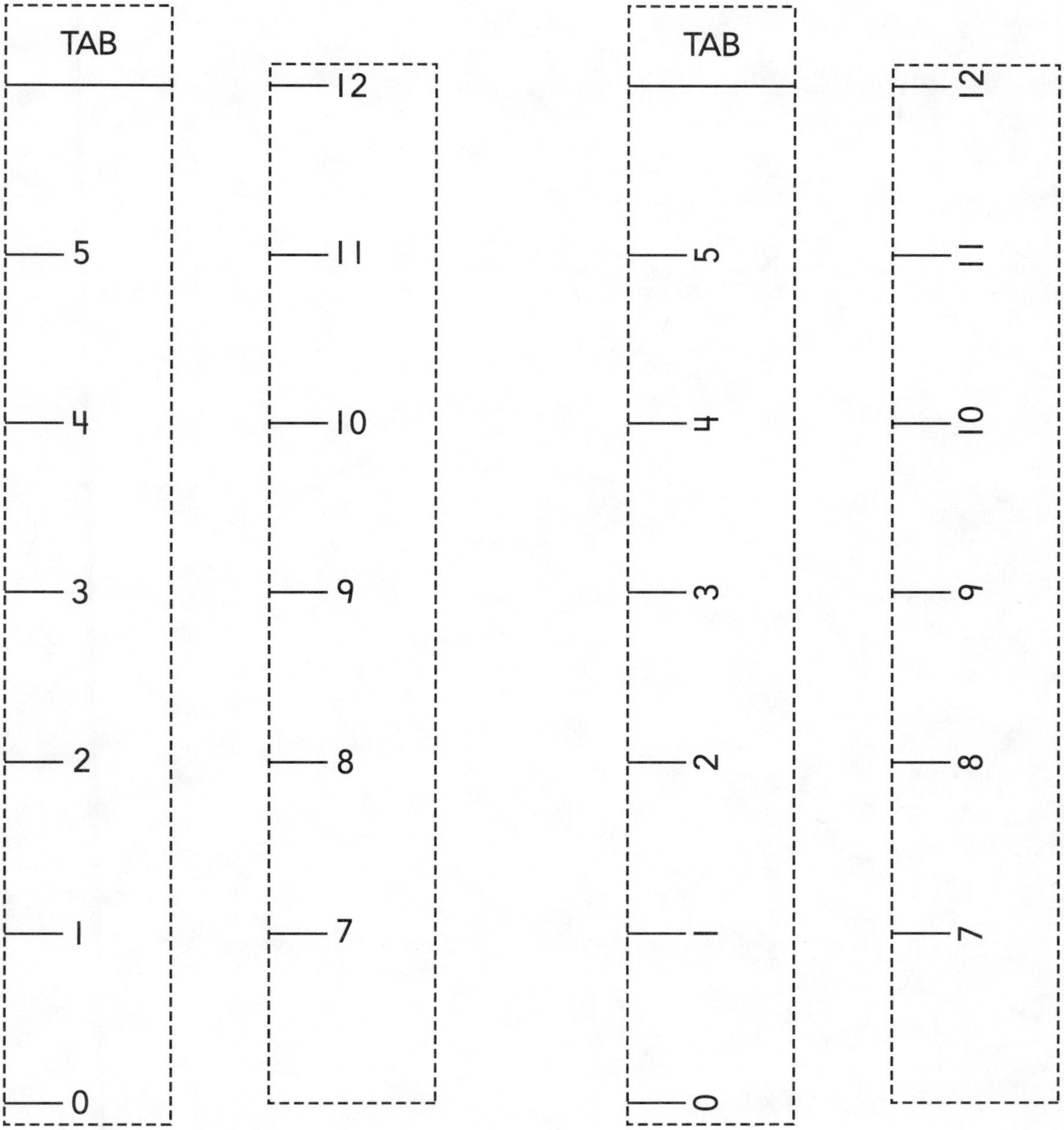

Content Standards **2.MD.A.1, 2.MD.A.2, 2.MD.A.3, 2.MD.D.9**
Mathematical Practices **MP2, MP3, MP5, MP6, MP7, MP8**

Inch Ruler

Name ______________________

Measure to the Nearest Inch

VOCABULARY
inch (in.)

To measure to the nearest **inch (in.)**, place the zero mark on your ruler at the left end of the object. Find the inch mark that is closest to the right end of the object.

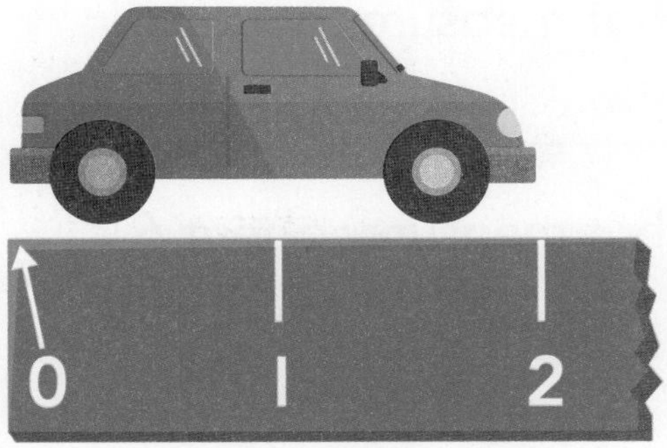

To the nearest inch, the length of this toy car is 2 inches.
Measure the length of each object below to the nearest inch.

1.  ______________

2. 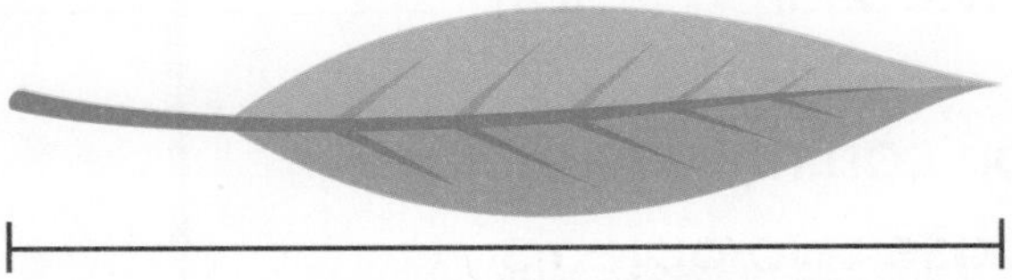 ______________

3.  ______________

4. Draw a horizontal line segment that is 2 in. long.

5. Draw a horizontal line segment that is 6 in. long.

Estimate and Measure in Inches

6 Describe a part of your hand that measures about 2 in.

____

7 Describe a part of your hand that measures about 1 in.

____

8 Describe a part of your hand that measures about 6 in.

____

Estimate and measure the length of each line segment.

9 |———————————|

Estimated length: ________ Measured length: ________

10 |—————————————————|

Estimated length: ________ Measured length: ________

11 Find four classroom objects that you can measure in inches and then in centimeters. Choose two objects with a length between 12 inches and 24 inches. Complete the table.

Object	Estimated length (in.)	Measured length (in.)	Measured length (cm)

Name ____________________

Make a Yardstick

Directions:

Step 1: Cut along the dashed lines.

Step 2: Place the sections in the correct order.

Step 3: Tape or glue together the sections at the tab.

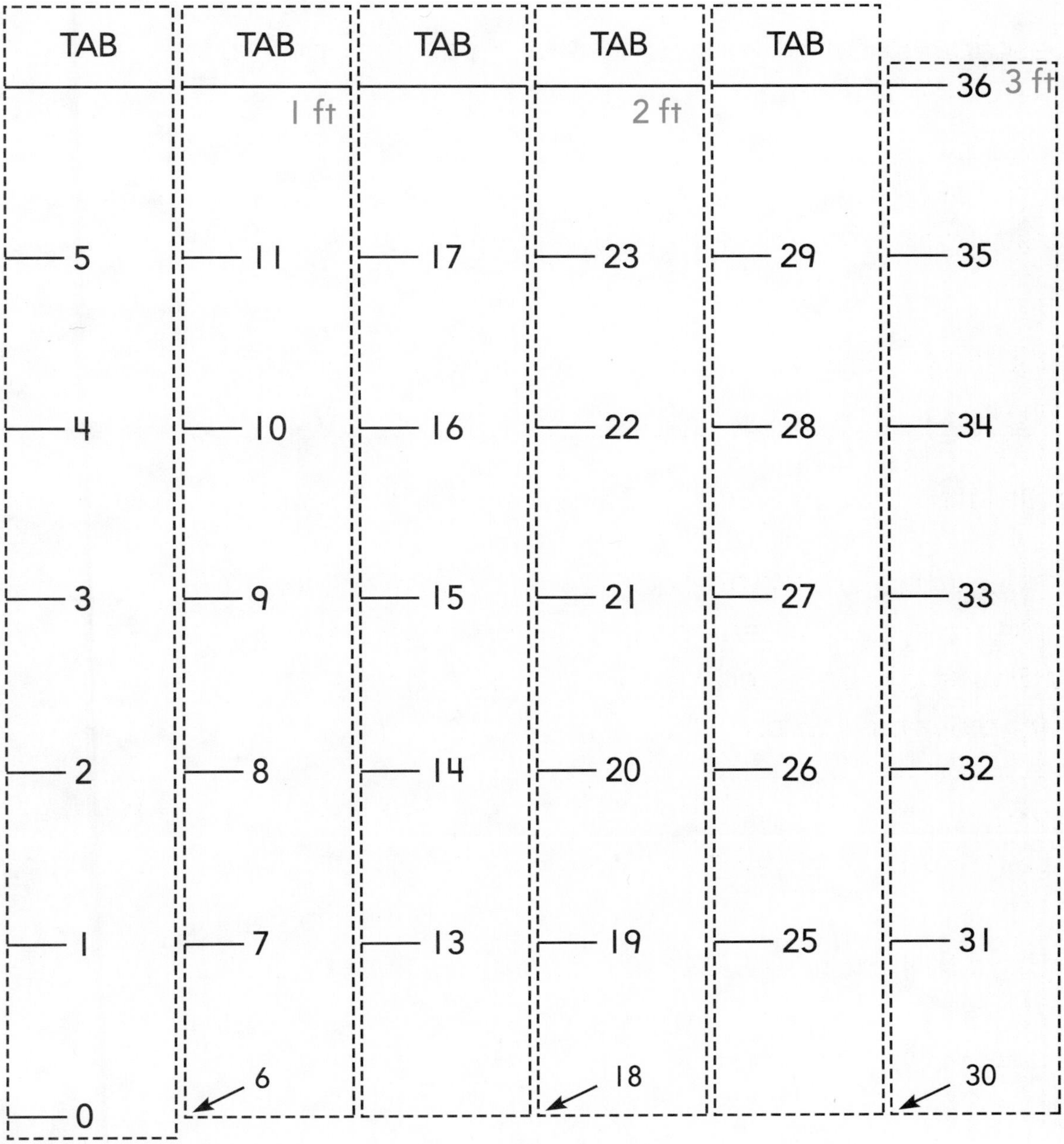

Name ______________________________

Measure in Feet and Yards

VOCABULARY
foot (ft)
yard (yd)

Find each length to the nearest **foot (ft)**.

12 width of your desk

____

13 length from your knee to your ankle

____

Find each length to the nearest **yard (yd)**.

14 height of the classroom door

____

15 length of a bookshelf

____

Measure each length to the nearest foot and to the nearest yard.

16 width of the classroom door

______________________ ft

______________________ yd

17 length of the classroom board

______________________ ft

______________________ yd

18 What do you notice about the numbers when you measure in yards instead of feet? Why?

____

____

Estimate and Measure Height

Estimate your height in inches. Then work with a partner to find your actual height.

19 Estimate: ______________________

20 Actual height: ______________________

Height in Centimeters and Inches

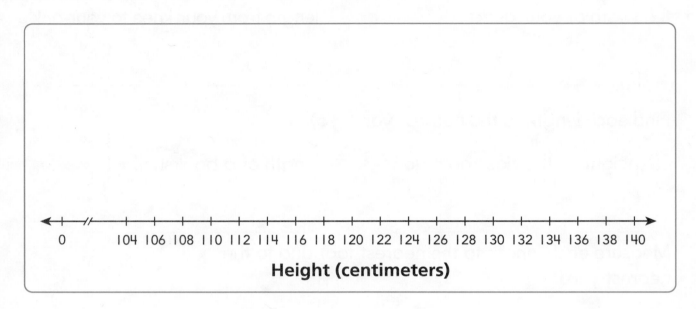

Draw a dot to show your height in centimeters.

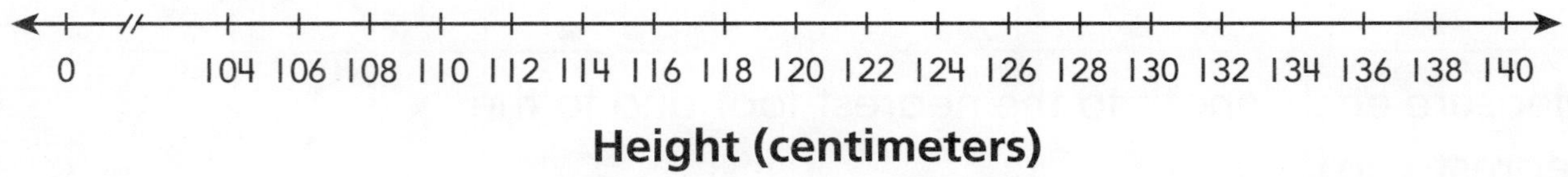

Draw a dot to show your height in inches.

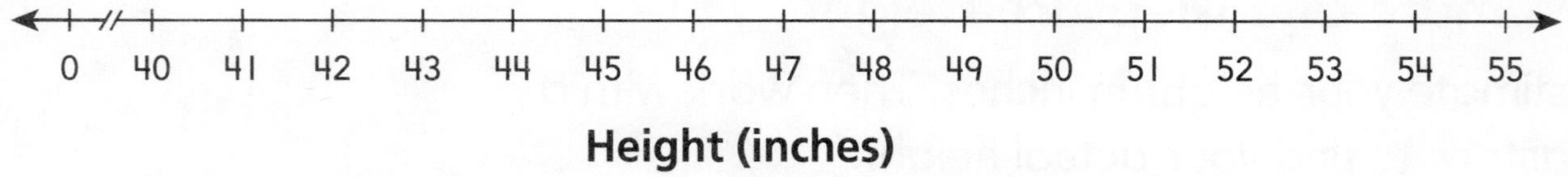

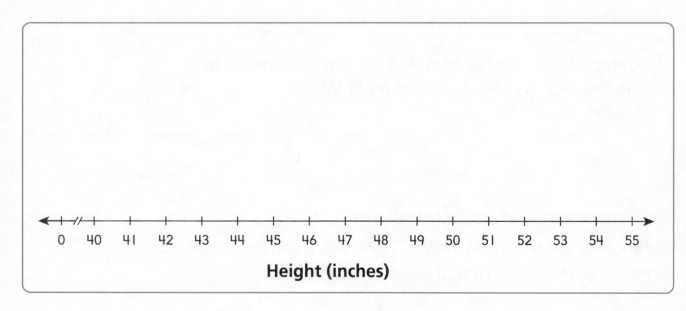

Check Understanding

Is a 20-inch piece of string *more* or *less* than 20 cm long? Explain how you know.

Name ______________________________

Lengths of Pencils

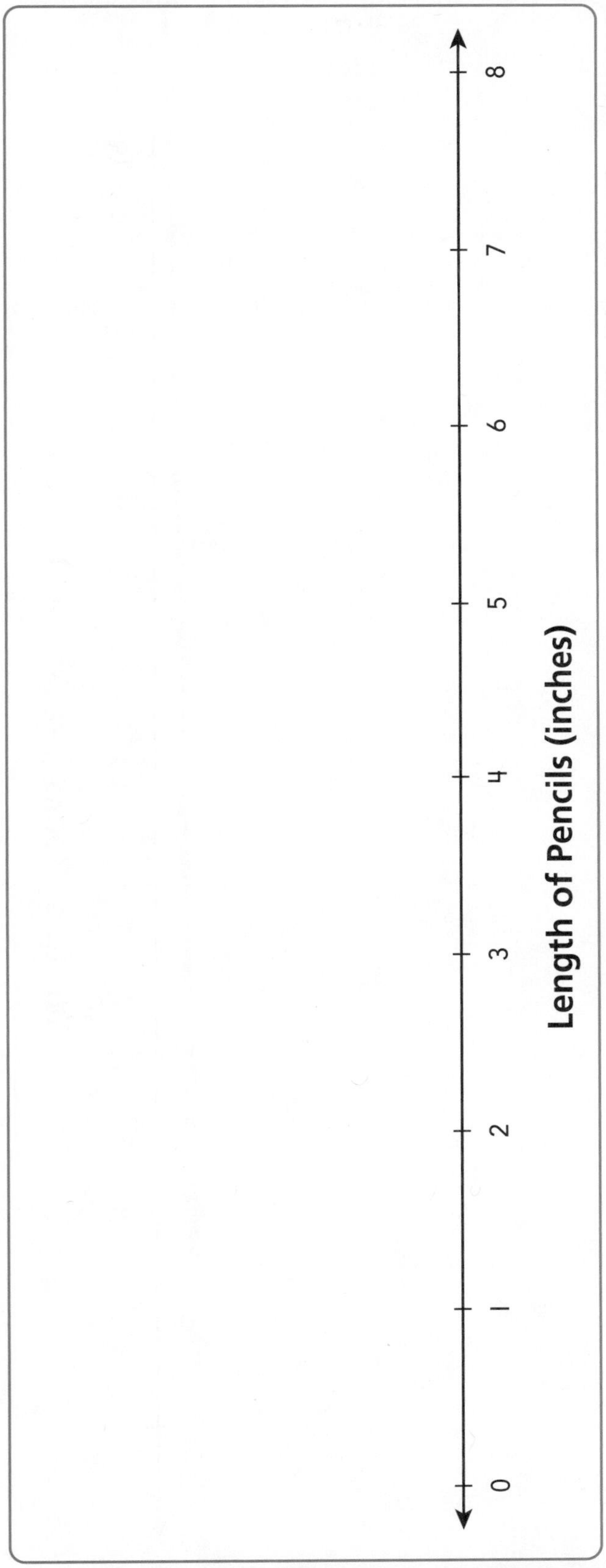

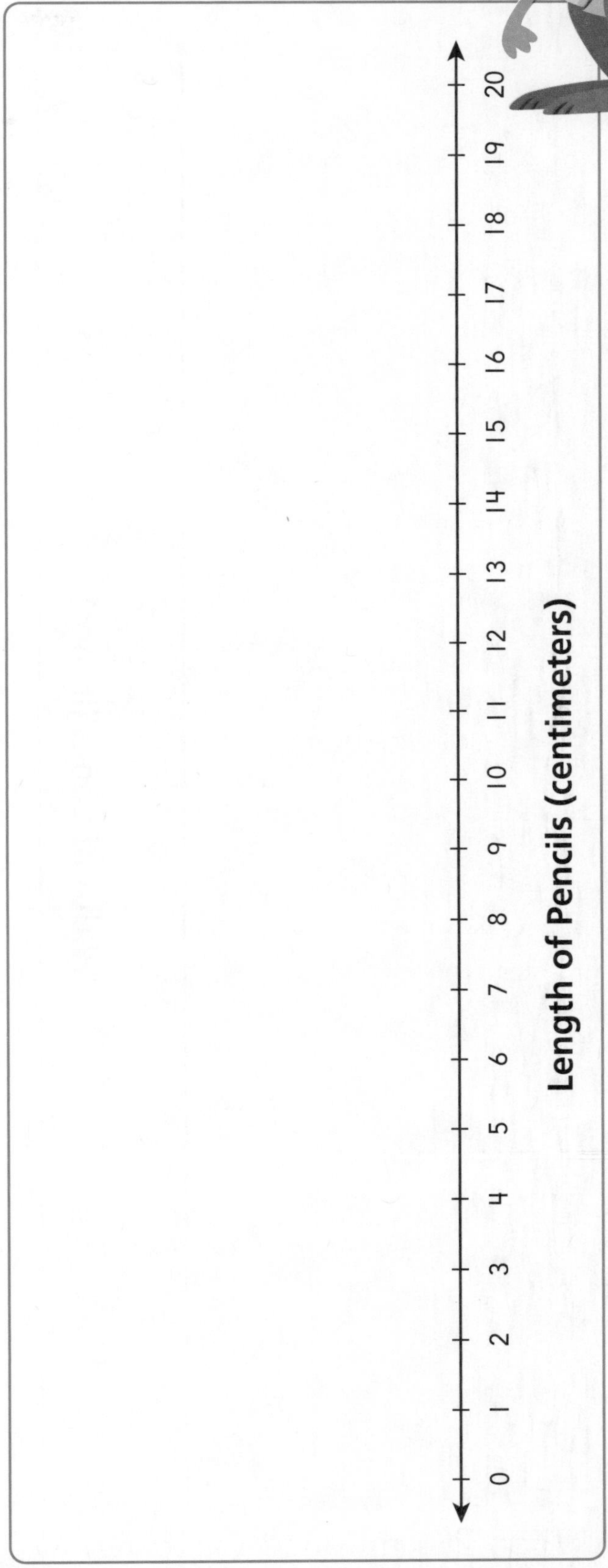

CC SS Content Standards **2.MD.A.1, 2.MD.A.2, 2.MD.A.3, 2.MD.D.9**
Mathematical Practices **MP2, MP4, MP5, MP7, MP8**

Widths of Books

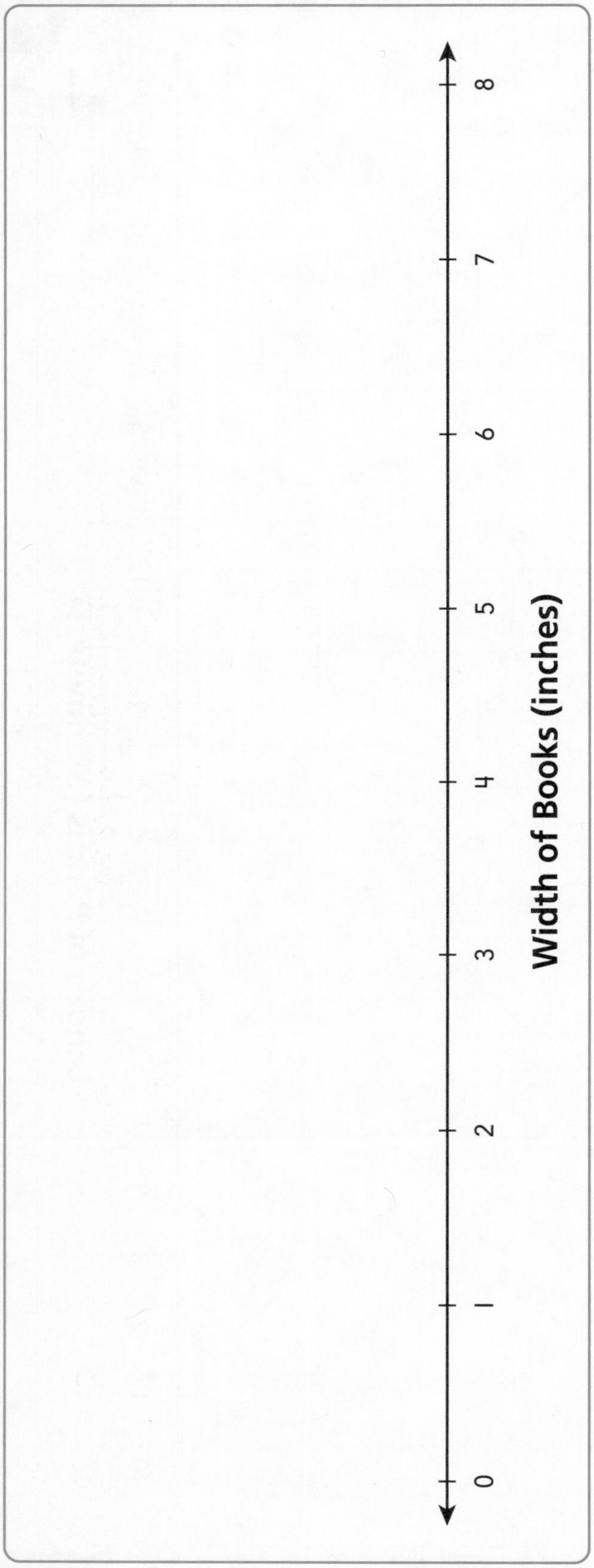

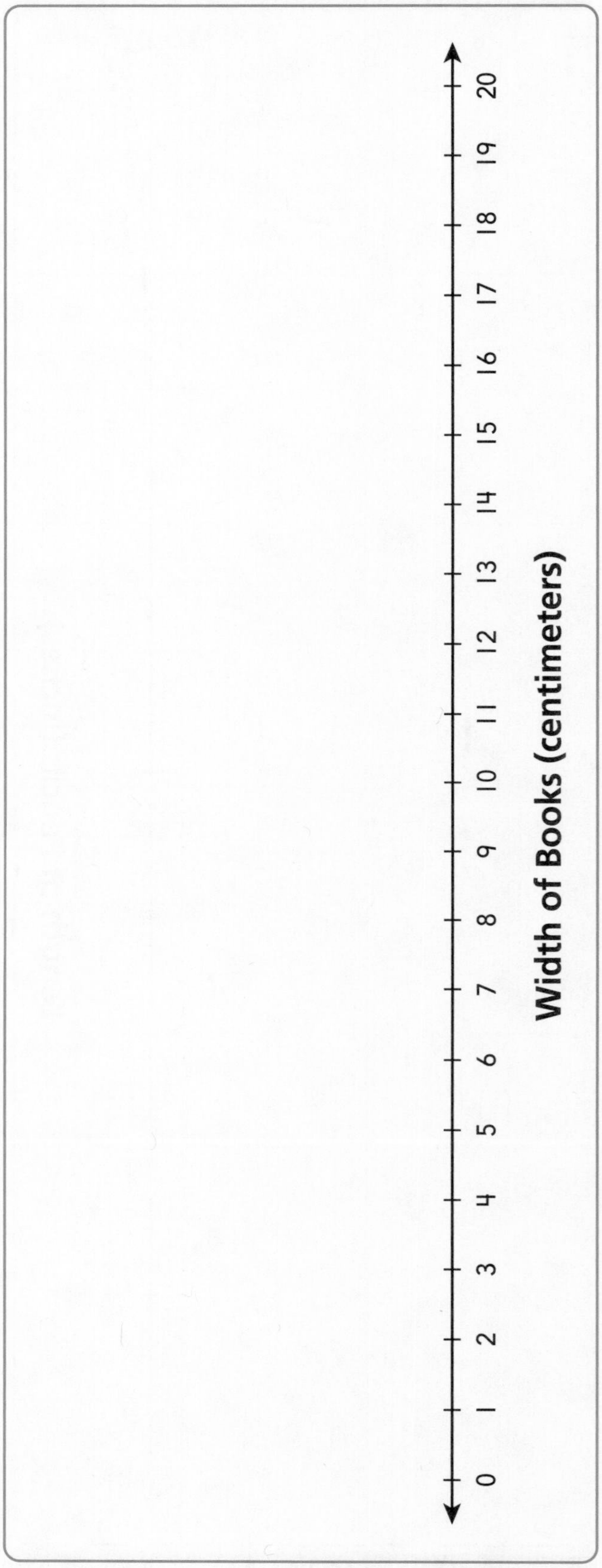

Name ___________________________________

Measurement Data on Line Plots

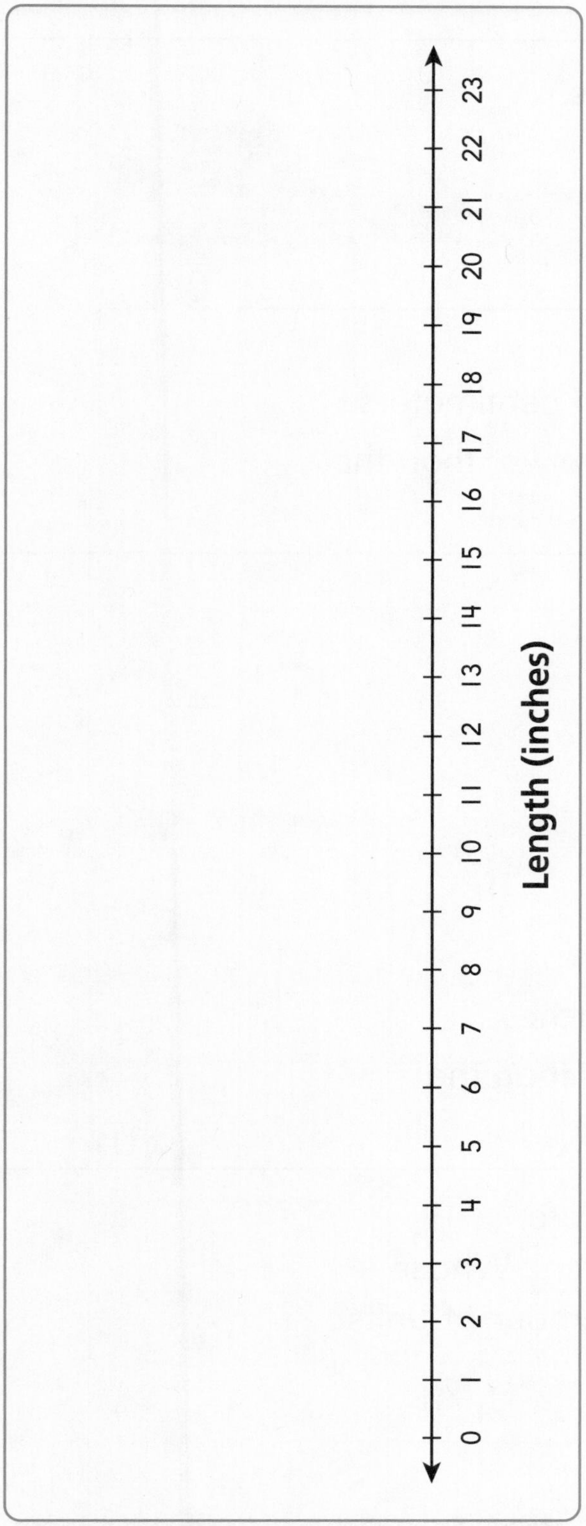

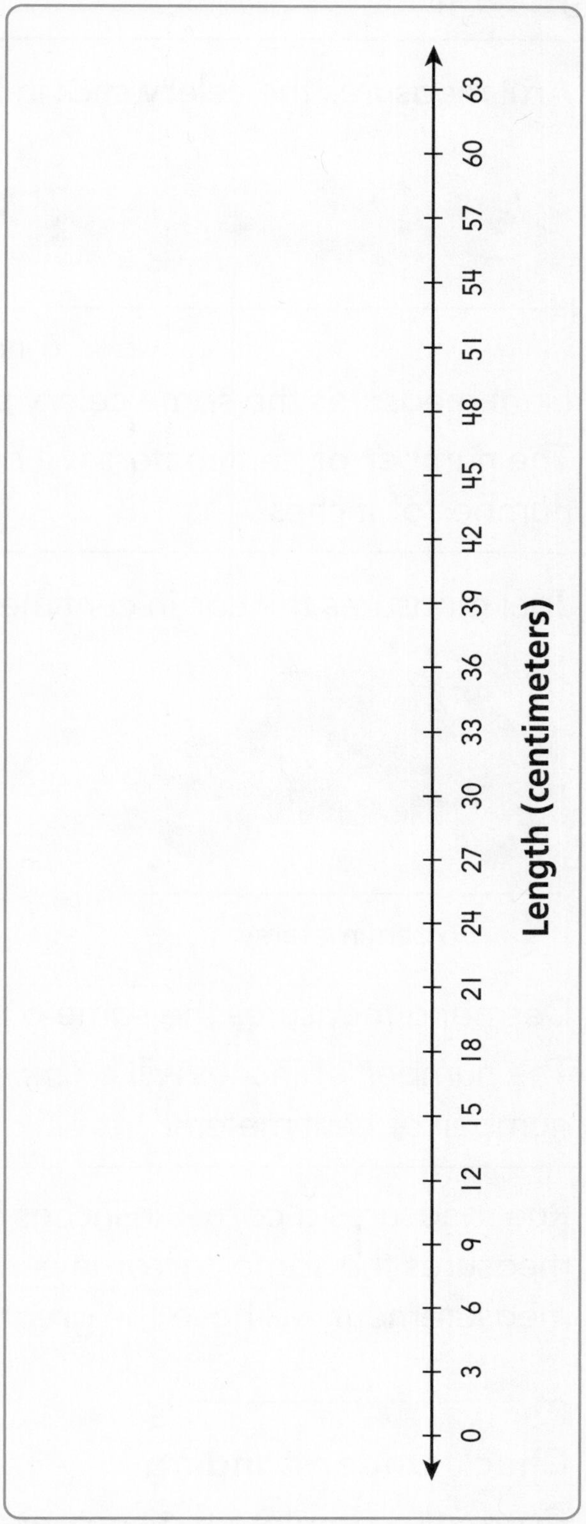

Compare Measurement Units

Ring *more* or *less*.

1 Arul measures the celery stick in inches.

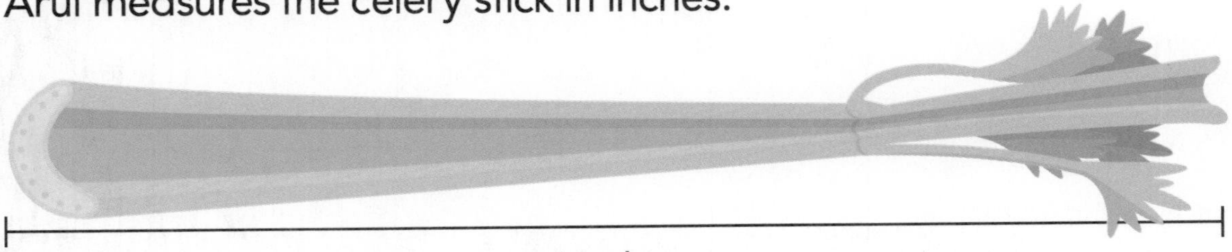

6 inches

Liam measures the same celery stick in centimeters.

The number of centimeters will be *more* *less* than the number of inches.

2 Jael measures the car in centimeters.

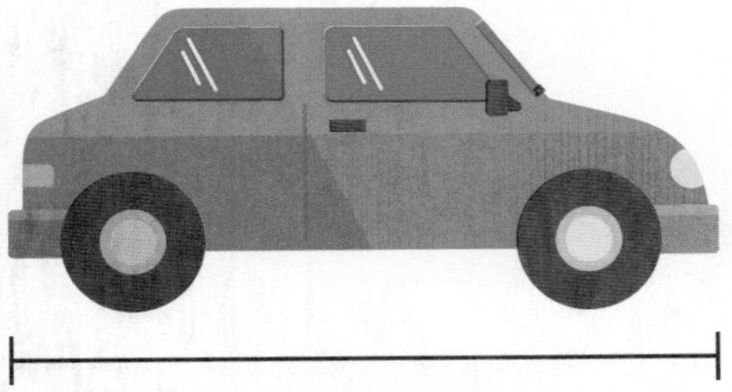

6 centimeters

Desmond measures the same car in inches.

The number of inches will be *more* *less* than the number of centimeters.

3 Rue measures a carrot in inches and Peter measures the same carrot in centimeters. Whose measurement will have the greater number of units?

____

Check Understanding

Correctly complete the sentence with *more* or *less*.

9 feet is ________ than 9 yards.

Name ____________________

Identify Quilt Shapes

A patchwork quilt is made by sewing pieces of cloth together. Look for shapes in these patchwork quilts.

1 Color each shape a different color.

Shape	triangle	quadrilateral	pentagon	hexagon
Color	red	orange	blue	yellow

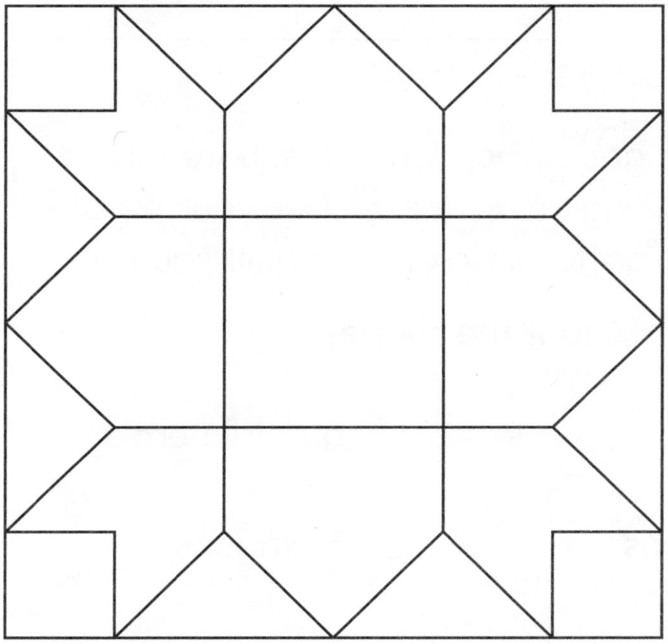

Make Quilts

2 Continue the pattern to complete this quilt square.

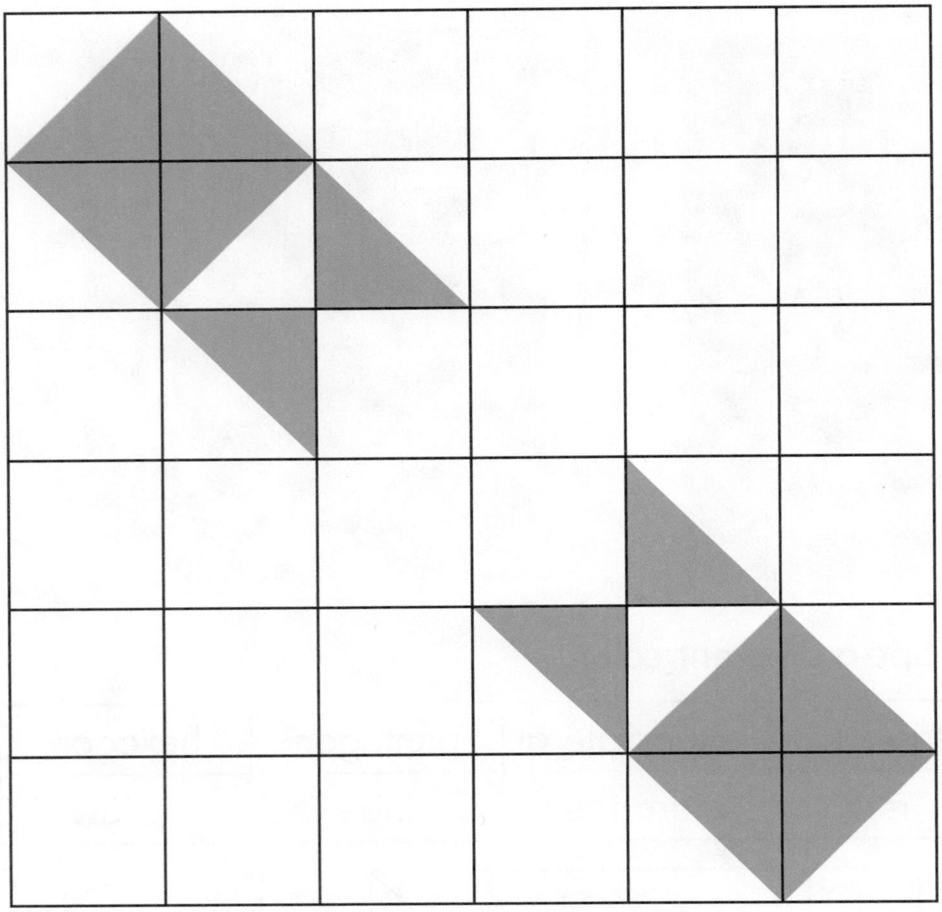

3 Use centimeter grid paper. Draw a square that is 16 centimeters long on each side. Use your square to make a quilt pattern. Color your quilt square.

When you finish, count the shapes.

_____ triangles _____ quadrilaterals

_____ pentagons _____ hexagons

Unit 3
Quick Quiz 2

Name ______________________ Date __________

Solve.

1. Estimate and then measure the length of the marker.

Estimate: ☐ inches

Measure: ☐ inches

2. Estimate and then measure the length of the chalk.

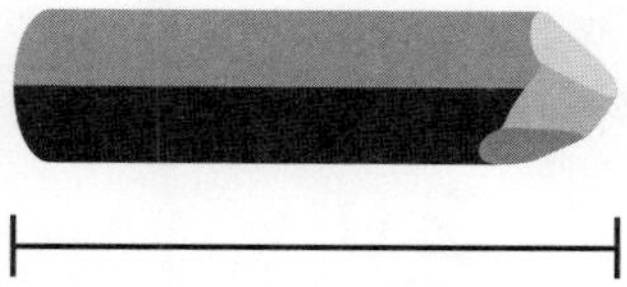

Estimate: ☐ centimeters

Measure: ☐ centimeters

3. Estimate the width of a desk in feet.

Estimate: ☐ feet

4. Describe a classroom object that measures about 2 meters.

____

5. Describe a classroom object that measures about 2 feet.

____

Name Date

PATH to FLUENCY

Add or subtract.

1. $4 + 1 = \square$

2. $11 + 9 = \square$

3. $9 + 7 = \square$

4. $12 - 4 = \square$

5. $10 - 8 = \square$

6. $17 - 10 = \square$

7. $\begin{array}{r} 14 \\ -\ \ 9 \\ \hline \end{array}$

8. $\begin{array}{r} 18 \\ -\ 14 \\ \hline \end{array}$

9. $\begin{array}{r} 20 \\ -\ \ 8 \\ \hline \end{array}$

10. $\begin{array}{r} 40 \\ +\ 20 \\ \hline \end{array}$

11. $\begin{array}{r} 48 \\ +\ 27 \\ \hline \end{array}$

12. $\begin{array}{r} 27 \\ +\ 32 \\ \hline \end{array}$

13. $\begin{array}{r} 69 \\ +\ 24 \\ \hline \end{array}$

14. $\begin{array}{r} 18 \\ +\ \ 2 \\ \hline \end{array}$

15. $\begin{array}{r} 54 \\ +\ 46 \\ \hline \end{array}$

Name ______________________ Date ______________

Measure each string to the nearest centimeter.
Then match the string to its length on the right.

1 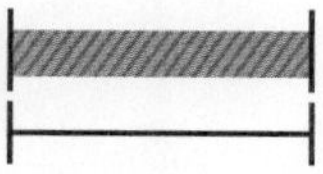 • • 6 cm

2  • • 2 cm

3 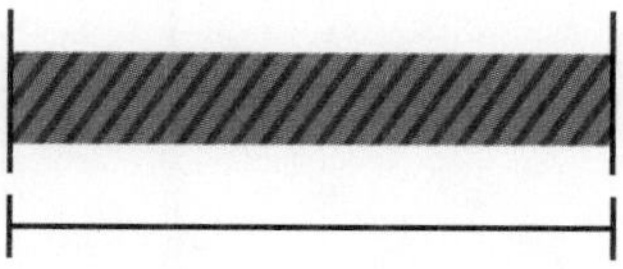 • • 3 cm

4  • • 5 cm

5  • • 4 cm

---

6 Show the lengths of the five strings on this line plot.

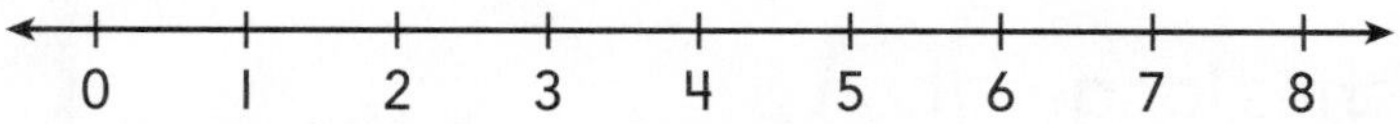

Length of Strings (centimeters)

How many strings are longer than 3 cm?

☐ strings

Name ____________________ Date ____________

7 Estimate the length of the eraser in inches.

Write your estimate.

about ☐ ____________
label

Measure the eraser to the nearest inch.
Circle the actual measure.

The eraser is 3 / 4 / 5 inches long.

---

8 Measure each pencil in inches.

☐ inches

☐ inches

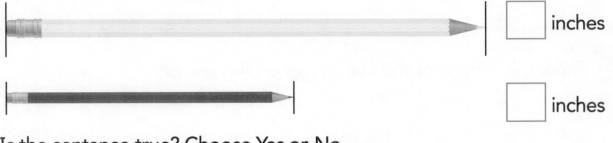

Is the sentence true? Choose Yes or No.

The yellow pencil is 2 inches longer than the blue pencil.	○ Yes	○ No
The yellow pencil is 1 inch longer than the blue pencil.	○ Yes	○ No
The blue pencil is 2 inches shorter than the yellow pencil.	○ Yes	○ No

Name ____________________ Date ____________

9 Draw each shape in the correct box below.

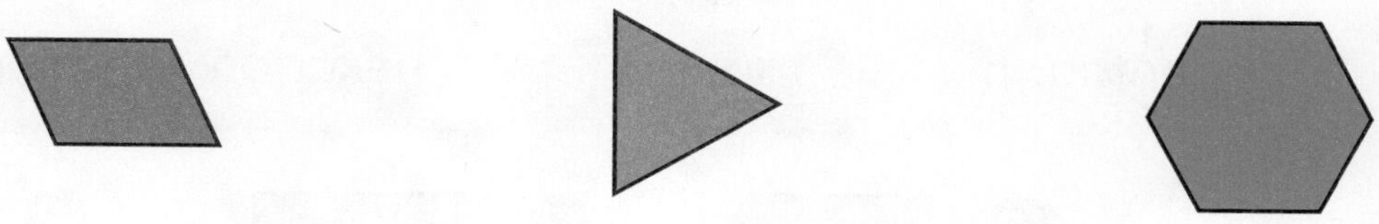

Has exactly 6 sides	Has exactly 4 angles	Has fewer than 4 angles

---

10 Measure the crayon in centimeters and in inches.

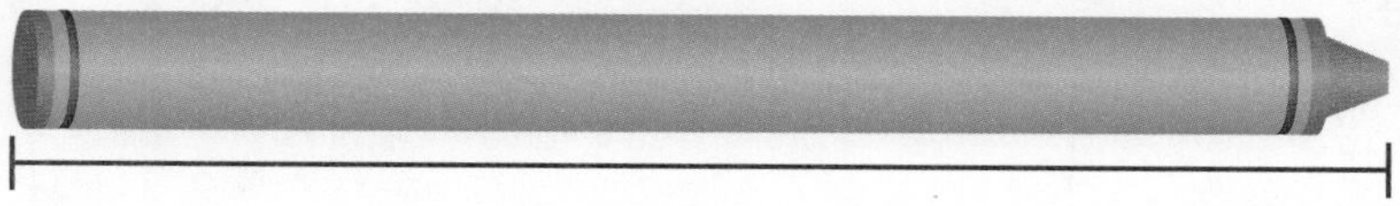

Circle the number or words in each box that makes the sentence true.

The crayon is [8 / 9 / 10] centimeters long.

The crayon is [3 / 4 / 5] inches long.

There are fewer [inches than centimeters / centimeters than inches] because [inches are bigger than centimeters. / centimeters are bigger than inches.]

Unit 3
Review/Test

Name ______________________________ Date ______________

Name the shapes using the words on the tiles.

cube | pentagon | triangle | hexagon | quadrilateral

11 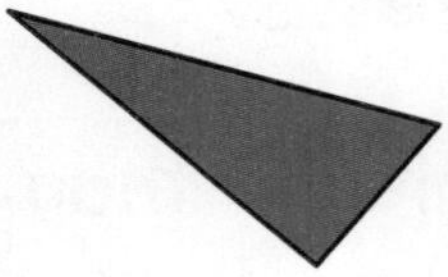

____

12 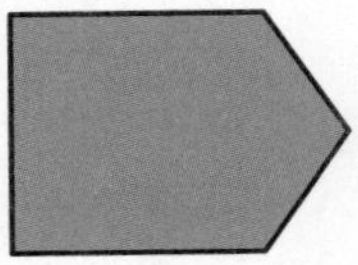

____

13 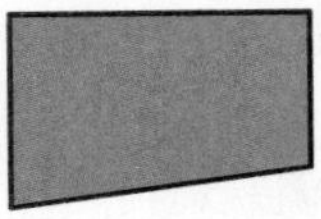

____

14 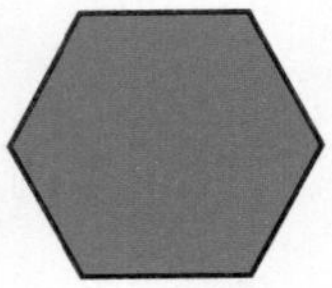

____

15 Complete the table. Use an inch ruler to measure.

Side	Estimate	Measure
EF		
FG		
GH		
HE		

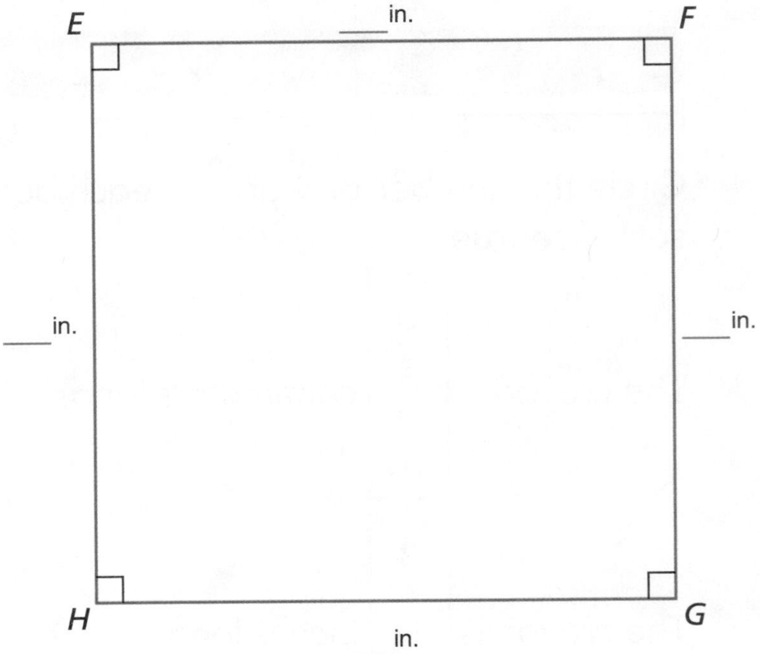

Find the distance around the square. Show your work.

The distance around the square is ☐ inches.

Unit 3
Performance Task

Name ______________________________

Setting Up the Table

8 people can sit at this table.	10 people can sit at this table.
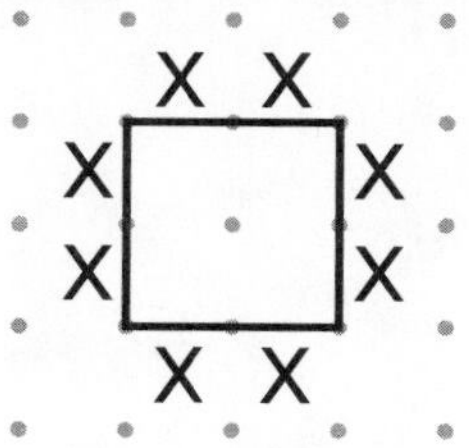	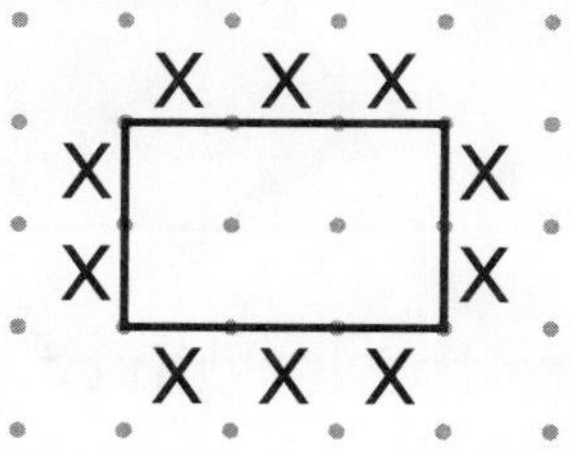

1. Draw a rectangular table that seats 12 people with no extra places.

2. Can the table be a square and seat exactly 12 people? Explain your answer.

____

____

____

3. Find the distance around the rectangular table you drew in centimeters and in inches.

__________ cm about __________ in.

Explain why the number of centimeters is different from the number of inches.

____

____

Name ____________________________

Caitlin is sitting at a table shaped like a quadrilateral. She uses an inch ruler to draw a model of the table.

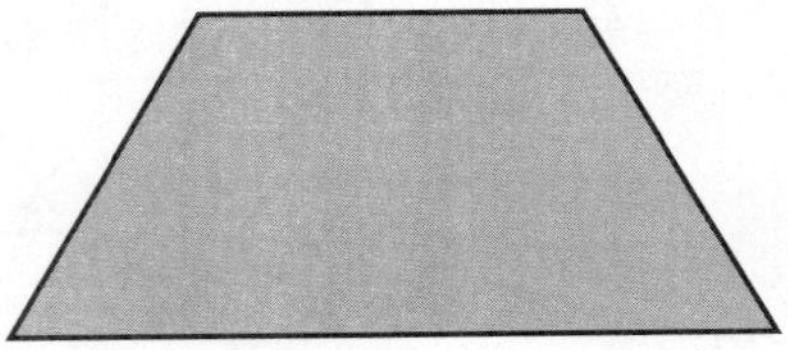

4 Measure the length of each side. Then find the distance around the table in Caitlin's drawing.

☐ in. + ☐ in. + ☐ in. + ☐ in. = ☐ in.

5 Mr. Evans puts two tables together to form a bigger table.

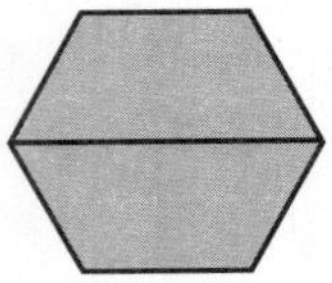

What shape is the table now? ____________

6 Draw another table connected to the table Caitlin drew. You can arrange them like Mr. Evans did, or choose an arrangement of your own.

What is the distance around your new bigger table? Show your work.

__________ inches

Addition and Subtraction Problem Types

	Result Unknown	Change Unknown	Start Unknown
Add To	Aisha has 46 stamps in her collection. Then her grandfather gives her 29 stamps. How many stamps does she have now? *Situation and Solution Equation:* $46 + 29 = \square$	Aisha has 46 stamps in her collection. Then her grandfather gives her some stamps. Now she has 75 stamps. How many stamps did her grandfather give her? *Situation Equation:* $46 + \square = 75$ *Solution Equation:* $\square = 75 - 46$	Aisha has some stamps in her collection. Then her grandfather gives her 29 stamps. Now she has 75 stamps. How many stamps did she have to start? *Situation Equation:* $\square + 29 = 75$ *Solution Equation:* $\square = 75 - 29$
Take From	A store has 43 bottles of water at the start of the day. During the day, the store sells 25 bottles. How many bottles do they have at the end of the day? *Situation and Solution Equation:* $43 - 25 = \square$	A store has 43 bottles of water at the start of the day. The store has 18 bottles left at the end of the day. How many bottles does the store sell? *Situation Equation:* $43 - \square = 18$ *Solution Equation:* $\square = 43 - 18$	A store sells 25 bottles of water during one day. At the end of the day 18 bottles are left. How many bottles did the store have at the beginning of the day? *Situation Equation:* $\square - 25 = 18$ *Solution Equation:* $\square = 25 + 18$

[1]A situation equation represents the structure (action) in the problem situation. A solution equation shows the operation used to find the answer.

Addition and Subtraction Problem Types (continued)

<table>
<tr><th></th><th>Total Unknown</th><th>Addend Unknown</th><th>Other Addend Unknown</th></tr>
<tr><td rowspan="2">Put Together/ Take Apart</td>
<td>A clothing store has 39 shirts with short sleeves and 45 shirts with long sleeves. How many shirts does the store have in all?
Math Drawing[2]:

Situation and Solution Equation:
39 + 45 = □</td>
<td>Of the 84 shirts in a clothing store, 39 have short sleeves. The rest have long sleeves. How many shirts have long sleeves?
Math Drawing:
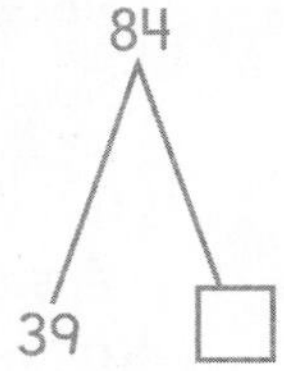
Situation Equation:
84 = 39 + □
Solution Equation:
84 − 39 = □</td>
<td>Of the 84 shirts in a clothing store, some have short sleeves. Forty-five have long sleeves. How many shirts have short sleeves?
Math Drawing:
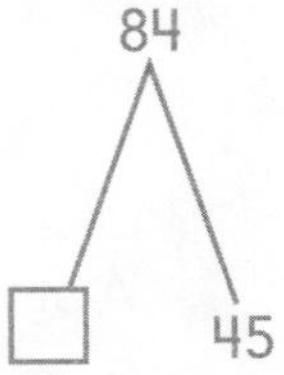
Situation Equation:
84 = □ + 45
Solution Equation:
□ = 84 − 45</td></tr>
<tr><td colspan="2">Both Addends Unknown is a productive extension of this basic situation, especially for small numbers less than or equal to 10. Such take apart situations can be used to show all the decompositions of a given number. The associated equations, which have a total on the left of the equal sign, help children understand that the = sign does not always mean makes or results in but always does mean is the same number as.</td>
<td>Both Addends Unknown
Pam has 24 roses. How many can she put in her red vase and how many in her blue vase?
Math Drawing:
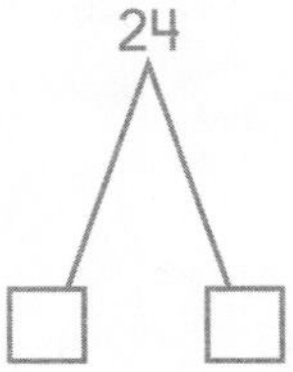
Situation Equation:
24 = □ + □</td></tr>
</table>

[2]These math drawings are called Math Mountains in Grades 1–3 and break-apart drawings in Grades 4 and 5.

Addition and Subtraction Problem Types (continued)

	Difference Unknown	Greater Unknown	Smaller Unknown
Compare[1]	Alex has 64 trading cards. Lucy has 48 trading cards. How many more trading cards does Alex have than Lucy? Lucy has 48 trading cards. Alex has 64 trading cards. How many fewer trading cards does Lucy have than Alex? *Math Drawing:* 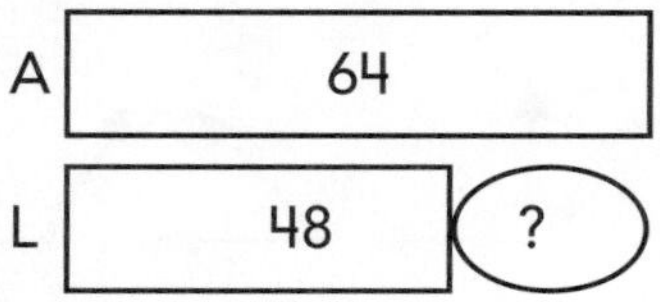 *Situation Equation:* 48 + □ = 64 or □ = 64 − 48 *Solution Equation:* □ = 64 − 48	**Leading Language** Lucy has 48 trading cards. Alex has 16 more trading cards than Lucy. How many trading cards does Alex have?	**Leading Language** Alex has 64 trading cards. Lucy has 16 fewer trading cards than Alex. How many trading cards does Lucy have?
		Misleading Language Lucy has 48 trading cards. Lucy has 16 fewer trading cards than Alex. How many trading cards does Alex have? *Math Drawing:* 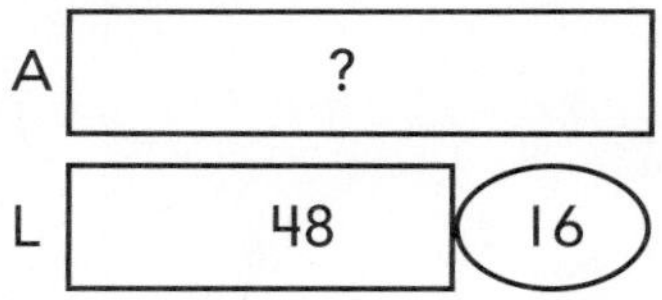 *Situation and Solution Equation:* 48 + 16 = □	**Misleading Language** Alex has 64 trading cards. Alex has 16 more trading cards than Lucy. How many trading cards does Lucy have? *Math Drawing:* 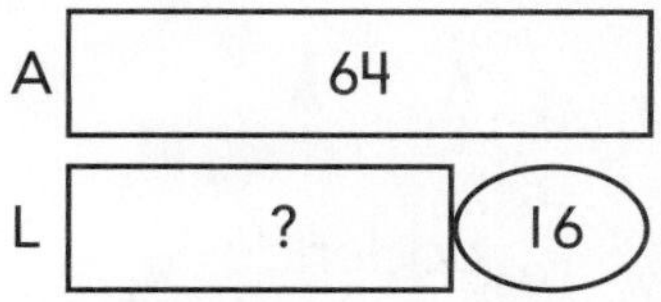 *Situation Equation:* □ + 16 = 64 or □ = 64 − 16 *Solution Equation:* □ = 64 − 16

[1] A comparison sentence can always be said in two ways. One way uses *more*, and the other uses *fewer* or *less*. Misleading language suggests the wrong operation. For example, it says *Lucy has 16 fewer trading cards than Alex*, but you have to add 16 cards to the number of cards Lucy has to get the number of cards Alex has.

5-groups*

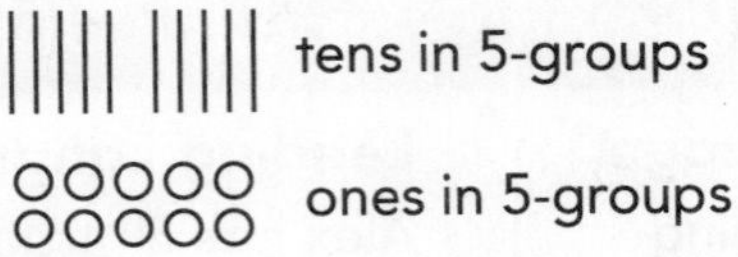

A

add

$4 + 2 = 6$

addend

$5 + 6 = 11$

↑ ↑

addends

Adding Up Method* (for Subtraction)

$$\begin{array}{r} 144 \\ -\ 68 \\ \hline 76 \end{array} \qquad \begin{array}{r} 68 + \ 2 = \ 70 \\ 70 + 30 = 100 \\ 100 + \underline{44} = 144 \end{array}$$

$\boxed{76}$

addition doubles*

Both addends (or partners) are the same.

$4 + 4 = 8$

A.M.

Use A.M. for times between midnight and noon.

analog clock

angle

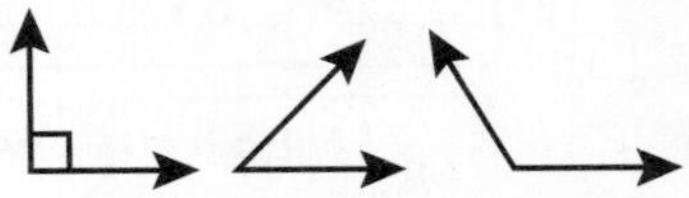

These are angles.

array

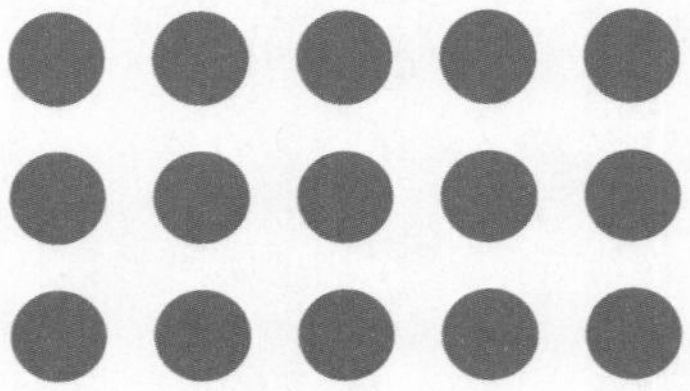

This rectangular array has 3 rows and 5 columns.

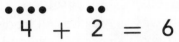

*A classroom research-based term developed for *Math Expressions*

B

bar graph

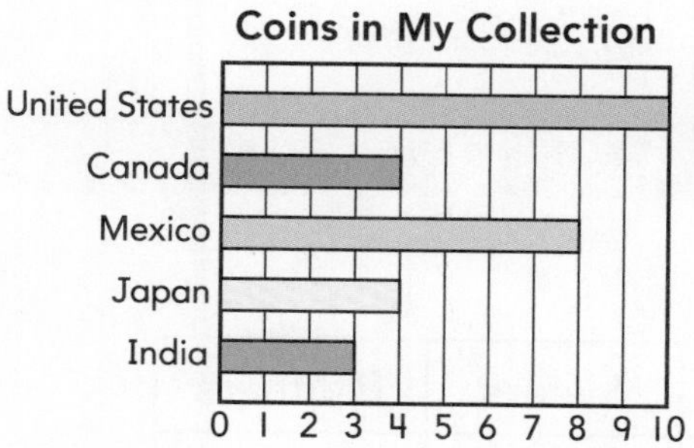

horizontal bar graph

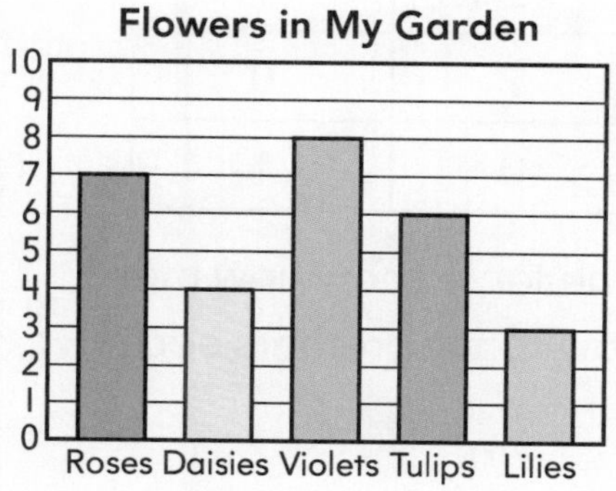

vertical bar graph

break-apart*

You can break apart a larger number to get two smaller amounts called break-aparts.

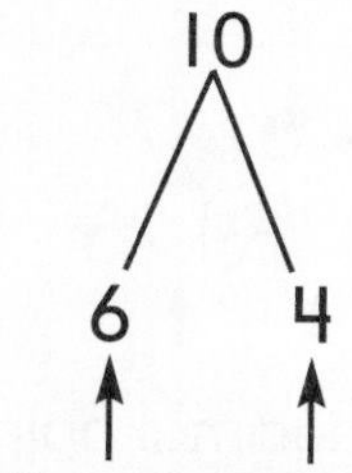

break-aparts of 10

C

cent

front back

1 cent or 1¢ or $0.01

centimeter (cm)

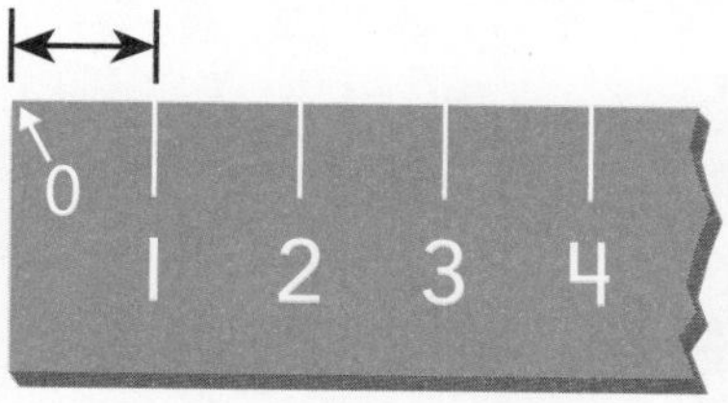

cent sign

56¢
↑
cent sign

clock

analog clock

digital clock

columns

This rectangular array has 4 columns with 3 tiles in each column.

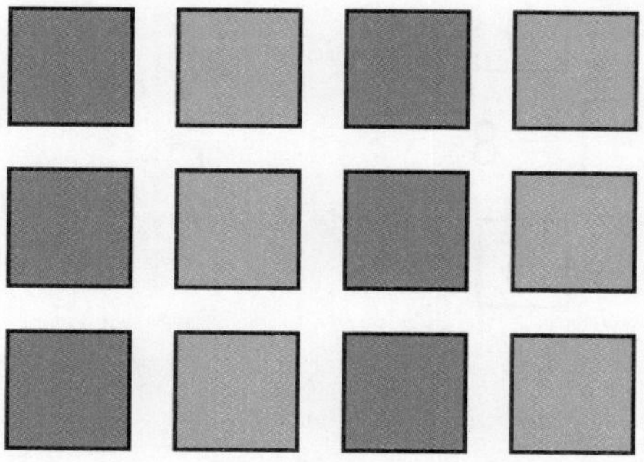

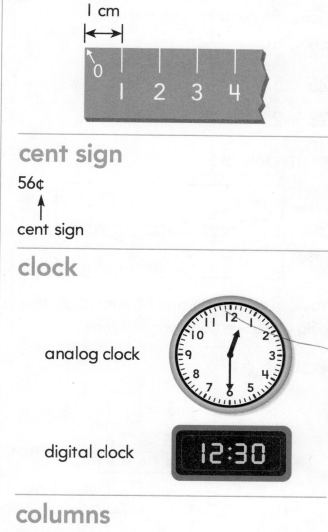

*A classroom research-based term developed for *Math Expressions*

compare numbers

Compare numbers using >, <, or =.

$52 > 25$

$25 < 52$

$25 = 25$

comparison bars*

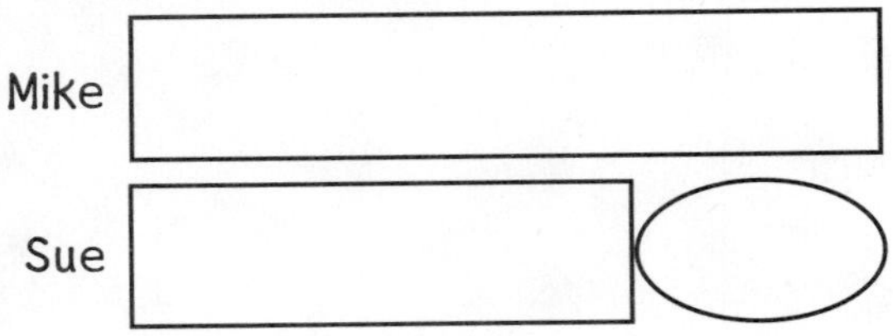

You can add labels and fill in numbers to help you solve *Compare* problems.

count all*

$5 + 3 = \square$

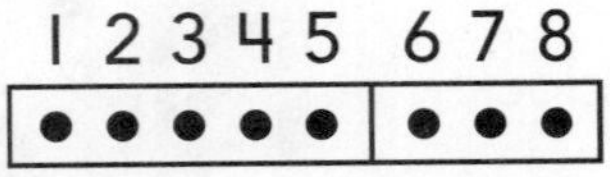

$5 + 3 = \boxed{8}$

count on

$5 + 3 = \boxed{8}$

$5 + \boxed{3} = 8$

$8 - 5 = \boxed{3}$

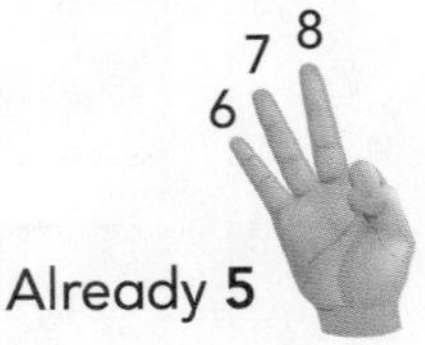

cube

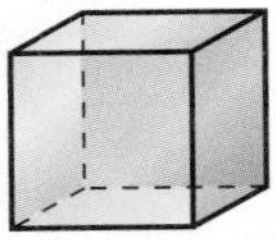

D

data

	Sisters	Brothers
Kendra	2	1
Scott	2	0
Ida	0	1

data (arrows point to Kendra's 2 and 1)

The data in the table show how many sisters and how many brothers each child has.

decade numbers*

10, 20, 30, 40, 50, 60, 70, 80, 90

decimal point

$4.25

↑

decimal point

diagonal

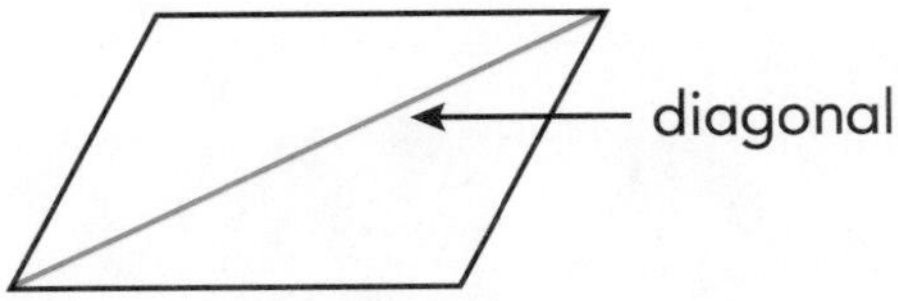

*A classroom research-based term developed for *Math Expressions*

difference

$11 - 3 = 8$

$$\begin{array}{r} 11 \\ -\ 3 \\ \hline 8 \end{array}$$

difference → 8 (and ↑ pointing to 8 in $11 - 3 = 8$)

digital clock

digits

0, 1, 2, 3, 4, 5, 6, 7, 8, 9

15 is a 2-digit number.

The 1 in 15 means 1 ten.

The 5 in 15 means 5 ones.

dime

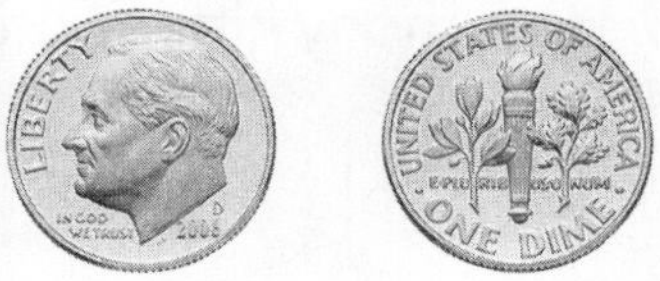

front back

10 cents or 10¢ or $0.10

dollar

100 cents or 100¢ or $1.00

front

back

dollar sign

$4.25

↑

dollar sign

doubles minus 1

7 + 7 = 14, so

7 + 6 = 13, 1 less than 14.

doubles minus 2

7 + 7 = 14, so

7 + 5 = 12, 2 less than 14.

doubles plus 1

6 + 6 = 12, so

6 + 7 = 13, 1 more than 12.

doubles plus 2

6 + 6 = 12, so

6 + 8 = 14, 2 more than 12.

E

equal shares

2 halves 4 fourths

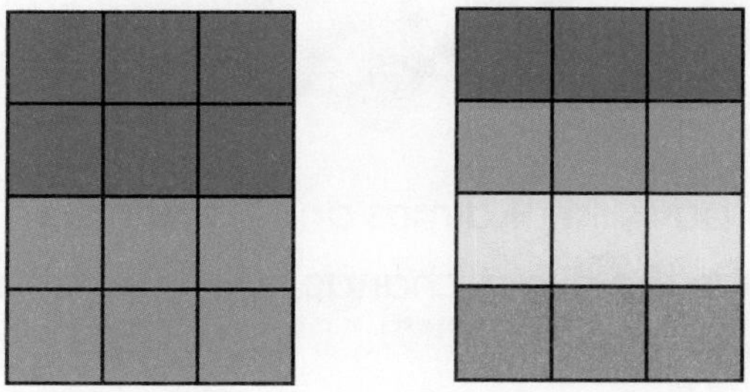

*A classroom research-based term developed for *Math Expressions*

equation

$4 + 3 = 7 \qquad 7 = 4 + 3$

$9 - 5 = 4 \qquad 4 + 5 = 8 + 1$

An equation must have an = sign.

equation chain*

$3 + 4 = 5 + 2 = 8 - 1 = 7$

estimate

Make a reasonable guess about how many or how much.

even

A number is even if you can make groups of 2 and have none left over.

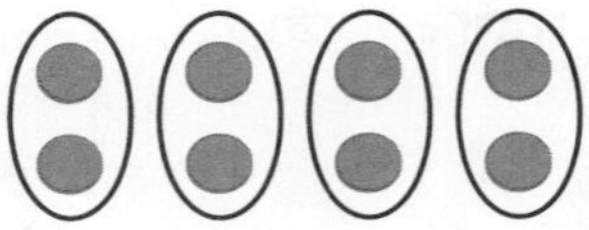

8 is an even number.

exact change

I will pay with 4 dimes and 3 pennies. That is the exact change. I won't get any money back.

expanded form

$283 = 200 + 80 + 3$

Expanded Method (for Addition)*

$$\begin{array}{rcr} 78 & = & 70 + 8 \\ +\ 57 & = & 50 + 7 \\ \hline & & 120 + 15 = 135 \end{array}$$

Expanded Method* (for Subtraction)

$$\begin{array}{rcl} 64 & = & \overset{50}{\cancel{60}} + \overset{14}{\cancel{4}} \\ -\ 28 & = & 20 + 8 \\ \hline & & 30 + 6 = 36 \end{array}$$

extra information

Franny has 8 kittens and 2 dogs. 4 kittens are asleep. How many kittens are awake?

$8 - 4 = \boxed{4}$

The number of dogs is extra information. It is not needed to solve the problem.

F

fewer

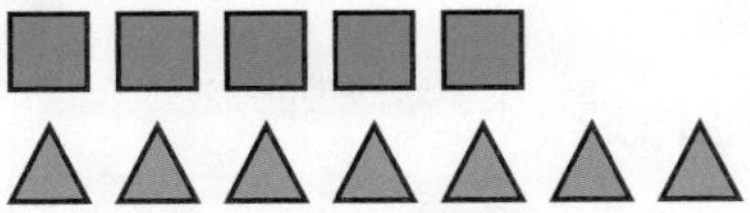

There are fewer ■ than ▲.

*A classroom research-based term developed for *Math Expressions*

foot (ft)

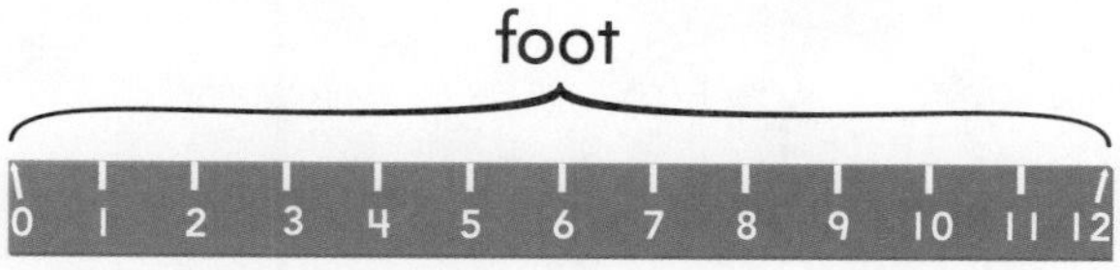

12 inches = 1 foot (not drawn to scale)

fourths

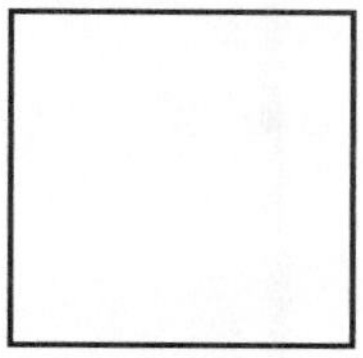

square

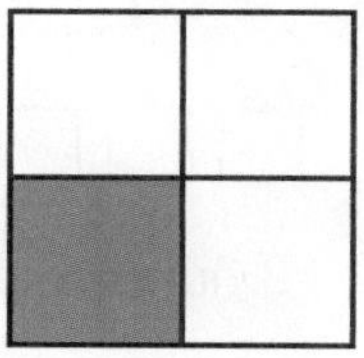

The picture shows 4 fourths. A fourth of the square is shaded.

G

greatest

25 41 63

63 is the greatest number.

group name*

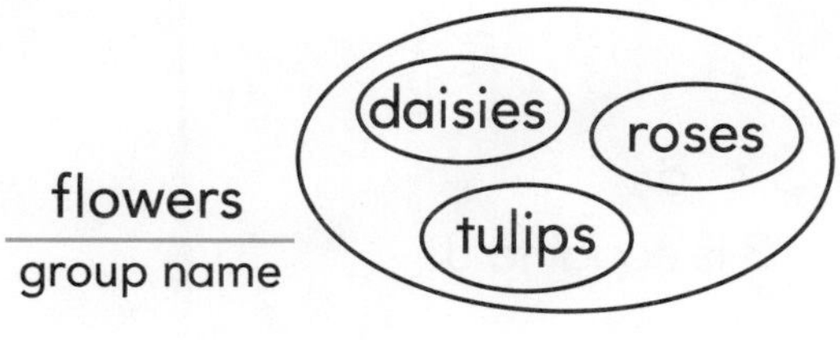

H

half hour

30 minutes = 1 half hour

halves

square

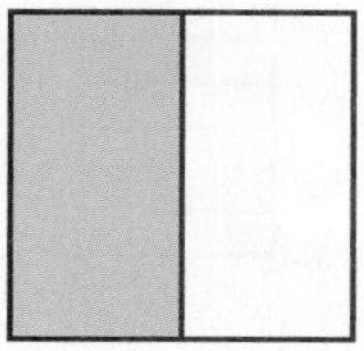

The picture shows 2 halves. A half of the square is shaded.

hexagon

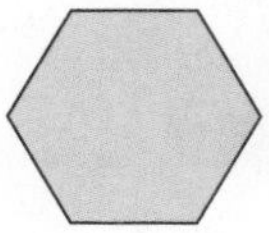

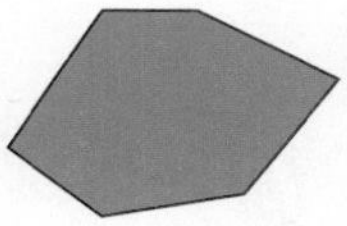

A hexagon has 6 sides and 6 angles.

*A classroom research-based term developed for *Math Expressions*

hidden information

Heather bought a dozen eggs. She used 7 of them to make breakfast. How many eggs does she have left?

$12 - 7 = \boxed{5}$

The hidden information is that a dozen means 12.

horizontal bar graph

horizontal form

$4 + 5 = 9$

horizontal line

hour

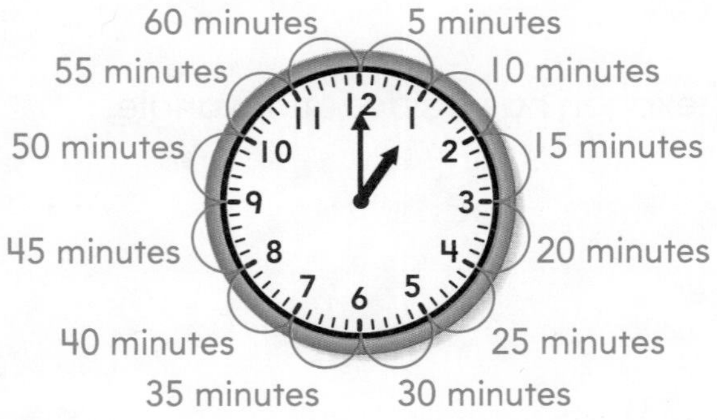

60 minutes = 1 hour

hour hand

hundreds

347 has 3 hundreds.

↑

hundreds

I

inch (in.)

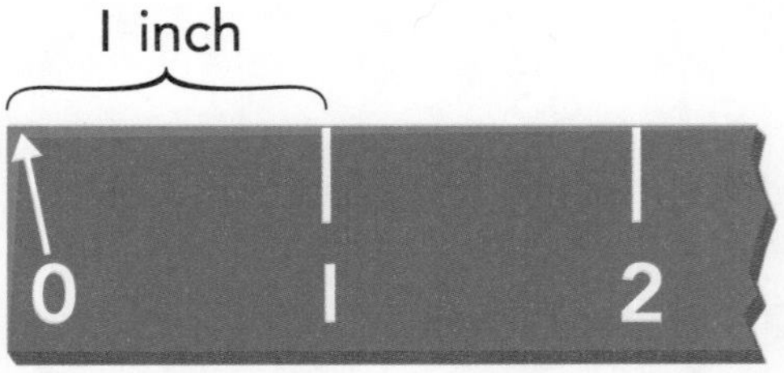

is equal to (=)

$5 + 3 = 8$

5 plus 3 is equal to 8.

is greater than (>)

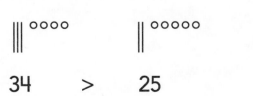

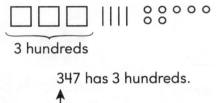

34 > 25

34 is greater than 25.

*A classroom research-based term developed for *Math Expressions*

is less than (<)

45 < 46

45 is less than 46.

L

least

14 7 63

7 is the least number.

length

The length of the pencil is about 17 cm.
(not to scale)

line plot

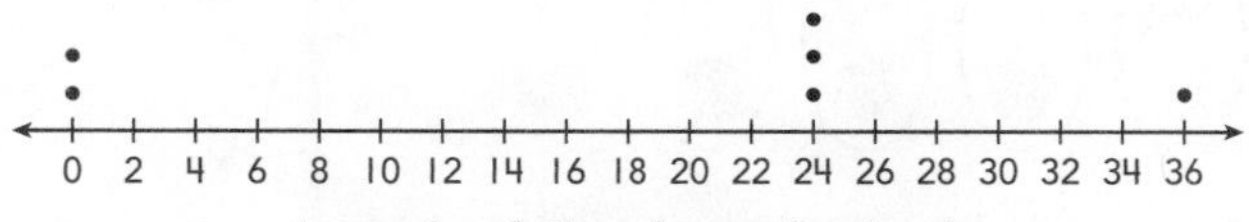

line segment

M

make a ten

8 + 6 = ☐

8 ●●|●●●●

10 + 4

10 + 4 = 14,

so 8 + 6 = 14

matching drawing*

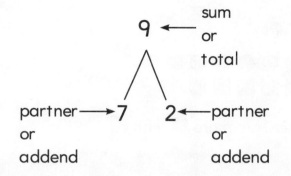

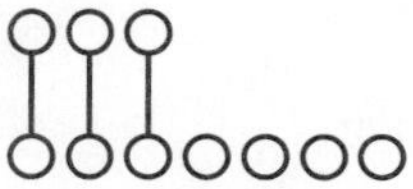

fewer

more

Math Mountain*

9 ← sum or total

partner → 7   2 ← partner

or addend   or addend

meter(m)

100 centimeters = 1 meter
(not drawn to scale)

minus

8 − 3 = 5

$$\begin{array}{r} 8 \\ -\ 3 \\ \hline 5 \end{array}$$

8 minus 3 equals 5.

minute

60 seconds = 1 minute

*A classroom research-based term developed for *Math Expressions*

minute hand

minute hand: points to the minutes

more

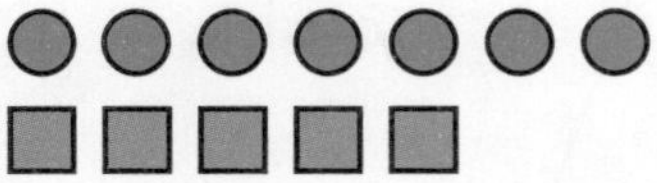

There are more ● than ■.

N

New Groups Above Method*

```
  1
  56
+ 28
----
  84
```

$6 + 8 = 14$

The 1 new ten in 14 goes up above the tens place.

New Groups Below Method*

```
  56
+ 28
--1-
  84
```

$6 + 8 = 14$

The 1 new ten in 14 goes below in the tens place.

nickel

front back

5 cents or 5¢ or $0.05

not equal to (≠)

$6 + 4 \neq 8$

6 + 4 is not equal to 8.

number line diagram

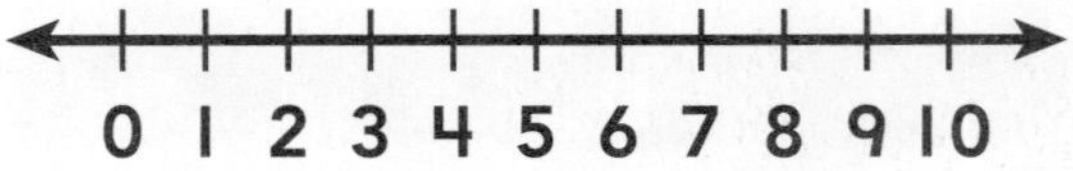

This is a number line diagram.

number name

12

twelve ← number name

O

odd

A number is odd if you can make groups of 2 and have 1 left over.

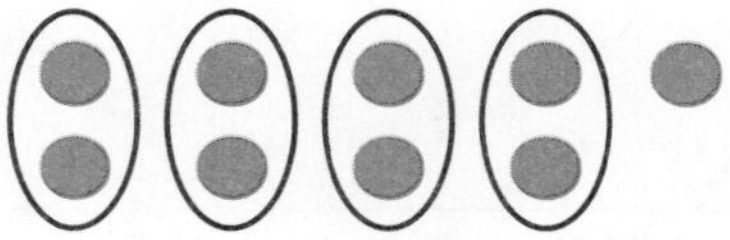

9 is an odd number.

ones

347 has 7 ones.

↑

ones

*A classroom research-based term developed for *Math Expressions*

opposite operations

Addition and subtraction are opposite operations.

$5 + 9 = 14$

$14 - 9 = 5$

Use addition to check subtraction. Use subtraction to check addition.

opposite sides

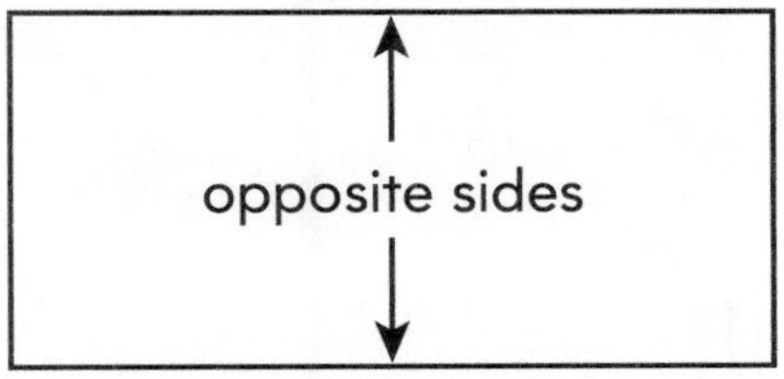

order

2, 5, 6

The numbers 2, 5, and 6 are in order from least to greatest.

P

pairs

A group of 2 is a pair.

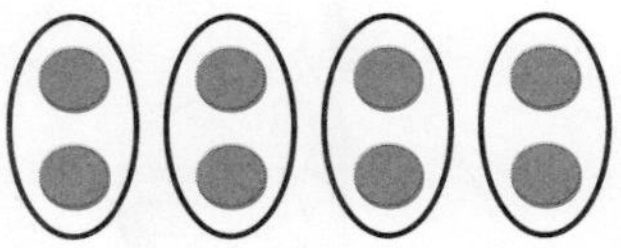

The picture shows 4 pairs of counters.

partner lengths*

partner lengths of 4 cm

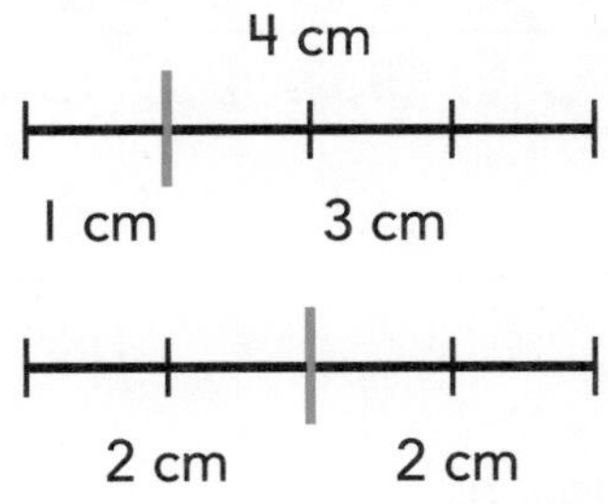

partners*

$9 + 6 = 15$

partners (addends)

pattern

This pattern shows counting by 2s.

2, 4, 6, 8, 10

penny

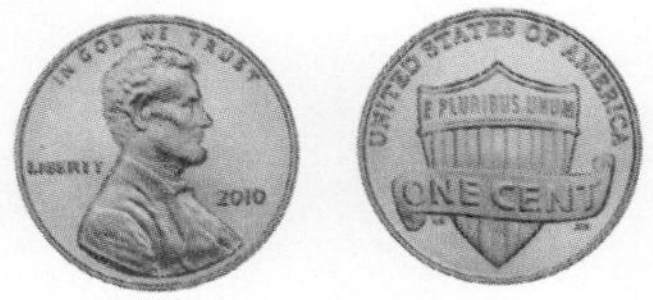

front back

1 cent or 1¢ or $0.01

pentagon

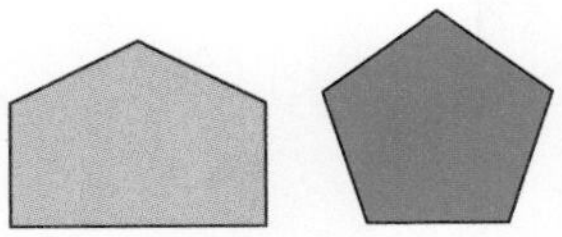

A pentagon has 5 sides and 5 angles.

*A classroom research-based term developed for *Math Expressions*

picture graph

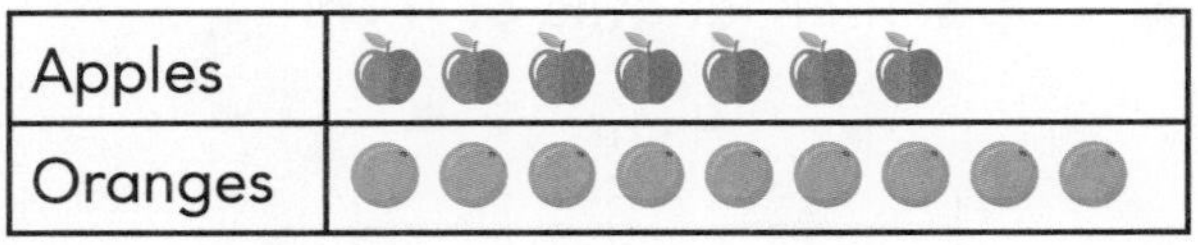

plus

3 + 2 = 5

3 plus 2 equals 5.

$$\begin{array}{r} 3 \\ +2 \\ \hline 5 \end{array}$$

P.M.

Use P.M. for times between noon and midnight.

proof drawing*

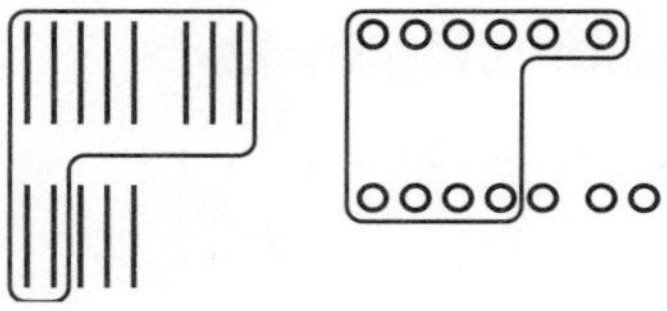

86 + 57 = 143

Q

quadrilateral

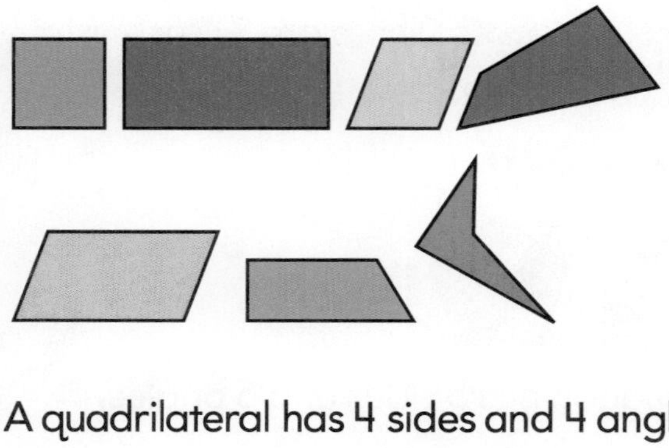

A quadrilateral has 4 sides and 4 angles.

quarter

front back

25 cents or 25¢ or $0.25

A quarter is another name for a fourth.

A quarter is a fourth of a dollar.

quick hundreds*

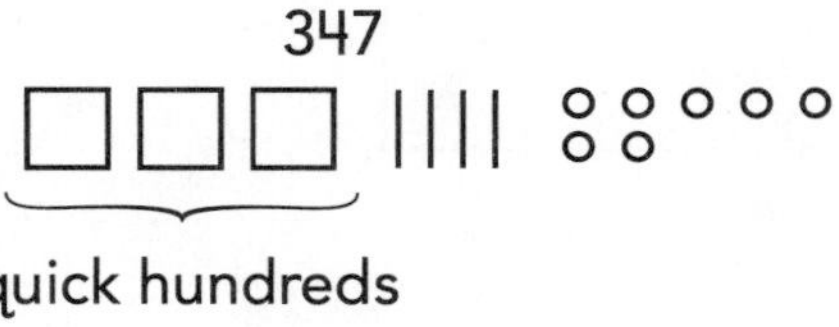

quick tens*

R

rectangle

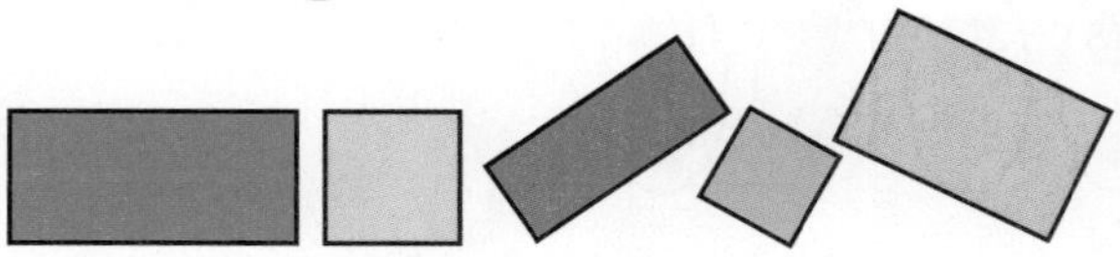

A rectangle has 4 sides and 4 right angles. Opposite sides have the same length.

rectangular prism

*A classroom research-based term developed for *Math Expressions*

right angle

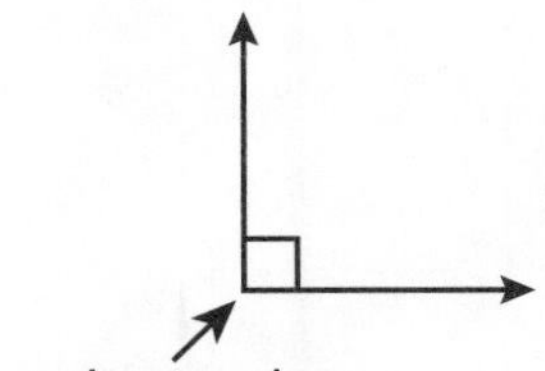

A right angle is sometimes called a *square corner*.

round

Express a number to the nearest ten or hundred. You can round down or round up.

$52 \longrightarrow 50 \qquad 278 \longrightarrow 300$

rows

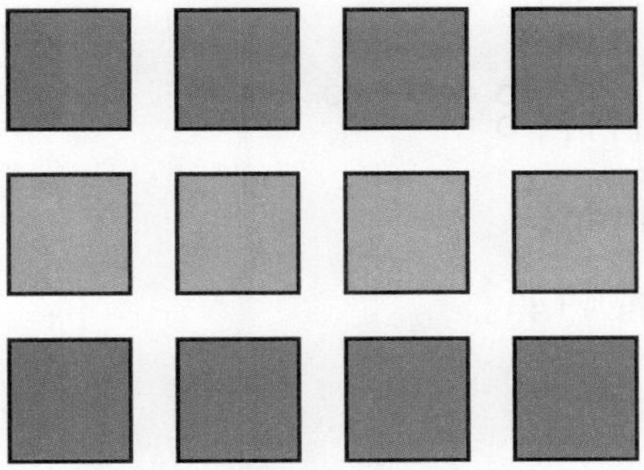

This rectangular array has 3 rows with 4 tiles in each row.

ruler

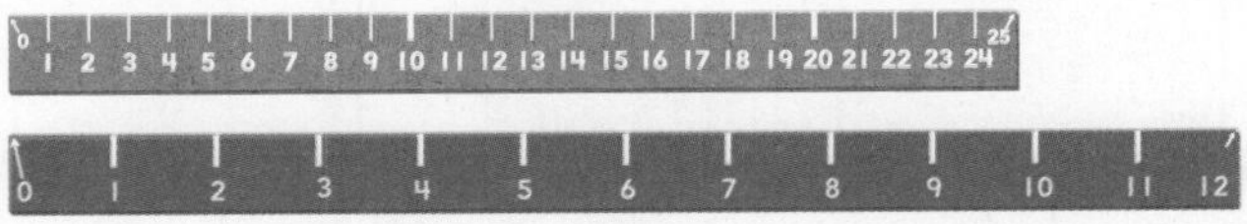

A ruler is used to measure length.

S

scale

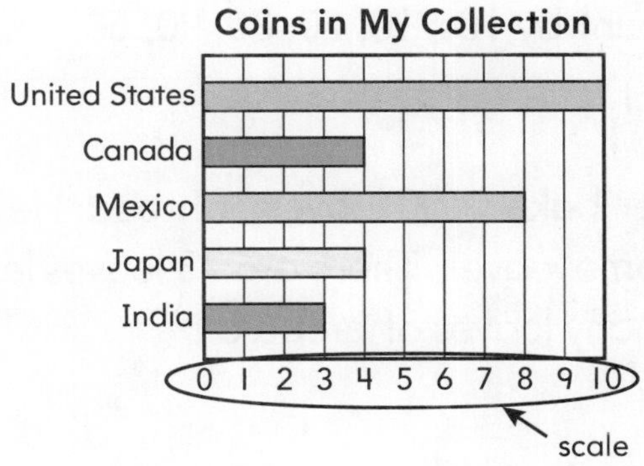

The numbers along the side or the bottom of a graph are the scale.

Show All Totals Method*

$$\begin{array}{r} 25 \\ +\,48 \\ \hline 60 \\ 13 \\ \hline 73 \end{array} \qquad \begin{array}{r} 724 \\ +\,158 \\ \hline 800 \\ 70 \\ 12 \\ \hline 882 \end{array}$$

situation equation*

A baker baked 100 loaves of bread. He sold some loaves. There are 73 loaves left. How many loaves of bread did he sell?

$100 - \square = 73$

situation equation

*A classroom research-based term developed for *Math Expressions*

skip count

skip count by 2s: 2, 4, 6, 8, . . .
skip count by 5s: 5, 10, 15, 20, . . .
skip count by 10s: 10, 20, 30, 40, 50, . . .

solution equation*

A baker baked 100 loaves of bread. He sold some loaves. There are 73 loaves left. How many loaves of bread did he sell?

$100 - 73 = \square$

solution equation

square

A square has 4 equal sides and 4 right angles.

subtract

$8 - 5 = 3$

subtraction doubles*

The subtrahend and the difference, or partners, are the same.

$8 - 4 = 4$

sum

$4 + 3 = 7$

$$\begin{array}{r} 4 \\ +\ 3 \\ \hline 7 \end{array}$$

sum

survey

When you collect data by asking people questions, you are taking a survey.

T

teen number

any number from 11 to 19

11 12 13 14 15 16 17 18 19

tens

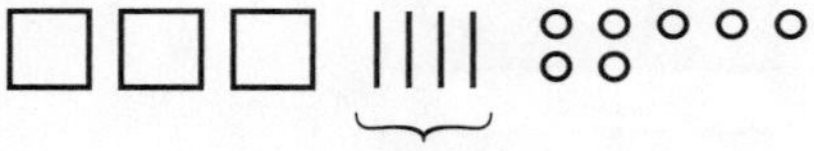

4 tens

347 has 4 tens.

tens

thirds

square

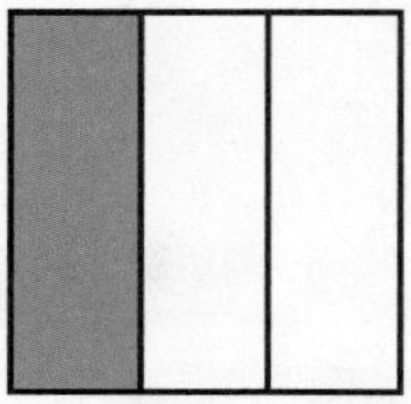

The picture shows 3 thirds. A third of the square is shaded.

*A classroom research-based term developed for *Math Expressions*

thousand

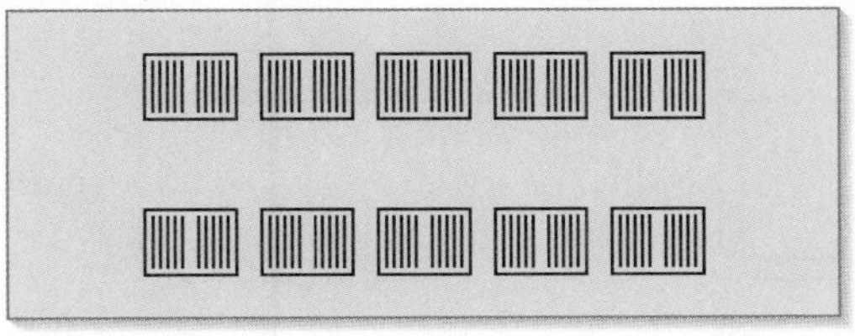

1,000 = 10 hundreds

total

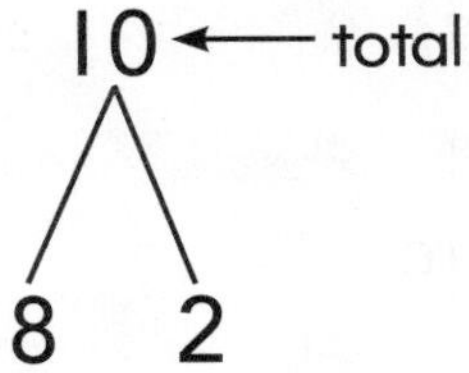

triangle

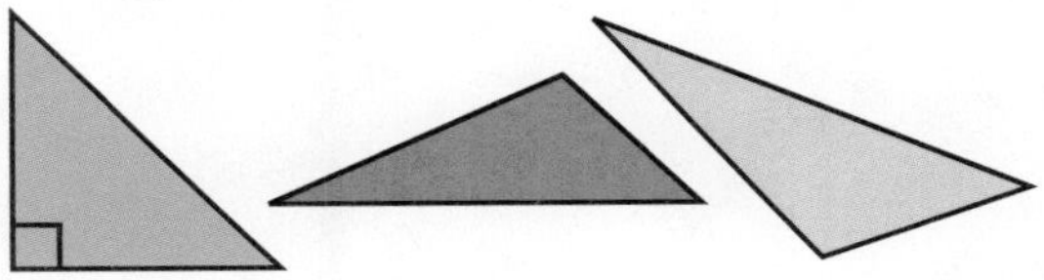

A triangle has 3 sides and 3 angles.

U

ungroup*

Ungroup when you need more ones or tens to subtract.

Ungroup First Method*

$$\begin{array}{r} 64 \\ -28 \\ \hline \end{array}$$

↑ ↑
yes no

1. Check to see if there are enough tens and ones to subtract.

$$\begin{array}{r} {\scriptstyle 5\,14} \\ \not{6}\not{4} \\ -28 \\ \hline \end{array}$$

2. You can get more ones by taking from the tens and putting them in the ones place.

$$\begin{array}{r} {\scriptstyle 5\,14} \\ \not{6}\not{4} \\ -28 \\ \hline 36 \end{array}$$

3. Subtract from either right to left or left to right.

unknown addend

3 + □ = 9

↑
unknown addend

unknown total

3 + 6 = □

↑
unknown total

V

vertical form

$$\begin{array}{r} 4 \\ +3 \\ \hline 7 \end{array}$$

*A classroom research-based term developed for *Math Expressions*

vertical bar graph

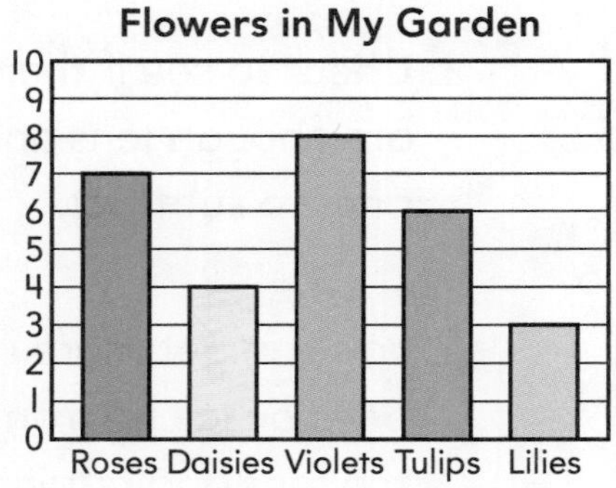

vertical line

view

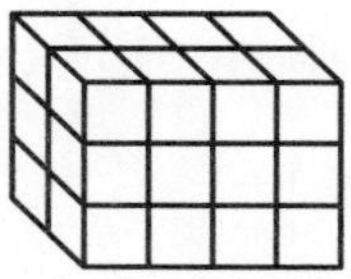

This is the side view of the rectangular prism above.

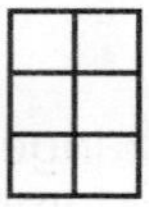

W

width

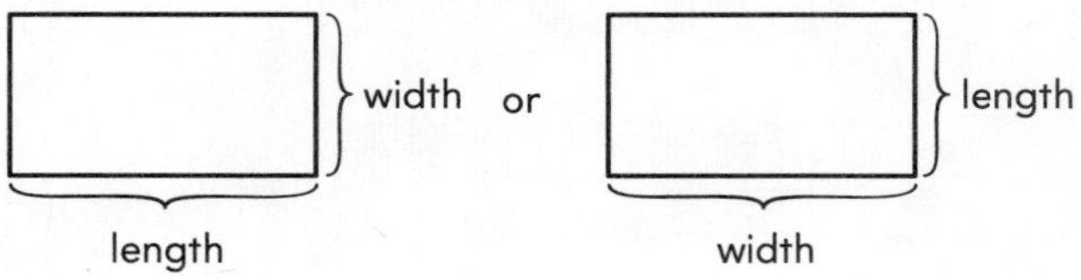

Y

yard (yd)

3 feet = 1 yard

(not drawn to scale)

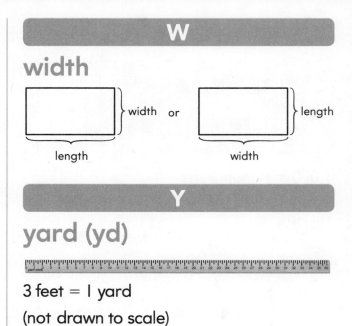

*A classroom research-based term developed for *Math Expressions*

2.OA Operations and Algebraic Thinking

Represent and solve problems involving addition and subtraction.		
2.OA.A.1	Use addition and subtraction within 100 to solve one- and two-step word problems involving situations of adding to, taking from, putting together, taking apart, and comparing, with unknowns in all positions, e.g., by using drawings and equations with a symbol for the unknown number to represent the problem.	Unit 1 Lessons 1, 2, 4, 9, 10, 11, 12, 13, 14, 15, 16, 17, 18, 19, 20, 21; Unit 2 Lessons 1, 2, 6, 7, 8, 15; Unit 4 Lessons 3, 4, 5, 12, 13, 14, 16, 17, 18, 19, 20, 21, 22, 23; Unit 5 Lessons 3, 4, 5, 6, 7, 9, 10; Unit 6 Lesson 15; Unit 7 Lessons 3, 4, 5
Add and subtract within 20.		
2.OA.B.2	Fluently add and subtract within 20 using mental strategies. By end of Grade 2, know from memory all sums of two one-digit numbers.	Unit 1 Lessons 1, 2, 3, 4, 5, 7, 8, 9, 10, 11, 12, 13, 14, 15, 16, 17, 18, 19, 20, 21; Unit 2 Lessons 2, 6; Unit 3 Lessons 1, 3, 4; Unit 4 Lessons 6, 13; Unit 5 Lessons 3, 4, 5, 6, 7, 8, 9, 10; Unit 7 Lesson 6
Work with equal groups of objects to gain foundations for multiplication.		
2.OA.C.3	Determine whether a group of objects (up to 20) has an odd or even number of members, e.g., by pairing objects or counting them by 2s; write an equation to express an even number as a sum of two equal addends.	Unit 1 Lessons 6, 7, 21; Unit 7 Lesson 1
2.OA.C.4	Use addition to find the total number of objects arranged in rectangular arrays with up to 5 rows and up to 5 columns; write an equation to express the total as a sum of equal addends.	Unit 7 Lessons 1, 6

■ Major ■ Supporting ■ Additional

2.NBT Number and Operations in Base Ten

Understand place value.

2.NBT.A.1	Understand that the three digits of a three-digit number represent amounts of hundreds, tens, and ones; e.g., 706 equals 7 hundreds, 0 tens, and 6 ones.	Unit 2 Lessons 1, 2, 3, 4, 5, 6, 7, 8, 9, 10, 11; Unit 4 Lessons 7, 8, 9, 10, 12; Unit 6 Lessons 1, 2, 3, 4, 10, 11, 12
2.NBT.A.1.a	Understand that the three digits of a three-digit number represent amounts of hundreds, tens, and ones; e.g., 706 equals 7 hundreds, 0 tens, and 6 ones. Understand the following as special cases: a. 100 can be thought of as a bundle of ten tens—called a " hundred."	Unit 2 Lessons 1, 2, 3, 4, 6, 7, 8, 9, 11; Unit 4 Lessons 3, 4, 7, 8, 9, 10, 12; Unit 6 Lessons 1, 4, 6, 7, 9. 10, 11, 13
2.NBT.A.1.b	Understand that the three digits of a three-digit number represent amounts of hundreds, tens, and ones; e.g., 706 equals 7 hundreds, 0 tens, and 6 ones. Understand the following as special cases: b. The numbers 100, 200, 300, 400, 500, 600, 700, 800, 900 refer to one, two, three, four, five, six, seven, eight, or nine hundreds (and 0 tens and 0 ones).	Unit 4 Lesson 7; Unit 6 Lesson 1
2.NBT.A.2	Count within 1000; skip-count by 5s, 10s, and 100s.	Unit 1 Lesson 6; Unit 2 Lessons 1, 2, 3, 12, 15; Unit 4 Lessons 1, 2, 15; Unit 5 Lesson 2; Unit 6 Lessons 1, 4
2.NBT.A.3	Read and write numbers to 1000 using base-ten numerals, number names, and expanded form.	Unit 2 Lessons 1, 2, 3, 4, 5; Unit 6 Lessons 1, 2, 4
2.NBT.A.4	Compare two three-digit numbers based on meanings of the hundreds, tens, and ones digits, using $>$, $=$, and $<$ symbols to record the results of comparisons.	Unit 2 Lessons 5, 15; Unit 5 Lesson 10; Unit 6 Lessons 3, 15

Major Supporting Additional

2.NBT Number and Operations in Base Ten

Use place value understanding and properties of operations to add and subtract.

2.NBT.B.5	Fluently add and subtract within 100 using strategies based on place value, properties of operations, and/or the relationship between addition and subtraction.	Unit 2 Lessons 2, 4, 13, 14, 15; Unit 3 Lesson 9; Unit 4 Lessons 1, 2, 3, 4, 5, 6, 11, 12, 13, 14, 15, 16, 17, 18, 19, 20, 21, 22, 23; Unit 5 Lessons 5, 8, 9; Unit 6 Lessons 3, 8, 10, 15; Unit 7 Lessons 3, 4, 5
2.NBT.B.6	Add up to four two-digit numbers using strategies based on place value and properties of operations.	Unit 2 Lessons 6, 8, 9, 10, 14, 15; Unit 4 Lessons 3, 5, 12, 15, 16, 17, 18; Unit 7 Lessons 4, 5
2.NBT.B.7	Add and subtract within 1000, using concrete models or drawings and strategies based on place value, properties of operations, and/or the relationship between addition and subtraction; relate the strategy to a written method. Understand that in adding or subtracting three-digit numbers, one adds or subtracts hundreds and hundreds, tens and tens, ones and ones; and sometimes it is necessary to compose or decompose tens or hundreds.	Unit 2 Lessons 4, 6, 7, 8, 9, 10, 11, 14, 15; Unit 3 Lesson 6; Unit 4 Lessons 3, 4, 5, 6, 7, 8, 9, 10, 12, 13, 15, 16, 17, 18, 19, 20; Unit 6 Lessons 2, 4, 5, 6, 7, 8, 9, 10, 11, 12, 13, 14, 15
2.NBT.B.8	Mentally add 10 or 100 to a given number 100–900, and mentally subtract 10 or 100 from a given number 100–900.	Unit 2 Lesson 4; Unit 4 Lesson 15; Unit 6 Lessons 2, 4
2.NBT.B.9	Explain why addition and subtraction strategies work, using place value and the properties of operations.	Unit 1 Lessons 1, 3, 4, 5, 7, 9, 10, 11, 16, 20; Unit 2 Lessons 2, 4, 6, 7, 8, 9, 10; Unit 4 Lessons 3, 4, 5, 6, 7, 8, 9, 10, 12, 14, 15, 16, 17, 18; Unit 6 Lessons 2, 5, 6, 7, 8, 9, 10, 11, 12, 13, 14, 15; Unit 7 Lessons 4, 5

2.MD Measurement and Data

Measure and estimate lengths in standard units.		
2.MD.A.1	Measure the length of an object by selecting and using appropriate tools such as rulers, yardsticks, meter sticks, and measuring tapes.	Unit 3 Lessons 1, 2, 3, 4, 6, 7, 8, 9; Unit 4 Lesson 23; Unit 7 Lesson 1
2.MD.A.2	Measure the length of an object twice, using length units of different lengths for the two measurements; describe how the two measurements relate to the size of the unit chosen.	Unit 3 Lessons 7, 8, 9
2.MD.A.3	Estimate lengths using units of inches, feet, centimeters, and meters.	Unit 3 Lessons 3, 4, 6, 7, 8; Unit 4 Lesson 23
2.MD.A.4	Measure to determine how much longer one object is than another, expressing the length difference in terms of a standard length unit.	Unit 3 Lessons 1, 2, 6; Unit 4 Lesson 23
Relate addition and subtraction to length.		
2.MD.B.5	Use addition and subtraction within 100 to solve word problems involving lengths that are given in the same units, e.g., by using drawings (such as drawings of rulers) and equations with a symbol for the unknown number to represent the problem.	Unit 4 Lesson 23; Unit 7 Lessons 3, 4, 5
2.MD.B.6	Represent whole numbers as lengths from 0 on a number line diagram with equally spaced points corresponding to the numbers 0, 1, 2, . . . , and represent whole-number sums and differences within 100 on a number line diagram.	Unit 7 Lessons 3, 5
Work with time and money.		
2.MD.C.7	Tell and write time from analog and digital clocks to the nearest five minutes, using a.m. and p.m.	Unit 5 Lessons 1, 2
2.MD.C.8	Solve word problems involving dollar bills, quarters, dimes, nickels, and pennies, using $ and ¢ symbols appropriately. *Example: If you have 2 dimes and 3 pennies, how many cents do you have?*	Unit 2 Lessons 11, 12, 15; Unit 4 Lessons 1, 2, 10; Unit 5 Lessons 3, 4

Major Supporting Additional

2.MD Measurement and Data

Represent and interpret data.

2.MD.D.9	Generate measurement data by measuring lengths of several objects to the nearest whole unit, or by making repeated measurements of the same object. Show the measurements by making a line plot, where the horizontal scale is marked off in whole-number units.	Unit 3 Lessons 6, 7, 8
2.MD.D.10	Draw a picture graph and a bar graph (with single-unit scale) to represent a data set with up to four categories. Solve simple put-together, take-apart, and compare problems using information presented in a bar graph.	Unit 5 Lessons 3, 4, 5, 6, 7, 8, 9, 10

2.G Geometry

Reason with shapes and their attributes.

2.G.A.1	Recognize and draw shapes having specified attributes, such as a given number of angles or a given number of equal faces. Identify triangles, quadrilaterals, pentagons, hexagons, and cubes.	Unit 3 Lessons 2, 3, 4, 5, 9; Unit 7 Lessons 1, 2, 4, 5
2.G.A.2	Partition a rectangle into rows and columns of same-size squares and count to find the total number of them.	Unit 7 Lessons 1, 6
2.G.A.3	Partition circles and rectangles into two, three, or four equal shares, describe the shares using the words *halves*, *thirds*, *half of*, *a third of*, etc., and describe the whole as two halves, three thirds, four fourths. Recognize that equal shares of identical wholes need not have the same shape.	Unit 5 Lesson 2; Unit 7 Lessons 1, 2, 6

MP1 Make sense of problems and persevere in solving them.

Mathematically proficient students start by explaining to themselves the meaning of a problem and looking for entry points to its solution. They analyze givens, constraints, relationships, and goals. They make conjectures about the form and meaning of the solution and plan a solution pathway rather than simply jumping into a solution attempt. They consider analogous problems, and try special cases and simpler forms of the original problem in order to gain insight into its solution. They monitor and evaluate their progress and change course if necessary. Older students might, depending on the context of the problem, transform algebraic expressions or change the viewing window on their graphing calculator to get the information they need. Mathematically proficient students can explain correspondences between equations, verbal descriptions, tables, and graphs or draw diagrams of important features and relationships, graph data, and search for regularity or trends. Younger students might rely on using concrete objects or pictures to help conceptualize and solve a problem. Mathematically proficient students check their answers to problems using a different method, and they continually ask themselves, "Does this make sense?" They can understand the approaches of others to solving complex problems and identify correspondences between different approaches.	Unit 1 Lessons 2, 3, 4, 5, 6, 7, 9, 10, 11, 12, 13, 14, 15, 16, 17, 18, 19, 20, 21 Unit 2 Lessons 1, 3, 4, 5, 6, 7, 8, 9, 11, 12, 13, 14, 15 Unit 3 Lessons 1, 3, 6, 9 Unit 4 Lessons 1, 2, 3, 4, 5, 6, 7, 8, 9, 10, 11, 12, 13, 14, 16, 17, 18, 19, 20, 21, 22, 23 Unit 5 Lessons 1, 3, 4, 5, 6, 7, 8, 9, 10 Unit 6 Lessons 1, 4, 5, 8, 9, 10, 11, 12, 14, 15 Unit 7 Lessons 1, 2, 3, 4, 5, 6

MP2 Reason abstractly and quantitatively.

Mathematically proficient students make sense of quantities and their relationships in problem situations. They bring two complementary abilities to bear on problems involving quantitative relationships: the ability to *decontextualize*—to abstract a given situation and represent it symbolically and manipulate the representing symbols as if they have a life of their own, without necessarily attending to their referents—and the ability to *contextualize*, to pause as needed during the manipulation process in order to probe into the referents for the symbols involved. Quantitative reasoning entails habits of creating a coherent representation of the problem at hand, considering the units involved, attending to the meaning of quantities, not just how to compute them, and knowing and flexibly using different properties of operations and objects.	Unit 1 Lessons 1, 5, 7, 8, 9, 10, 11, 14, 21 Unit 2 Lessons 1, 3, 4, 5, 6, 7, 8, 9, 11, 12, 13, 14, 15 Unit 3 Lessons 1, 2, 3, 7, 8, 9 Unit 4 Lessons 1, 2, 3, 4, 5, 6, 7, 8, 9, 10, 11, 12, 13, 15, 17, 19, 20, 22, 23 Unit 5 Lessons 1, 2, 3, 5,10 Unit 6 Lessons 1, 2, 4, 10, 15 Unit 7 Lessons 1, 2, 3, 4, 5, 6

MP3 Construct viable arguments and critique the reasoning of others.	
Mathematically proficient students understand and use stated assumptions, definitions, and previously established results in constructing arguments. They make conjectures and build a logical progression of statements to explore the truth of their conjectures. They are able to analyze situations by breaking them into cases, and can recognize and use counterexamples. They justify their conclusions, communicate them to others, and respond to the arguments of others. They reason inductively about data, making plausible arguments that take into account the context from which the data arose. Mathematically proficient students are also able to compare the effectiveness of two plausible arguments, distinguish correct logic or reasoning from that which is flawed, and—if there is a flaw in an argument—explain what it is. Elementary students can construct arguments using concrete referents such as objects, drawings, diagrams, and actions. Such arguments can make sense and be correct, even though they are not generalized or made formal until later grades. Later, students learn to determine domains to which an argument applies. Students at all grades can listen to or read the arguments of others, decide whether they make sense, and ask useful questions to clarify or improve the arguments.	Unit 1 Lessons 1, 2, 3, 4, 5, 6, 7, 8, 9, 10, 11, 12, 13, 14, 15, 16, 17, 18, 19, 20, 21 Unit 2 Lessons 1, 2, 3, 4, 5, 6, 7, 8, 9, 10, 11, 12, 13, 14, 15 Unit 3 Lessons 1, 2, 3, 4, 5, 6, 7, 8, 9 Unit 4 Lessons 1, 2, 3, 4, 5, 6, 7, 8, 9, 10, 11, 12, 13, 14, 15, 16, 17, 18, 19, 20, 21, 22, 23 Unit 5 Lessons 1, 2, 3, 4, 5, 6, 7, 8, 9, 10 Unit 6 Lessons 1, 2, 3, 4, 5, 6, 7, 8, 9, 10, 11, 12, 13, 14, 15 Unit 7 Lessons 1, 2, 3, 4, 5, 6

MP4 Model with mathematics.	
Mathematically proficient students can apply the mathematics they know to solve problems arising in everyday life, society, and the workplace. In early grades, this might be as simple as writing an addition equation to describe a situation. In middle grades, a student might apply proportional reasoning to plan a school event or analyze a problem in the community. By high school, a student might use geometry to solve a design problem or use a function to describe how one quantity of interest depends on another. Mathematically proficient students who can apply what they know are comfortable making assumptions and approximations to simplify a complicated situation, realizing that these may need revision later. They are able to identify important quantities in a practical situation and map their relationships using such tools as diagrams, two-way tables, graphs, flowcharts and formulas. They can analyze those relationships mathematically to draw conclusions. They routinely interpret their mathematical results in the context of the situation and reflect on whether the results make sense, possibly improving the model if it has not served its purpose.	Unit 1 Lessons 10, 11, 12, 13, 14, 15, 16, 17, 18, 19, 20, 21 Unit 2 Lessons 1, 4, 6, 7, 11, 12, 14, 15 Unit 3 Lessons 6, 7, 8, 9 Unit 4 Lessons 1, 3, 4, 5, 7, 10, 12, 13, 18, 19, 20, 21, 23 Unit 5 Lessons 3, 5, 8, 9, 10 Unit 6 Lessons 9, 11, 14, 15 Unit 7 Lessons 3, 6

MP5 Use appropriate tools strategically.	
Mathematically proficient students consider the available tools when solving a mathematical problem. These tools might include pencil and paper, concrete models, a ruler, a protractor, a calculator, a spreadsheet, a computer algebra system, a statistical package, or dynamic geometry software. Proficient students are sufficiently familiar with tools appropriate for their grade or course to make sound decisions about when each of these tools might be helpful, recognizing both the insight to be gained and their limitations. For example, mathematically proficient high school students analyze graphs of functions and solutions generated using a graphing calculator. They detect possible errors by strategically using estimation and other mathematical knowledge. When making mathematical models, they know that technology can enable them to visualize the results of varying assumptions, explore consequences, and compare predictions with data. Mathematically proficient students at various grade levels are able to identify relevant external mathematical resources, such as digital content located on a website, and use them to pose or solve problems. They are able to use technological tools to explore and deepen their understanding of concepts.	Unit 1 Lessons 3, 6, 20, 21 Unit 2 Lessons 1, 2, 3, 4, 5, 8, 12, 13, 14, 15 Unit 3 Lessons 1, 2, 3, 5, 6, 7, 8, 9 Unit 4 Lessons 1, 2, 3, 4, 7, 8, 9, 11, 18, 23 Unit 5 Lessons 1, 2, 5, 10 Unit 6 Lessons 1, 2, 5, 7, 10, 15 Unit 7 Lessons 1, 2, 3, 6

MP6 Attend to precision.	
Mathematically proficient students try to communicate precisely to others. They try to use clear definitions in discussion with others and in their own reasoning. They state the meaning of the symbols they choose, including using the equal sign consistently and appropriately. They are careful about specifying units of measure and labeling axes to clarify the correspondence with quantities in a problem. They calculate accurately and efficiently, expressing numerical answers with a degree of precision appropriate for the problem context. In the elementary grades, students give carefully formulated explanations to each other. By the time they reach high school they have learned to examine claims and make explicit use of definitions.	Unit 1 Lessons 1, 2, 3, 4, 5, 6, 7, 8, 9, 10, 11, 12, 13, 14, 15, 16, 17, 18, 19, 20, 21 Unit 2 Lessons 1, 2, 3, 4, 5, 6, 7, 8, 9, 10, 11, 12, 13, 14, 15 Unit 3 Lessons 1, 2, 3, 4, 5, 6, 7, 8, 9 Unit 4 Lessons 1, 2, 3, 4, 5, 6, 7, 8, 9, 10, 11, 12, 13, 14, 15, 16, 17, 18, 19, 20, 21, 22, 23 Unit 5 Lessons 1, 2, 3, 4, 5, 6, 7, 8, 9, 10 Unit 6 Lessons 1, 2, 3, 4, 5, 6, 7, 8, 9, 10, 11, 12, 13, 14, 15 Unit 7 Lessons 1, 2, 3, 4, 5, 6

MP7 Look for and make use of structure.

Mathematically proficient students look closely to discern a pattern or structure. Young students, for example, might notice that three and seven more is the same amount as seven and three more, or they may sort a collection of shapes according to how many sides the shapes have. Later, students will see 7×8 equals the well remembered $7 \times 5 + 7 \times 3$, in preparation for learning about the distributive property. In the expression $x^2 + 9x + 14$, older students can see the 14 as 2×7 and the 9 as $2 + 7$. They recognize the significance of an existing line in a geometric figure and can use the strategy of drawing an auxiliary line for solving problems. They also can step back for an overview and shift perspective. They can see complicated things, such as some algebraic expressions, as single objects or as being composed of several objects. For example, they can see $5 - 3(x - y)^2$ as 5 minus a positive number times a square and use that to realize that its value cannot be more than 5 for any real numbers x and y.	Unit 1 Lessons 1, 2, 3, 5, 6, 9, 13, 17, 18, 19, 21 Unit 2 Lessons 1, 2, 3, 4, 6, 10, 11, 12, 15 Unit 3 Lessons 1, 3, 4, 5, 7, 8, 9 Unit 4 Lessons 1, 2, 7, 13, 17, 19, 21, 23 Unit 5 Lessons 2, 6, 7, 10 Unit 6 Lessons 4, 12, 13, 15 Unit 7 Lessons 2, 6

MP8 Look for and express regularity in repeated reasoning.

Mathematically proficient students notice if calculations are repeated, and look both for general methods and for shortcuts. Upper elementary students might notice when dividing 25 by 11 that they are repeating the same calculations over and over again, and conclude they have a repeating decimal. By paying attention to the calculation of slope as they repeatedly check whether points are on the line through (1, 2) with slope 3, middle school students might abstract the equation $(y - 2)/(x - 1) = 3$. Noticing the regularity in the way terms cancel when expanding $(x - 1)(x + 1)$, $(x - 1)(x^2 + x + 1)$, and $(x - 1)(x^3 + x^2 + x + 1)$ might lead them to the general formula for the sum of a geometric series. As they work to solve a problem, mathematically proficient students maintain oversight of the process, while attending to the details. They continually evaluate the reasonableness of their intermediate results.	Unit 1 Lessons 2, 6, 7, 21 Unit 2 Lessons 5, 10, 11, 15 Unit 3 Lessons 1, 2, 7, 8, 9 Unit 4 Lessons 4, 8, 13, 23 Unit 5 Lesson 10 Unit 6 Lessons 2, 4, 7, 8, 12, 15 Unit 7 Lessons 2, 6

A

B

C

D

E

N

Q

R

S

T

Be an Illustrator

Illustrator: Josh Brill

Did you ever try to use shapes to draw animals like the platypus on the cover?

Over the last 10 years Josh has been using geometric shapes to design his animals. His aim is to keep the animal drawings simple and use color to make them appealing.

Add some color to the platypus Josh drew. Then try drawing a cat or dog or some other animal using the shapes below.

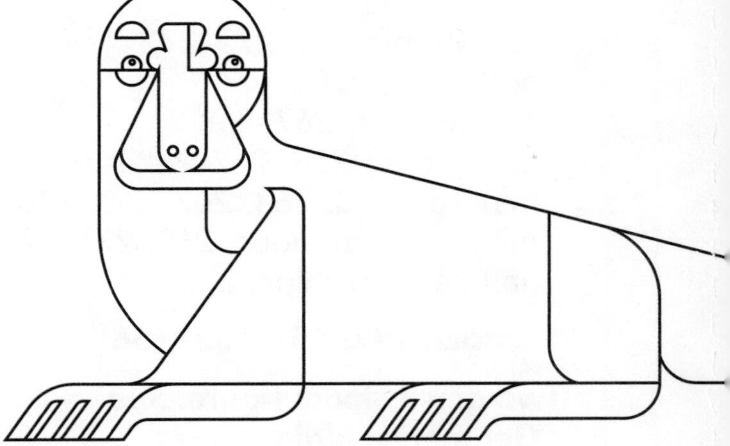

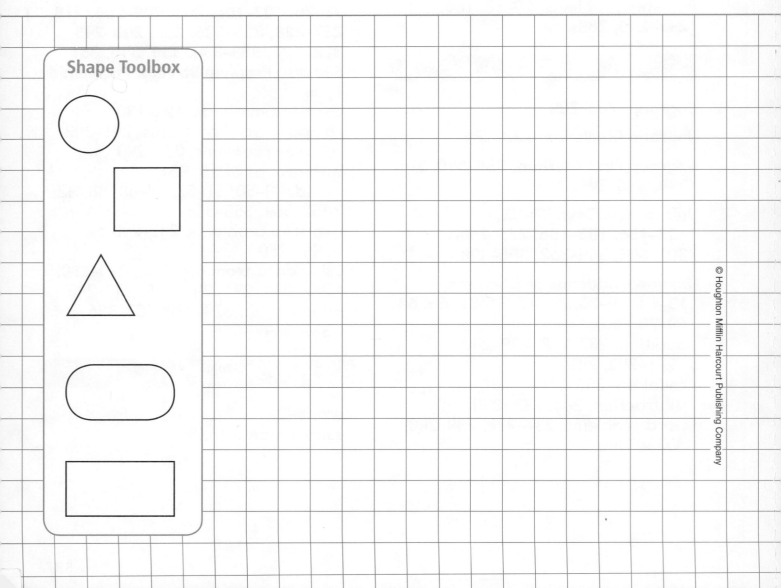

Shape Toolbox

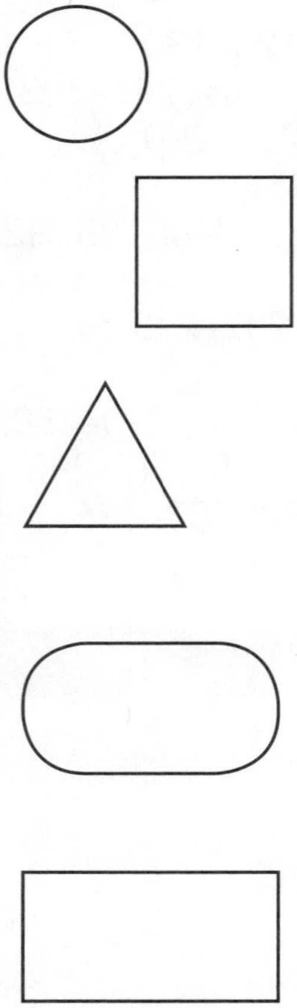